We Are What We Celebrate

We Are What We Celebrate

Understanding Holidays and Rituals

EDITED BY

Amitai Etzioni and Jared Bloom

WITHDRAWN

New York University Press

NEW YORK AND LONDON

NEW YORK UNIVERSITY PRESS
New York and London
www.nyupress.org

Library of Congress Cataloging-in-Publication Data
We are what we celebrate : understanding holidays and rituals /
edited by Amitai Etzioni and Jared Bloom.
p. cm.
Includes bibliographical references and index.
ISBN 0–8147–2226–1 (cloth : alk. paper)
ISBN 0–8147–2227–X (pbk. : alk. paper)
1. Holidays.   2. Ritual.   3. Family.   4. Community life.
I. Etzioni, Amitai.   II. Bloom, Jared, 1981–
GT3930.W37   2004
394.2673—dc22   2004015245

New York University Press books are printed on acid-free paper,
and their binding materials are chosen for strength and durability.

Manufactured in the United States of America
c 10 9 8 7 6 5 4 3 2 1
p 10 9 8 7 6 5 4 3 2 1

Contents

Part I

Introduction

Chapter 1

Holidays and Rituals
Neglected Seedbeds of Virtue

Amitai Etzioni

On May 27, 1999, the board of the National Association of Securities Dealers (the parent organization of NASDAQ) announced that it planned to open an evening trading session for stocks between 5:30 p.m. and 9:00 or 10:00 p.m. NASDAQ president Richard Ketchum added, "there may come a day when we trade 24 hours."[1] Actually, a "24/7 week" was already at hand. People can trade stocks and much else twenty-four hours a day, seven days a week (including holidays), on the Internet. In a society that has made economic advancement a key value while downgrading others, people dedicate more and more of their time to work and commerce, and less to family, community, and holidays. Although the per capita hours in the formal workweek have not increased much, many people work overtime and take work home, and, above all, more members of the family now work outside the household.

The rise of cyberspace presents a qualitative jump in the scope of opportunities to work and trade because it knows neither clock nor calendar nor holidays. For those who seek to trade or labor within the Internet's rapidly expanding confines, any time is as good as any other. While in the "old" pre-Internet world, banks still closed at certain hours on certain days, rapidly rising e-banks are operational at all times. And while some shops stay open late-nights and weekends, only on the Internet can one safely assume that time, day, and date do not matter. There is no day of rest for the Internet mailman; email flows into one's PC nonstop. In short, cyberspace has no Sabbath—nor Christmas nor Yom Kippur. Cyberspace stands to eradicate whatever remains of "institutionalized" barriers, that is, those that are used to separate and protect the sacred from the profane, the social and spiritual from labor and commerce.

In examining these transformations in society's attitudes toward work, rest, and holidays, the family dinner is a fine indicator of the changes that have taken place, as well as a ritual of importance. Once upon a time, many families sat down for dinner together at a set time. All members of the family were expected to be present. Family discussions and normative deliberations took place.[2] (True, in many earlier societies, there were no set meals. And in 1950s America, the conversation over dinner may have been dominated by the father or his views and may have reinforced values that few would seek to uphold today.) In recent years, increasingly it seems, families rarely dine together, due in part to conflicting schedules and changing roles within families (the movement of women into the workforce, etc.).[3] And if they do, they often watch TV while they eat.

In reaction to this trend, some efforts have been made to restore traditional holidays. One day before the announcement of the board of NASDAQ, the Central Conference of American Rabbis, the board that guides Reform Jews, voted to call on its members to return to the observance of traditional rituals such as observing the Sabbath, wearing a skullcap, and keeping kosher.[4] Numerous other religious groups, including almost all Christian denominations, have initiated drives to renew religious commitment among their members through increased dedication to holidays and rituals.

Efforts to secure more room for family, community, religious life, and holidays rarely seek to simply restore tradition. They often do not constitute a simple call for a return to the past, to observe rituals and tenets "because that's the way we've always done things" or "because that is the way the Lord or the scripture commands." Instead, society faces still *more* choice; its members are challenged to examine which rituals they will adapt and which new rituals they will develop to protect the "sacred" from the profane. These efforts include such innocuous steps as defining places where cell phones will be turned off and declaring that bringing laptops to places of worship is inappropriate. (Amtrak now has a "silent" car on some of its trains.)[5] More important, efforts may include restoring the Sabbath as a day of rest and reflection and restoring the family dinner, or perhaps dedicating one day of the week to "family time," which could be reserved for family activities.

If one needs a symbol for the growing need to choose one's rituals instead of merely following or reinstating traditional rituals, it may be the family dinner. Unless NASDAQ traders plan to have dinner at 11:00 p.m.

or so, they are extremely unlikely to share a meal with their families on weekdays—unless they choose to miss the evening session. Most other members of society have long faced the decision of whether, given their busy households and conflicting schedules, they should plan to come together for dinner—at least on some agreed days of the week. Indeed, additional deliberate choices are involved: Those who seek weekday dinners that are occasions where family members can truly communicate with one another must formulate "policies" on matters such as turning off the TV, not answering the phone, and staying at the table until an agreed time. The same now increasingly holds for weekends and holidays.[6]

Selective observance, rather than a simple return to tradition, has become the norm. This is evident when one compares those rituals various individuals and groups seek to uphold or adapt versus those they choose to abandon. These are decisions that are increasingly made on the basis of what seems meaningful to the contemporary generation rather than on what is handed down from earlier ones. Observing the Sabbath thus may well be one of those rituals that many find meaningful because they see the virtue of securing time away from economic activities. At the same time, the Jewish tradition of women purifying themselves in a public bathhouse (*mikvah*) after they menstruate may well be one of those rituals that lack the same contemporary conviction for most.

I am not suggesting that tradition will play no role. It is one major source of options that people consider, but it is not the depository of the answer. In effect, religion can be viewed as a place where earlier approaches have been preserved so that members of contemporary societies may reembrace them. Contemporary individuals do so not merely because that is the way they are commanded by religious authorities or because it is what they have learned from their forefathers and mothers, but because they find elements of these traditions compelling and meaningful. The way people plan weddings these days is a case in point. Various alternative rituals are considered, from traditional nuptials to newly composed vows, tailored to the particular couple.[7]

Some of these decisions people are able to render as individuals and as families, for instance, whether or not—and when—to attend church. Other choices, though, require communal dialogues and shared decisions, for instance, whether committee and board meetings, which are increasingly conducted via email, will be conducted only on workdays and during "regular" hours (whatever that means) or whether they will go the way of twenty-four-hour stock trading.

Thus, editing and limited reengineering of holidays (rituals included) take place constantly, drawing on both new designs and old patterns. How effective this is, and can be, is a major subject for social scientists, as it currently remains largely unstudied.

Social scientists have long focused on the family as the institution that initiates the socialization process, and, in this context, much attention has been paid to the effects of family composition and structure and of the rise of other childcare institutions on the outcomes of socialization. Considerable attention has also been accorded to schools as agents of socialization. (In the past few decades, leaders and members of society at large have addressed these matters using code words such as "family values" and "character education.") Many social scientists have also studied the role of communities (and within them, voluntary associations and places of worship) and national societies as *seedbeds of virtue,* that is, as places that cultivate normative behavior.

In sharp contrast, social scientists have given little consideration over the past decades to the function of holidays and rituals in general and to their role as seedbeds of virtue in particular. The term "holiday" does not even appear in the index of the sixteen volumes of the otherwise rich and elaborate *International Encyclopedia of Social Sciences* (1968); it is not listed in the indexes of the *American Sociological Review* or the *American Journal of Sociology* from 1975 to 1995, nor can the term be found in the *Encyclopedia of Sociology* (1992). There is also no entry for "holiday" in the *Encyclopedia of Community* (2003).

This book seeks to contribute to the development of a theory of holidays. (For the purposes of this work, the term "holidays" is used to encompass both holidays *and* rituals because rituals generally serve the same basic role as holidays in society. Select cases may demand that we distinguish between the two terms; when such cases arise, we will do so.) Holidays are defined as days on which custom or the law dictates a suspension of general business activity in order to commemorate or celebrate a particular event.[8] They are symbolic in the sense that their essential elements (activities, foods, rules) cannot be substantively explained—the connection between these elements and the holiday they belong to is arbitrary. Just as a nation's flag evokes much more reverence than the piece of cloth it is made of, so does a glass of wine used during religious rituals evoke much more reverence than one consumed in a bar.

Holidays and rituals are repetitive rather than one-time events. A demonstration that occurs once will turn into a ritual only if repeated over several years, in basically the same format. In this limited sense, rituals are part of tradition. They reaffirm communal bonds (although they may reaffirm some bonds at the same time that they undermine others); they are concerned with normative dimensions of society (because they all reinforce some values); and they are dramatic in the sense that in order to communicate effectively they employ narratives, displays, or some other three-dimensional, theaterlike performance.[9]

This book starts by examining Émile Durkheim's well-known contributions and then suggests ways in which they may need to be extensively modified in order to further develop a more comprehensive theory.[10] This volume also raises theoretical issues not directly addressed by Durkheim. To proceed, we draw on public accounts, personal observations, and findings culled from studies by contemporary social scientists, either previously published or specifically prepared for a conference that inspired this volume.[11] (These papers focus on Western, especially American, society. The study of the same issues in other kinds of societies requires a separate undertaking.)

Because Durkheim's work has been systematically analyzed, well reviewed, and effectively summarized, very little is to be gained by a reanalysis of Durkheim here.[12] The main relevant points, following Durkheim's functional approach, are merely listed briefly:

(a) Profane (secular), routine, daily life—the conduct of instrumental activities at work and the carrying out of household chores—tends to weaken shared beliefs and social bonds and enhance centrifugal individualism. For societies to survive these centrifugal, individualistic tendencies, they must continuously "re-create" themselves, by shoring up commitments to one set of shared ("common") beliefs and practices.

(b) Rituals provide one major mechanism for the re-creation of a society in which members worship the same objects and share experiences that help form and sustain deep emotional bonds among the members.

(c) The specific elements of rituals, as well as the objects that are worshiped or celebrated in rituals—be they colored stones, woodcuts, or practically anything else—have no intrinsic value or meaning. It is the society that imbues these objects with significance, and, thus endowed, the objects become the cornerstones of the integrative rituals built around them.

Viewed this way, religious services on weekends serve to reinforce the commitments that have been diluted during the week. Holidays, in this context, are seen as *supraweekends,* as especially strong boosters of commitments and bonds.[13]

To put it in more Weberian terms, on weekdays, which are dedicated to work and commerce, people tend to abandon their commitments to shared values and communities; during holidays these commitments and shared values are reaffirmed. Hence, when holidays deteriorate, so do moral and social order. Durkheim hypothesizes that rituals (the term he uses rather than "holidays") correlate negatively with societal disintegration (defined as excessive individualism).[14] This statement, we shall see, can serve only as a first approximation. Actually, the relationships between holidays and the reinforcement of values and bonds is much more complex than Durkheim's theory suggests. But before I can both build on this theoretical foundation and seek to modify it, a brief methodological note.

Holidays as "Global" Indicators

Holidays have a special methodological merit that makes them particularly attractive to students of societies: They provide indicators that help us to ascertain the attributes of large collectives. In studying societies, social scientists often rely on measurements based on aggregate data about myriads of individuals, objects, or transactions such as public-opinion polls, economic statistics, and census data.[15] For various reasons not explored here, such aggregated data are best supplemented with indicators that tap directly into collective attributes of the macro social system being studied, sometimes referred to as "global" measurements.[16] For instance, in order to characterize a polity it is useful not only to determine the voting and alienation rates of millions of citizens but also to establish whether there are two dominant political parties or numerous small ones and whether there is a written constitution. These are significant macro (or "system") attributes not derivable from data about the attributes of citizens or from other aggregates.

In studying the belief systems of a society by using global indicators, researchers have drawn on various cultural products, such as books considered to "typify" a particular group (e.g., novels by William Faulkner as a reflection of the "mind" of the South) or major speeches by public leaders (e.g., those of Martin Luther King Jr. or Louis Farrakhan as representations of the African-American community). Using such cultural products as indicators seems unavoidable when one deals with earlier periods such as ninth-century feudalism in France, from which only a very limited amount of such material is available. However, for contemporary societies, cultural products are available in huge quantities and their contents vary greatly. Hence, choosing a particular book, movie, or speech as indicative of a period and system of beliefs is often difficult to justify, and analyzing all of them (or even a random sample) is an onerous task (even when setting aside questions that arise from trying to determine the proper universe to be sampled, such as whether one should include imported books and movies). In contrast, the ways holidays are celebrated—whether their focus is nationalist, militarist, or religious; whether they are dominated by merchandising and conspicuous consumption or dedicated to public service; whether they take place in people's homes or in public spaces; and so on—offer effective and parsimonious global indicators. Moreover, data about the ways holidays are celebrated in a particular society are often not available for countries in which one can neither conduct reliable public-opinion polls nor collect other kinds of aggregate data, such as Tibet.

Using holidays as sociological indicators might be rather misleading if the focus is only on the content of the occasions, for instance, how religious or secular they are. To the extent possible, it is desirable to determine the rough number of the participants, the extent of their involvement, and any specific attributes that distinguish them from other members of a society. For instance, observation of a Promise Keeper ritual in 1997 revealed that most who attended were male and white.[17]

To point to the merits of observing holidays as a source of data and insight into the belief systems of a society is not to argue that such data are fully accurate or can be relied upon as the sole source of evidence. Holidays, like other cultural products, tend to offer a somewhat refractory reading of society.[18] Thus, one cannot rely on the finding that many in India watch MTV to conclude that they are becoming Americanized. Indeed, studies show that when members of different ethnic groups watch the same TV program, they see rather different things.[19] Nor can one necessarily conclude that because Times Square in New York City and several other such sites in major cities are crowded with jubilant people on New Year's Eve, the country is in a happy mood. I merely suggest that observations about holidays provide one important and relatively accessible source of global data about the beliefs and other attributes of a given society. The resulting readings, like those of other indicators, need to be compared with other sources of data.

Finally, it should be noted that, unlike many other measurements (GDP levels, for instance), which are social science constructs or artifacts, holidays are both a social phenomenon of considerable sociological interest in their own right as well as a source of data on a society at large. Hence, those who study holidays reap a double benefit: They advance our understanding of a set of specific social phenomena, and they cast light on the community or society in which they are celebrated. All this suggests that holidays deserve much more sociological attention than they have received in recent decades and points to the merits as well as the limits of using holidays as macrosociological indicators.

Holidays as Socialization Agents

To move beyond the Durkheimian starting point, one must recognize that Durkheim basically treats all rituals (holidays included) as if they are of one kind, in the sense that they all fulfill one societal "function": fostering integration by reinforcing shared beliefs.[20] To put the same proposition in somewhat different sociological terms, holidays serve to socialize members of a society as well as to reaffirm their commitments to values, and as such, holidays serve to sustain the integration of society. (Socialization, it is widely recognized, is not limited to the young; adults are continuously socialized in the sense that social processes and resources are dedicated to recommit adults to existing beliefs or introduce them to new ones.)

Although there is no reason to doubt that all holidays, to some extent, serve a socializing function, I suggest that (a) different holidays play different societal roles—indeed, no two holidays serve the same societal role—and (b) not all holidays are integrative. (The last proposition assumes that one holds constant one's frame of reference; a holiday may be integrative for one group or another but may not be integrative for the society at large, as Durkheim suggests.)

To proceed, one must first note that there is no agreed-upon typology of holidays to draw on, let alone one based on the societal roles fulfilled by various holidays. Some scholars have arranged holidays by the seasons they mark; others have called attention to each holiday's role in the lives of the individuals involved (rather than to the societal roles of holidays); still others see holidays as largely rooted in history.[21] I attempt here to provide a typology based on the varying societal roles fulfilled by different holidays.

Probably the most important distinction among holidays from this viewpoint is between those that use narratives, drama, and ceremonies to directly enforce commitments to shared beliefs—which I shall refer to as *recommitment holidays*—and those that fulfill this role indirectly by releasing tensions that result from the close adherence to beliefs, which I term *tension management holidays*.[22] One and the same holiday may work in both ways, but my own very preliminary and informal survey suggests that, in those societies I am familiar with, each holiday serves in one way more than in the other. (However, such a primacy is changeable over time, as we shall see below.)

Recommitment holidays are most familiar; they are the ones that Durkheim had in mind, and they are commonly associated with his integration thesis. Easter and Passover are typical holidays of recommitment. Easter dramatizes and extols the essential message of Christianity: the resurrection of Christ, the joy and fulfillment of redemption, and the rebirth and reaffirmation of faith. The holiday is marked by specific and elaborate rituals such as services at sunrise and the use of rousing music to celebrate the Resurrection. Passover is built around the reading of the Haggadah, a narrative openly dedicated to socialization with a special focus on children. The Passover Seder ritual is rich with symbols that entail reaffirmation of one's commitment to the beliefs of political liberty, deliverance by a supernatural force, and the perseverance of Judaism as a distinct cultural identity and tradition. The implied sociological-Durkheimian hypothesis is that those who share the particular Christian or Jewish beliefs at issue and who participate in these holidays will be more committed to the shared beliefs and institutions of their respective communities after participation than they were before. (To test this proposition by comparing the intensity of beliefs of those who participate in said rituals to the intensity of beliefs of those who do not participate is somewhat more difficult, due to the effects of self-selection.)[23]

While holidays of recommitment are expected to directly serve socialization and societal integration, holidays of tension management are expected to serve societal integration indirectly and therefore pose a higher risk of malfunction. Holidays of tension management include New Year's Eve, Mardi Gras, Purim, Oktoberfest, and their equivalents in other cultures. (Whether or not Halloween belongs in this category is a matter of considerable conjecture, which cannot be resolved here.[24] April Fools' Day also belongs in this category, although it is hardly a holiday.) During these holidays, mores that are upheld during the rest of the year are suspended to allow for indulgence, and some forms of behavior usually considered asocial, and hence disintegrative, are temporarily accepted.

Anthropologists report that in some societies there are holidays in which daughters-in-law are permitted to insult their mothers-in-law. New Year's office parties are known for suspending mores against excessive consumption of alcohol and sexual infidelity. During Mardi Gras in New Orleans, thousands of students expose themselves on the balconies in the French Quarter. Jews, usually warned against interrupting their studies of scripture for idle chatter and even for appreciation of aesthetic beauty, are allowed to play games on Purim.

In theory, tension management holidays are expected to indirectly contribute to the reinforcement of shared beliefs and institutions by releasing tension that results from conformity to societal beliefs and the behavioral prescriptions they entail. The underlying theoretical assumption is that people cannot be fully socialized and that sublimation will not be fully successful. Therefore, the reasoning follows, there will be a significant and accumulative residue of alienation to all commitments, even if they are not imposed by some foreign power or cultural or political elite.[25] Occasional release of this tension is expected to enhance socialization (and resocialization).

The extent to which tension management holidays, which tend to occur every few months, actually serve to vent tension, or at least keep it at a low level, has, as far as I can establish, not been a subject of empirical study. There seems to be no systematic evidence that people who return to work after New Year's Day have a stronger commitment to their duties than before, although Jack Santino suggests that people do return to work "psychologically refreshed" after the holidays. (He does not suggest how long such "refreshment" lasts.)[26] The proposition that holidays fulfill such a role should be treated as a hypothesis rather than a finding.

Tension management holidays that set clear time limits are expected to be more integrative than those that do not. ("Time limits" refer to points in time after which participants are expected to return to the conformist modes of behavior that reflect shared societal beliefs.) It is as if society fears that once its members experience the raw satisfaction that results from suspended mores, members might be reluctant to return to the tighter restraints of their social roles. (A similar point has been made about people recovering from an illness who are reluctant to return to work because of the "secondary gains" of being sick, that is, being legitimately exempted from numerous duties such as working and attending to household chores. Physicians—and rules governing sick pay—are used to curb such tendencies.)[27] Thus, Mardi Gras is followed by a recommitment on Ash Wednesday. New Year's Eve is followed in the United States by one day of vacation (New Year's Day), but there is a clear expectation that on the following day people must return to work. Several religions set a clear time limit on mourning and for the conclusion of other rituals, as Judaism does at the end of the Sabbath. In contrast, for secular mourning there is no clear time limit.

Bachelor and bachelorette parties, which presumably serve to vent tension on the eve of weddings, are bounded by the wedding date itself. They also provide a telling case of how "tension management" holidays may cause tension rather than relieve it. Weddings in contemporary America are not fraught with the same level of tension they may have generated in earlier generations, but conduct in these rituals that violates norms, especially infidelity, can cause tension in the marriages that follow. Similarly, New Year's Eve office parties may now offer less tension relief than they did in earlier generations, as work relations have grown more informal and less hierarchical. These parties can, however, *generate* a considerable amount of tension if behavior strays beyond the norms to a greater extent than is allowed, as in practically all tension management holidays. Teasing the boss may be acceptable; going off on a public drunken tirade about his or her misconduct may not be, and so on.

The relative importance that a society attaches to recommitment versus tension management holidays is an indicator of the state of its value integrity and enforcement. In Israel, during the pioneering days when commitments to hard work and the common good were paramount—especially in the collective settlements, as well as in earlier, more religious periods in the Jewish diaspora—value reinforcement holidays were much celebrated, while those of the tension management variety were given short shrift. Passover was a major holiday during both of these eras, while Purim was notably less important.

As stated previously, the Passover Seder is used to retell and share with children the importance of freedom, as well as other values, through the reading of the Haggadah, the holiday's main text. (These readings vary according to which Jewish group has revised the particular Haggadah used. There are homosexual, feminist, and socialist Haggadot aside from the traditional ones, though all serve to reinforce values.) As in all holidays and rituals, Passover uses symbols to communicate its lessons. These symbols are concentrated around the items arranged on the Seder plate, which stand for the bitterness of slavery (bitter herbs), the sweetness of redemption (*charoset*), and the "passing over" of the Israelites when the Egyptians were struck by the tenth plague (lamb shank bone). The lineup and significance of these items varies somewhat from community to community. Many feminists, for instance, add an orange to the plate, a practice that began as a rejoinder to a rabbi who stated that women belong on the *bimah* (dais for leading prayers) the way "an orange belongs on the Seder plate."

Purim, in contrast, is a quintessential tension management holiday. The holiday begins with a reading of the Megillah, a scroll containing the Book of Esther. However, the reading of the Megillah is no solemn affair. Children and adults may come in costume, and whenever the name of the villain of the story is read aloud, the congregation hisses, stomps their feet, or shakes noisemakers. Once the reading of the Megillah concludes, celebrants are expected to consume alcoholic drinks—according to tradition, one is supposed to become so intoxicated that he cannot distinguish between Haman, the villain, and Mordecai, the heroic cousin of Esther.

Over recent decades, as commitment to traditional kibbutz values has declined in Israel, Purim has moved up at least a notch or two, if not more, in Israelis' esteem. Passover is still a major holiday, but not as central as it used to be. While we don't have a holiday in the United States whose decline in importance exactly parallels that of Passover in Israel, Halloween, like Purim, has escalated in importance over the last few decades—during the same years that the seedbeds of virtue are said to have thinned out.[28]

As with all historical comparisons, if one uses changes in the relative weight of recommitment versus tension management holidays as an indicator of the state of the values of the community or society involved, one's observations will be affected by the baseline used, that is, whatever earlier period one chooses to compare to current or more recent events. Thus, compared to the 1950s, holidays in the contemporary United States may well seem less oriented toward recommitment and more toward tension management, but this observation will change if one uses, say, the 1850s as one's baseline. Elizabeth Pleck notes that tension management holidays (which she calls "carnivalesque") used to be much more prevalent during the eighteenth and nineteenth centuries: There were shooting matches at Christmas, gander pulling on Shrove Tuesday or Easter Monday, and sexual orgies on Pinkster. She views the decline of rowdy, bawdy celebrations over the last two centuries as the result of a decreasing willingness of the middle class to tolerate "routine rowdiness as a form of cathartic release among the lower orders, especially lower-class men."[29] This attitude grew out of middle-class Victorian conventions, an increasing focus on family privacy, and the general rise of holidays as "domestic occasions." With the decline of the carnivalesque celebrations came the rise of home- and family-centered American rituals such as Thanksgiving.[30]

Gary Cross's essay in this volume is an illustration of the ways in which the very nature of holidays themselves can transform over time. Cross traces the evolution of American holidays from their "carnivalesque" beginnings to the "child-centered" rituals that we see today. He argues that nineteenth-century reforms have made contemporary American holidays, which tend to focus on the innocence of "the wondrous child," unrecognizable from the rowdy celebrations of the nation's past.

In other words, when recent times are compared to the 1850s, one finds that tension management holidays have *declined* and that those of the reinforcement variety have *increased*. That is, as we change the baseline, so changes the magnitude of difference between the baseline period and recent and/or current times. Nonetheless, whatever baseline one uses, holidays can still inform us about changes in the level of recommitment and tension in a given society.

In testing the preceding hypotheses, and others that follow, one must take into account that while holidays are largely of one kind or the other, they are not pure types. A recommitment holiday may include some opportunities for indulgence and suspension of mores (for instance, those entailed in work), and tension management holidays may include some recommitment (for instance, prayers), but the dominant activities tend to be of one kind or the other.

Unity, Diversity, and Relations among the Parts

Critics may question whether a functional analysis of holidays biases the analysis in a conservative direction. Indeed, the analysis so far has focused on one societal role, that of evolving and sustaining commitments to prevailing societal beliefs and the behavioral expectations they entail. We shall see below that holidays also serve as opportunities for societal change, by providing occasions to symbolize and embody new conceptions of social relations and entities. This is illustrated in the development of new roles for women in religious holidays, especially for rituals in the home.

I turn next to show that holidays can and are employed to strengthen commitments to a great variety of societal entities rather than only to uphold the dominant society's values; these entities include social movements, ethnic or racial groups, deviant religious denominations, and still other societal entities that challenge established regimes or seek to form new societies.[31] Like pipelines, holidays are largely indifferent to the content of the normative "flows" they facilitate.

Although for a preliminary approximation it might suffice to propose that various attributes of holidays (such as their prevalence, number of participants, and the strength of recommitment that they evoke) correlate negatively with societal disintegration, this proposition must be further specified. Because many, if not all, holidays may have some kind of an integrative function, I hypothesize that numerous holidays that help integrate some societal entities have the opposite effect on others. Returning to my starting point, to the work of Durkheim, one notes that he focuses on the integrative function of rituals for whole societies and for societies that did not have significant internal divisions, at least none that he recognized. This approach is best understood if one takes into account not only the utilitarian and individualistic bodies of thought Durkheim was challenging, but also that his empirical base observations were drawn from studying Australian totemism. That is, he was dealing with a very small society with a high level of homogeneity and integration.

A theory of holidays applicable to complex societies needs to abandon the assumption that holidays are necessarily unifiers of societies and specify which social entities they are serving. Instead, it should be assumed that (a) while holidays do include an integrative mechanism, this mechanism may work to solidify social groups and not necessarily a whole society (indeed, an examination of the holidays of a given society can serve as an indicator of the level of unity of that society), (b) the integrative effects of holidays on the society will depend on the relationships among such groups and between the groups and the society-at-large, which can vary from confrontational to complementary, and (c) these relationships can in turn be changed, and tensions "worked through," during holidays.[32] Some illustrative observations, which give some preliminary and limited support for the preceding propositions, follow.

An example of a holiday that encompasses and unifies most members of a community is provided by observations of the celebrations of

Passover in early small and homogeneous Israeli kibbutzim. In contrast, in contemporary American society, one finds—in addition to some holidays that are widely, although not universally, shared on a national level (e.g., Memorial Day)—numerous holidays that are specific to one religious group or another (e.g., Christmas and Hanukkah), to one ethnic group or another (e.g., St. Patrick's Day, Kwanzaa, Cinco de Mayo, Chinese New Year), or, much less often, to a particular socioeconomic class (May Day).[33]

If there were systematic evidence indicating whether or not all these various differences in the ways holidays are practiced by various social entities have increased or decreased over a specific period (for instance, during the second half of the twentieth century) in a given society, this would provide a global indicator of the extent to which that society, in that period, had become more fragmented or more unified. For instance, one would expect that the rising diversity and intergroup tension in American society since 1960 would be reflected in a rising diversity in the way holidays are celebrated by various ethnic and racial groups. Lacking systematic evidence to this effect, one must either rely on casual and informal observations or regard the preceding statements as strictly theoretical propositions.

Holidays can serve to modify the relationships between societal parts and the whole, to the extent that such a whole exists. In some ceremonies, conscious and systematic efforts are made to ensure that a particular group holiday does not undermine the commitment to the whole. One symbolic expression of the commitment to the whole is to display flags during parades, ceremonial speeches, and prayers. When a group in the United States seeks to reinforce its members' commitments not only to the group but also to the society at large, the celebrants often display both ethnic flags (e.g., Italian) and the Stars and Stripes.[34] Most speakers, religious functionaries, and community leaders—if the said disposition is sought—are careful to include ". . . and God bless America" or some other such expression to indicate their loyalty to the whole, stressing that their group upholds dual loyalties, and hence, its particularistic commitments do not conflict with its commitment to the larger national society.

Ellen Litwicki's analysis of ethnic celebrations in Chicago between 1876 and 1918 (chapter 12 in this volume) provides a telling example of the tension that exists between ethnicity and assimilation. Drawing much of her evidence from ethnic newspapers, Litwicki makes a compelling case that these groups used holiday celebrations to consciously represent both their ethnic history and their loyalty to the United States, creating what she refers to as "mutually reinforcing identities."

Cinco de Mayo offers a different view of the way holidays reflect diversity within a society. The holiday commemorates the Mexicans' defeat of the French at the Battle of Puebla on May 5, 1862. Over the past decades, Mexican immigrants and Mexican Americans have begun to celebrate Cinco de Mayo in growing numbers. A traditional celebration of the holiday once typically involved a dance, which was preceded by a civic program including speeches highlighting the historical significance of the holiday, poems expressing Mexican patriotism, and/or theatrical reenactments.

Through the 1950s, such celebrations were held in a few states in the southwestern United States. With the rise of the Chicano movement, the celebration of Cinco de Mayo was expanded and transformed into a more general celebration of ethnic heritage and an opportunity to advance the political goals of a particular ethnic group. The holiday was increasingly promoted as more than the commemoration of a battle in a war for Mexican independence; it was also a celebration of shared culture and heritage that would "galvanize group emotions and affirm group identity."[35] Schools in areas with large Mexican-American populations began to use the occasion of Cinco de Mayo to incorporate Hispanic events and traditions into their curricula. Chicano student activists at colleges and universities organized Cinco de Mayo events that paired traditional festive elements such as a fiesta and dancing with features meant to reinforce cultural identity (ballet folkloricos, mariachi music, and teatros) and political solidarity (displays of politically based art and speeches addressing current political issues and the significance of the holiday for all colonized peoples).[36]

Yet Cinco de Mayo's transformation into a major festival of ethnic pride has now been superseded by a second transformation: into a holiday with cross-cultural appeal. By the 1980s, Cinco de Mayo festivals could be found in twenty-one U.S. states, and the holiday is now known and celebrated across the United States. It has been increasingly embraced not only by non-Mexican Hispanics but also by non-Hispanic Americans. At a typical Cinco de Mayo celebration in Oklahoma City, an observer found the scene "perplexing." On the one hand, much of the music, food, and souvenirs he encountered seemed typically Mexican. On the other hand, "The sea of Chicano and non-Chicano faces, the tacos, Cokes and corndogs [he] passed suggested Cinco de Mayo was on the verge of becoming another Fourth of July."

Today, some would say that Cinco de Mayo's relationship with Mexico is like St. Patrick's Day's relationship with Ireland. The holidays' ethnic roots are still clear, but both have become genuinely American rituals: American companies sponsor Cinco de Mayo parties in the western and southwestern United States, and supermarkets and other retailers offer Mexican and Hispanic goods to mark the occasion.[37] As with St. Patrick's Day, celebration of Cinco de Mayo in its country of origin is fairly subdued. Cinco de Mayo rituals that have become de rigueur in the United States—huge, often multi-day parties, with fried food, alcoholic drinks, mariachi music, and, generally, a carnival atmosphere—are practically unknown in Mexico.[38]

Clearly not all particularistic holidays are celebrated in such a dual (group- and society-building) manner. Some group celebrations are disintegrative for the society as a whole, are openly oppositional and challenge the societal mores and symbols, or even serve as outright expressions of a breakaway from the societal whole or from some other group. Native Americans, especially the Wampanoag, have used Thanksgiving as a protest holiday, a day of fasting and mourning.[39] Several New York City schools also adopted this protest perspective, teaching children that Thanksgiving marks a day on which "'strange looking' people . . . landed in the family's backyard and proceeded to ransack their homes, cut down their trees, kill their pets, and take tomatoes from their gardens."[40] Intense debates about Columbus Day mark similar societal divisions, with some seeing the day as a recognition of a great discovery by the man who opened the door for the creation of the American society, while others view the day as a celebration of a brutal killer and conqueror who should not be lionized.[41]

Francesca Polletta's essay in this volume looks at the relationship between holidays and protest, especially with respect to public demonstrations during holiday celebrations. She finds that public rituals provide ripe opportunities for dissenters to communicate that they are staying true to the values of the holiday while other celebrants are not. She goes on to argue that this dissension can actually breed unity by welcoming disagreement.

Kwanzaa was originally a protest holiday of sorts, invented by black nationalist Maulana Karenga in the 1960s as an alternative to Christmas and to help American blacks reconnect with their African ancestry and protect themselves from domination by white values and the holidays that enforce them. According to his own account, Karenga took the name "Kwanzaa" from the Swahili phrase *matunta ya kwanza*, meaning "first fruits." Karenga's authoritative book, *The African American Holiday of Kwanzaa*, explains that the holiday is a harvest festival that celebrates seven core values, over the course of seven days (December 26 through January 1). A menorah-like ornament called a *kinara* holds seven candles, which are to be lit in sequence to honor each value: unity, self-determination, collective work and responsibility, cooperative economics, purpose, creativity, and faith. The last night of the holiday, December 31, is a time when families gather for a communal feast (*karamu*). All these elements, according to Karenga, are meant to foster values and principles that represent traditions from all regions of Africa in an effort to "reaffirm African culture" and, in conjunction with this, serve as a "political act of self-determination."[42]

The early promoters of Kwanzaa were members of US, a group that included political activists such as Karenga and LeRoi Jones, who is now known as the radical poet Amiri Baraka.[43] (Baraka gained notoriety for his poem "Somebody Blew Up America," which suggested that Israelis received advance warning of the September 11 attack on the World Trade Center.)

However, over time, Kwanzaa has become more mainstream. In the past twenty years, stores have begun to sell Kwanzaa cards, wrapping paper, teddy bears, and cookbooks. Kwanzaa celebrations have moved from the home to churches, community centers, and schools.[44] And many schools have incorporated Kwanzaa into their multicultural curricula.

In her enlightening essay in this volume, Anna Day Wilde examines the evolution of Kwanzaa from a protest-driven holiday into a mainstream cultural celebration for the African-American community. She argues that the development of Kwanzaa into a "middle-class holiday" is consistent with the notion of multiculturalism, whereby middle-class blacks attempt to reconnect with their African roots while still trying to integrate themselves into a "pluralist" society.

Holidays can also be used to work out a new relationship between society and a member group and, in the process, advance and ritualize a change in the beliefs of those involved. That is, integration is achieved as Durkheim would expect but in a way he did not consider: by changing the beliefs around which society congeals. (The point is not that Durkheim did not recognize changes in symbols and rituals, but that his theory did not allow for changes in the level of societal integration that are achieved, in part, by changing the content of holidays, as is hypothesized here.) Some illustrative examples follow.

The establishment of a holiday honoring the late Martin Luther King Jr. has been an ongoing source of contention. Initially, the idea that there should be a holiday marking Martin Luther King Jr.'s birthday was met with considerable opposition, especially from conservatives, including President Ronald Reagan. But after fifteen years of considerable lobbying by civil rights groups, the government declared King's birthday a federal holiday in 1986. Those opposed to declaring the day an official holiday generally offered either an economic argument ("we can't afford to give workers another paid holiday") or an argument that Martin Luther King Jr., as an individual, was not worthy of having his own holiday.[45] Such contentions were generally rejected by proponents of the new federal holiday, who often claimed that objections to Martin Luther King Jr. Day were rooted in racism.[46]

Many states initially resisted establishing King's birthday as an official holiday and were only gradually won over. Kentucky and North Dakota recognized the day, but not as a paid holiday. Conservative Arizona was particularly slow to join the other states in this regard. New Hampshire chose to follow its individualistic streak and declared a Civil Rights Day in place of King's birthday. South Carolina's legislature finally agreed to recognize the day as a state holiday in 2000—but the state's House of Representatives amended the legislation to remove King's name, instead calling the day, like New Hampshire, "Civil Rights Day." Other states recognized Martin Luther King Jr. Day, but not as a paid holiday.[47]

While many believe that Martin Luther King Jr. Day is the first "African-American holiday" that is also a holiday for all Americans (in contrast to, say, Kwanzaa or Emancipation Day), some African Americans remain wary of attempts to universalize King's identity, and, at the same time, the holiday is still more actively celebrated by African Americans than by whites.[48] Debates persist today about whether the holiday should be focused on Martin Luther King Jr.'s advancement of black civil rights in particular or whether it should be a time for more-general consideration of the need for tolerance of diversity.

The process that led to the inauguration of Martin Luther King Jr. Day, as well as its implications, are explored in Matthew Dennis's essay in this volume. Beyond providing an important historical account of the process, Dennis also explores the motivations and emotions that guided both sides of the debate.

A much more successful example of how holidays can allow us to work through an intergroup difference can be seen in the participation of Vietnam veterans in parades and other activities on Veteran's Day. Initially, the refusal of large segments of society to treat Vietnam veterans as returning heroes or as individuals who served their country on par with those who fought in the First and Second World Wars caused many to be reluctant to participate in these parades. Nor could Vietnam veterans expect a warm welcome from other veterans who did march.[49] However, as the rift over Vietnam gradually healed in the early 1990s, Vietnam veterans participated much more often in these parades, were more warmly received by the public at large and by other veterans, and felt more positive about participating in these national ceremonial occasions.[50] In Chicago in 1994, Mayor Richard Daley conducted a ceremony that officially honored Vietnam veterans.[51] In 1995, the city council of Berkeley, California, once a center of anti–Vietnam War protests, held a commemoration on Veteran's Day honoring those who fought in the Vietnam War.[52]

The extent to which the entire holiday calendar (or cycle) is shared by a given society tends to be representative of the degree to which that society is integrated and unified. It follows that groups seeking to establish a firm boundary between themselves and the rest of society would be inclined to eschew this holiday calendar.[53] This is true, for instance, for various Amish communities, in which holidays serve to reinforce group identity as well as to emphasize separation from other societal groups and the larger national community. The Amish calendar does not include such public holidays as George Washington's Birthday, Martin Luther King Jr. Day, Memorial Day, the Fourth of July, and Labor Day. (The Amish do recognize Thanksgiving and New Year's Day, in addition to holy days that are not recognized by many other Americans, including Easter Monday, Pentecost Monday, Ascension Day, and a Second Christmas on December 26.)

All this suggests that, to advance a theory of holidays, one must strongly modify Durkheim's notion that holidays serve to integrate a *society* and recognize that, while they may solidify various social groups, the relationships of these groups to the societal whole may vary from being highly complementary, and hence integrative, to being rather conflictive and *dis*integrative. The relationship may range from being one in which a group is self-aware and well-defined, yet deeply integrated into a more encompassing whole, to one characterized by hostile relations or even civil war (Kurds in Turkey, for instance). Additionally, groups that started as conformist may draw on reinterpretation of holidays to aggrandize their distinctiveness, while hostile subgroups—and the societies in which they are situated—may reformulate holidays as part of the reconstruction of society, its core beliefs, and its relation to member groups.

In short, (a) whether or not a given holiday is integrative cannot be assumed by merely observing that a holiday is celebrated, even if it is well attended and celebrants are deeply involved. In addition, one needs to specify the reference unit: Which entity is being integrated, the society as a whole, some other social entity, or both? (b) the nature of the relationship between this entity and the society needs to be examined, as reflected in the given holiday, and (c) one needs to introduce a dynamic perspective that calls attention to the fact that holidays that originally integrated a group into society as a whole may change to undermine that bond or that holidays that originally served to divide may help work through differences to enhance not only the internal integration of a particular group but also the integration of the society as a whole.

Public versus Private Holidays

Durkheim assumes that holidays are public events, in the sense that members of tribes assemble as one group in one space, and the rituals involved are shared by and visible to one and all. It follows that this integrative function cannot be served, at least not as well, if holidays are celebrated privately by individuals (or their families) in their huts, shanties, or suburban homes, and not in public squares, parade grounds, or other points of assembly.

Durkheim's hypothesis finds some initial support in numerous reports of communal celebrations of holidays in nonliterate tribes as well as in Western societies, at least in the pre-industrial era. In eighteenth-century rural America, when society was more homogeneous and most communities were much smaller than contemporary ones, holidays were often celebrated in public spaces. For example, a typical Fourth of July celebration centered on a parade that ended up in a church, where the crowd was blessed and shared a communal meal.[54] Marriages were also communal occasions, not family events.

David Procter's essay in this volume is a case study of a contemporary community celebration in Kansas known as Victorian Days. In observing and evaluating the behavior of the festival's celebrants, Procter shows that the planning and celebration of these days helps to create a sense of "civic communion."

In contrast, in recent decades, families or other small groups have celebrated more holidays in private homes.[55] The Fourth of July is now often observed at private picnics, outings with friends or co-workers, or in back-yard barbecues, as the holiday has become less focused on commitment to the national community. Thanksgiving is reported to have initially been observed as a communal holiday that Pilgrims and Native Americans cele-brated together, but since that time it has become mainly a family holiday.

Still, it is far from established that the privatization of holidays is neces-sarily disintegrative. There is some support for the hypothesis that private rituals can engender recommitment to the society at large in the same way publicly shared rituals do and that some holidays can encompass both the private and the public. (Talcott Parsons, for instance, suggests that holi-days can be integrative even if celebrated privately as long as the commit-ment to the society at large is recognized.)[56]

By and large, though, one can still determine a sort of private/public ratio of holidays and assess which side is gaining and which is losing in a given period or in a particular society. Religions, for instance, differ in the extent to which they rely on rituals that take place in public spaces, such as Sunday rituals in churches or Sabbath in synagogues, as compared to those that build on family-based rituals that take place in private homes, or a mix of both. Easter, for instance, is more public than Passover. Christ-mas and Hanukkah mix both public and private rituals, but the balance between their two fronts has changed over the decades, strengthening the private and truncating the public.

Even in those shared, communal events that remain popular, some evi-dence suggests that the outward appearance of what Victor Turner called *communitas*[57] (fellowship) does not reflect actual bonding. For instance, one might expect public celebrations of the kind that take place during Mardi Gras to create a sense of communal well-being or "emotional fu-sion" in the large, diverse group of celebrants who gather for the festivities. In order to determine whether festival and carnival environments actually promote a transformation in the ways people relate to one another, William Jankowiak and Todd White observed group interactions in New Orleans on several occasions: Mardi Gras week, a Christmas parade, a "nonfestival Saturday evening," and Fat Tuesday.[58] The researchers ob-served individuals alone and in different group formations (dyads, triads, or larger groupings), and they recorded different types of behavior (con-versing, touching, hand holding, kissing, gift exchanging). They also noted "unusual behavior." On all occasions, there was very little interaction be-tween noncostumed strangers.[59] Many of the public interactions that were observed hardly indicate the warmth of *communitas*: Sexual catcalls, particularly from men to women, were especially prominent. The few other out-group interactions were not much deeper than requests for directions. The greatest amount of out-group interaction (interactions between strangers) occurred when one or more of the individuals was in costume or when there was an exchange of beads (during Mardi Gras). The costumes and beads of the Mardi Gras ritual functioned as "material props" that seemed to ease out-group conversation and other interaction.[60] However, even on Fat Tuesday, the people who gathered in New Orleans remained a basically anonymous crowd of spectators, observing a parade behind police barricades and reaffirming their relationships with the people they knew before they arrived.[61] All this points to the need to specify under what conditions public holidays generate the kind of communal bonding (what Robert Putnam calls "social capital")[62] one often assumes to take place merely because the holiday is celebrated in public rather than in private spaces. Moreover, there is some reason to suggest that the retreat from public activities to more atomized experiences is further extended even within private spaces.

A related question is whether the increased privatization of holidays reflects an adaptation of holidays to the decline in the level of integration in society or vice versa—whether the privatization of holidays helped cause a decline in societal integration, as Durkheim would have it, or whether both take place simultaneously, reinforcing each other. The observations that are available tend to suggest that an increase in privatization is much more affected by societal factors than the other way around. Among the factors cited are a decline in public safety, an increase in the level of heterogeneity, and the decline of close (or "primary") relations in growing cities.[63] We can see this, for instance, in the recent transformation of Halloween. While the modern American Halloween was always something of a tension management holiday, it was also a holiday that affirmed the vitality and stability of a community. In recent decades, however, for many children, trick-or-treating no longer entails walking from house to house in their own neighborhood, knocking on doors, begging for candy, and being welcomed by people who know them. Often parents are afraid to let their children wander around after dark and/or do not know or trust their neighbors. Some parents drive their children to malls, which have taken advantage of parents' fears by offering "alternative" Halloween activities. Other parents drive their children across town to a safer neighborhood. Thus, what was once a holiday centered on interactions within the local community has become a more private and/or anonymous experience.

That is, the increase in private holiday celebrations is said to reflect a general decline in the bonding that ties small social entities to a society and in the level of individual commitments to the society. It also reflects a growing loyalty to particularistic groups (ethnic, religious, etc.), small intimate social circles, and an emphasis on personal achievement and interests. It is no surprise, then, that individualism rose between 1960 and 1990 in American society, the same years during which holidays have become less public.[64]

It should also be noted that since 1990, following increased concern about the rising level of individualism and the decline of public spaces, limited attempts have been made to restore the public nature of holidays. For instance, a community in Ontario, California, annually sets up a two-mile-long table, around which many members of the community, from divergent social backgrounds, are reported to picnic together on the Fourth of July.[65] Furthermore, there are some reports about a rise in efforts to celebrate holidays in "artificial" extended families for single parents, other singles, gays and lesbians, and still others who seek communities that are more extensive than their households, especially during holidays.[66] Following the decline of crime in major cities in the United States, there has been some return to the old, more communitarian patterns and a decline in paranoia; very few parents brought apples and candy to be x-rayed to avoid razor blades in the first years of the twenty-first century as compared to the 1980s. That is, as the American society has begun, roughly as of 1990, to restore its communal elements, one witnesses some attempts to shore up the public elements of holidays.

A major factor that deeply affects both public and private holidays— both the balance between the two as well as the values expressed and undermined by them—is the profit motive, especially in its institutionalized form. It deeply affects almost everything, from the ways weddings and funerals are carried out to the ways in which Christmas is celebrated; it creates new holidays on which one is expected to send and receive greeting cards; and it elevates material goods and undermines spirituality. This increasing commodification of holidays is not further studied here, both despite and because of its prominence. Its effects are already very well known, making commercialization arguably the only aspect of this subject that is well covered.[67] Even so, this trend deserves a whole new and separate analysis, especially one focused on how to restore less-materialistic rituals.

The Significance of the Holiday Cycle

To advance a sociological theory beyond Durkheim's work, one must determine the sociological significance of the fact that in most, if not all, societies holidays are repeated over time and in the same sequence. While I was unable to find a comparative study directly focused on this point, an informal survey of numerous cultures suggests that a fixed and annual sequence of holidays is one of the most robust observations one can make based on cross-cultural comparisons, in the sense that it can be seen in societies that differ a great deal on numerous other accounts.[68]

The question for the sociologist is: What is the societal significance of the particular sequence in which holidays are arranged? To suggest that holidays follow the climatic seasons per se may be true, but it casts little sociological light on the matter, unless one uncovers the social reasons why some seasons are ritualized while others are ignored.[69]

One interesting sociological hypothesis that has been advanced in this context deals with what might be called holiday subcycles. For instance, Theodore Caplow (whose essay, drawn from the seminal Middletown study, is included in this volume) notes that holidays focused on children—Christmas, for instance—are preceded and followed by festivities that are built around aggressive, sexual, adult themes (e.g., Christmas is preceded by office parties and followed by New Year's Eve) and that major holidays are organized in a particular sequence in order to emphasize specific values at specific times of the year.[70] We have already noted the difference between recommitment and tension management holidays; the hypothesis should be added here that these two kinds of holidays will alternate, rather than holidays of one kind being followed by more of the same.

The underlying assumption of both Caplow's team's observation and the hypothesis advanced here is that the service to various societal needs is arranged in a sequence so that after one need is attended to, attention to the other gains predominance. The question of this hypothesis, developed on the basis of informal observation of a few holidays, can be extended to all holidays. It requires a macroanalysis of societal needs to determine if they are all served by one holiday or another. Only after this is completed can one seek to determine whether societies whose holidays are "properly" sequenced show a lower level of social tension, a higher level of integration, and a greater commitment to their shared values than societies whose holidays are out of sequence for one reason or another, perhaps as a result of the attempts at social engineering introduced by totalitarian governments or, more recently, by religious fundamentalist ones.[71]

Restructuring of Gender and Kinship Roles: A Lagging Sector

Durkheim, dealing with small homogeneous societies, assumed that they were monolithic; he characterized whole societies either as well integrated or as suffering from a lack of integration. However, for complex societies, it should be hypothesized that change in some sectors will lag after developments in others. And, based on some very preliminary and informal observations, outlined below, a plausible hypothesis is that holidays tend to lag rather than lead societal change, and the more they lag the more they hinder rather than advance societal integration. The reason is that some members of society are likely to be more involved in the leading segment of society (for instance, those younger than fifty years of age) while others might be more involved in the lagging segments (those sixty-five years of age or older). Hence, the greater the sectorial lag, the more tension one would expect between the social groups involved.

This hypothesis can be illustrated by changes in women's roles in the preparation for and celebration of holidays. Women's roles in holidays seem to have been akin to their roles in other parts of the socialization and moral reinforcement institutional infrastructure. Thus, in relatively traditional American society—in the 1950s, for instance—women were charged with preparing the celebratory meals, shopping for gifts, promoting the holiday spirit, and so on.[72] Similar accounts are available from some earlier periods; for instance, the Pilgrim dinner, to which native Americans were invited and which laid the foundation for the first Thanksgiving in 1623, is reported to have been prepared exclusively by women.[73]

As the feminist movement started to challenge women's roles in the 1960s, their holiday roles were also recast—but these changes seem to have lagged behind other changes in society, and there is a significant measure of regression toward traditional mores during holidays. There is some evidence to support the preceding statements: Even in those households where women work outside the home and husbands assume some household and childcare responsibilities, women still do a disproportionate share of the inviting, planning and preparing, cooking, and serving of holiday meals; and above all, women are expected to ensure the warm glow of the holiday spirit.[74]

Elizabeth Pleck's chapter in this volume, cited numerous times throughout the book, is an examination of family-centered holiday rituals, including the role of women within them and how these roles have varied over time and between ethnic groups. She argues that the domestication of holidays thrusts women into the role of "queen of the home," while also stressing the importance of status and wealth in ritual celebrations.

All this is not to suggest that changes in women's societal roles have not been reflected in the internal structure of holidays. Some women lead religious services in both communal and home-based rituals in several religious denominations, and some have been ordained for posts from which they previously had been excluded; a fair number of Jews have added Bat Mitzvah (for girls) to Bar Mitzvah and rituals for naming girls to parallel the Bris. In Jewish congregations, there have been several attempts to edit sexist language out of traditional texts, for instance, by reading "she" (or alternating between "she" and "he") whenever the Lord is referred to as masculine.

We also find fewer differences between the genders in nonreligious rituals. Bachelorette parties have become increasingly raunchy—even as some bachelor parties have grown tamer. One popular activity at contemporary bachelorette parties is the "racy scavenger hunt." In this party "game," the bride-to-be is required, for example, to approach men on the street and ask them for a condom or to procure a piece of underwear from the man wearing it.[75]

One of the most indicative changes in the way holidays are celebrated and rituals are performed is the splitting of traditional gender roles, which reflects changes in the structures of the nuclear family and, more widely, kinship structures. Whereas formerly only one father-role and one mother-role existed, there are now several versions of each, referred to as "natural" versus "social" fathers, parents versus stepparents, "biological grandparents" versus step-grandparents, and so on. The increasing complexity of roles and relations is reflected in the inclusion in family holidays of a large number of people who are related neither by blood nor by marriage, but by former marriages, which one wit has half-jokingly called the "ex-kinship structure."

A considerable etiquette has developed for addressing who "gives away" the bride (i.e., the natural father or the stepfather) and the place of the natural mother during the wedding ceremony, as well as in rituals such as confirmations and B'nai Mitzvah when there is a stepmother. These examples indicate role changes, as the society is struggling to come to terms with new gender, and related family, structures. However, since these changes are not widely recognized, codified, or institutionalized, they are lending further support to the hypothesis that the internal restructuring of holidays lags behind other major societal changes and, hence, hinders rather than serves integration, as the adaptation of one part of the society—holidays—lags behind the others.

The essay by Mary Whiteside in this volume details, from a psychological perspective, the role of family rituals in creating kinship connections within families that include remarried parents. Her main thesis is that holidays are critical times during which the futures of remarried families (in terms of their similarity to "normal" nuclear families) are shaped and reinforced.

Editing and Engineering Holidays

Durkheim often treats societies and their holidays as given or as evolving under the impact of unfolding historical and social forces, and not as subject to deliberate societal change.[76] Modern societies, though, are to some extent engineered and are subject to public policies that attempt to change the relations among racial, ethnic, and economic groups. Hence, there have been numerous attempts by public authorities (and by others) to create or change holidays.

Diana Muir's essay in this volume offers a fine example of this process, as she recounts the efforts of American governors and other leaders to introduce Thanksgiving to their constituencies during the nineteenth century. As she explains, the holiday of Thanksgiving, which was historically opposed by theologians, was spread not by popular practice but by the decisions of public leaders.

Modifications of holidays both reflect changes in values and power relations and help to formulate and ensconce changes in values and power; such efforts can range from attempts to modify them on a relatively small scale, which I refer to as the editing of holidays, to attempts to create wholly new holidays—i.e., to engineer novel ones. Changes in the texts used during prayers in places of worship (e.g., making them gender neutral to reflect the decrease in gender inequality) are typical editorial changes; the introduction of Martin Luther King Jr. Day constitutes the engineering of a new holiday.

Given that holidays tend to rely on the legitimization of tradition and on affective attachment founded on shared memories and histories, a question arises that is of much interest to those who study social change: Do holidays lose some or all of their power to reinforce commitments to values if they are extensively edited, let alone vastly reengineered?[77] It is an issue that has been long debated in numerous religious bodies, tribal councils, and national parliaments.

Since religions are typically more traditional than secular ideologies (if only because the latter tend to have significantly shorter histories), one promising place to start the examination of the limits and opportunities of the social reengineering of holidays is to ask whether recasting is less subversive of the legitimacy of secular holidays than it is for religious ones. (It should be noted in passing that, although Durkheim recognizes the difference between religious rituals carried out by nonliterate tribes and those national holidays that Robert Bellah analyzed as examples of "civil" religion, to Durkheim these are but two forms of religion, fulfilling the same essential integrative function. For Durkheim, while a society could replace God as the source of sacredness, this did not secularize the icons, cults, and rituals the society endowed in this peculiar manner. They were all sacred.)[78]

In contrast, contemporary social scientists might well find it necessary to draw a distinction between holidays that are built around sacred religious objects and those that surround revered secular objects, including days that mark national liberations, independence, armistices, or civic occasions such as New Year's Eve. Like many other typologies, reference here is not to pure types but to the dominant elements of each category of holidays. Thus, a secular holiday may include some prayers, but the main focus of the objects held in special awe and the values dramatized and ritualized are secular. In the same vein, a largely religious holiday may include some secular elements.

A question arises, then, as to which type of holidays can be more readily reengineered without undermining their legitimacy. I suggest as a hypothesis that religious holidays can be more readily redesigned, without losing their legitimacy, than secular ones. There follows some observations that support this hypothesis, but they should not serve as a substitute for the evidence that has yet to be collected and analyzed.

In the Soviet Union, continuous, systematic, and deliberate efforts were made to secularize holidays and to engineer new ones. Christmas and Easter were abolished in 1920, and November 7 (the anniversary of the founding of the Bolshevik government) and May 1 (the day celebrating the unity of labor) were introduced as holidays. In 1929, the Sunday Sabbath was abolished to create a six-day workweek. Gift exchanging was moved to New Year's Eve, and a secular "Father Frost" replaced Santa Claus.[79] These efforts were widely resisted. Despite the fact that they were banned, religious holidays continued to be observed by millions, and not always in secrecy. Sunday Sabbath was restored in 1940. And while the Soviet regime did not survive, the celebration of religious holidays did.[80]

When traditional holidays are edited (as opposed to new ones being manufactured), and when the changes introduced are in line with changes in widely held values and social needs, especially religious ones, modifications are much more effective. A case in point is the Catholic Church's shift from the use of Latin during mass to the use of the vernacular, symbolizing a move from the devotion to strong universalism to a greater openness to local cultural differences, as part of a much larger attempt to downgrade the central role of authority and place greater emphasis on communal elements of the Church. These principles also guided the decision, as communicated through Vatican II, to allow priests in the Roman Catholic Church to face the congregation during the Eucharist portion of the mass, whereas traditionally they performed these rites with their backs to the congregants.

Traditional Jewish holidays were profoundly changed by Conservative and Reform Jews attempting to make the religious rituals more accessible to congregations whose members by and large did not understand Hebrew. Their members were also less willing to participate in prolonged rituals, insisted on some measure of gender equality, and otherwise sought to reconcile their Jewish commitments with other normative agendas.[81] (For instance, many modern versions of the Haggadah drop or reinterpret a line that calls on God to wreak his vengeance on "other" people.)

In another example, the Iranian observance of the Muslim holy day of Chelum, which memorializes the martyrdom of the Imam Hussein, involves a rather violent ritual: self-flagellation with heavy, hydra-headed whips. However, in Tehran today, this ritual is more like a well-stylized dance. Young men step in a circle to the tune of pleasant repetitive music, gently waving small whips, with which they symbolically touch their well-protected backsides.[82] This is not the only Iranian holiday that has changed. Iranian scholars have suggested that the overwhelming majority of young Iranians (70 percent of the population is under age thirty) neither fast during Ramadan nor pray five times each day, as required by religious law. The transformations of these rituals may help us to understand larger changes in Iranian society.

Although debates continue within these and other religious groups about the appropriateness of deliberate efforts to redesign holidays—and there have been some efforts to restore traditional features—many of the new modes of celebrations are widely followed and considered legitimate.

Other editing of holidays includes the recasting of Thanksgiving, transforming it from a Yankee holiday, primarily celebrated in the North, into a national holiday after the Civil War and from a holiday celebrated on different days in different states—requiring annual proclamations by various governors—to one that is fully institutionalized and celebrated on the same day nationwide.[83]

Establishing the extent to which holidays can be deliberately edited and new ones engineered, and the comparative effectiveness of various ways and means of such endeavors, is particularly significant in light of a challenge posed by historian John R. Gillis. He argues that American holidays, rituals, and myths are lagging behind reality—that they represent a distorted view of a society that is long gone, especially the notion that there was and ought to be one "traditional" kind of family. He argues—drawing on Marxist and Freudian ideas about the possibility of developing a higher level of consciousness—for a profound recasting of our core myth (and hence, our holidays and rituals), toward a formulation that provides a higher level of reality-testing and a more genuine expression of our true feelings and psychic needs.[84] One may argue that this is what is taking place, under the influence of various consciousness-raising and reeducation drives, despite opposition by traditional groups.

My hypothesis is that holidays can be edited, and even new ones manufactured, as long as they either reflect changes in values and power relations within a society or advance these changes without moving too far away from the evolving trends. Thus, as race relations improved and we witnessed a decrease in segregation and inequality (I choose my words carefully), Martin Luther King Jr. Day gradually gained acceptance. It is hard to imagine this holiday being introduced, say, in 1950, let alone in earlier generations.

In Conclusion

Holidays and rituals provide a valuable tool for a sociological analysis of societies both because they reflect various attributes of societies and their major constituting social entities (i.e., they are effective macro indicators) and because they serve to modify these attributes (i.e., they constitute forces of societal change). To develop such an analysis, suggestions are provided for a sociological theory of holidays that, in several instances, significantly modifies Durkheim's hypotheses and adds factors that he did not consider.

The main propositions that arise from the discussion are:

(a) If one uses the society as the frame of reference, tension management holidays are expected to be less integrative than holidays of recommitment. Although both might contribute to the integrative state of a societal entity, tension management holidays are more prone to foster antisocial behavior.

(b) A theory of holidays will benefit from taking into account that one and the same holiday may have different effects on the integration of the society at large than it does on the integration of some member units. For instance, some ethnic holidays strengthen the communal bonds of member units but undermine societal integration, while other holidays help to reinforce not merely the integration of the member units but also their relationship to the society at large. Moreover, a holiday that started as fragmenting may serve as a societal process that helps work through conflicts among the member units and the society at large.

(c) The extent to which holidays that have been previously celebrated in public are privatized is expected to correlate with the rise of diversity in society—unless countervailing efforts to shore up societal bonds are effectively introduced.[85] Moreover, the privatization of holidays that used to be public will undermine societal integration, in conflict with Durkheim's expectation that all holidays will serve to enhance integration.

(d) The particular reasons holidays are arranged in a given repeated sequence (or cycle) in a given society are not known. A preliminary hypothesis suggests that holidays follow the sequences observed in order to serve various societal needs, so that sooner or later most or all needs are attended to. For this reason, for instance, tension management holidays and holidays of recommitment tend to alternate instead of a group of one kind being followed by a group of the other.

(e) Religious authorities may be more effective than secular authorities at deliberately changing holidays without alienating large numbers of their followers.

(f) Changes in gender and kinship roles during holidays are expected to lag behind changes in these roles in other institutional sectors, undermining the integrative role of holidays.

(g) Holidays can be extensively edited and new ones engineered if these changes either reflect societal changes in values and power relations or advance these changes but are not "too far" ahead of them or do not otherwise diverge from them.

In short, once we abandon Durkheim's assumption of a close, positive correlation between the occurrence of and participation in holidays and societal integration, we are on our way to laying the foundations for a much richer, nuanced, and empirically valid theory of holidays.

NOTES

1. Ianthe Jeanne Dugan, "24-Hour Stock Trading Moves Closer; Nasdaq Board Approves Adding Evening Session," *Washington Post*, May 28, 1999, A1.

2. For a brief discussion of the family meal as an agent of socialization, see James H. S. Bossard, "Family Table Talk—An Area for Sociological Study," *American Sociological Review* 8, no. 3 (1943): 295–301.

3. See Ida Harper Simpson, "The Disappearance of the Family Meal and the Epidemic of Obesity," presented at the annual meeting of the Southern Sociological Society, 2003.

4. Central Conference of American Rabbis, "A Statement of Principles for Reform Judaism Adopted at the 1999 Pittsburgh Convention," May 1999, available at http://ccarnet.org/platforms/principles.html (accessed on January 27, 2004).

5. "A Hard Cell," *Washington Post*, October 11, 2002, T34.

6. For an account of the decline of the Sabbath, as well as prospects for its future, see Judith Shulevitz, "Bring Back the Sabbath," *New York Times Magazine*, March 2, 2003, F50.

7. For an overview of common wedding rituals and traditions, including wedding vows, see Barbara Jo Chesser, "Analysis of Wedding Rituals: An Attempt to Make Weddings More Meaningful," *Family Relations* 29, no. 2 (1980): 204–209.

8. *American Heritage Dictionary of the English Language*, 3rd ed. (Boston: Houghton Mifflin, 1996), 862. Steven Lukes defines ritual as "*rule-governed activity of a symbolic character which draws the attention of its participants to objects of thought and feeling which they hold to be of special significance*" (italics in original). Steven Lukes, "Political Ritual and Social Integration," *Sociology* 9 (1975): 291.

Robert Goodin offers a more simplistic notion of rituals, defining them as any formal procedure that involves a "solemn performance." Robert E. Goodin, "Rites of Rulers," *British Journal of Sociology* 29, no. 3 (1978): 282.

9. See Loring Danforth, *Firewalking and Ritual Healing: The Anastenaria of Greece and the American Firewalking Movement* (Princeton, NJ: Princeton University Press, 1989); Abraham Rosman and Paula G. Rubel, *Tapestry of Culture: An Introduction to Cultural Anthropology* (New York: McGraw-Hill, 1995); and Conrad Kottack, *Cultural Anthropology,* 8th ed. (Boston: McGraw-Hill, 2000).

10. Émile Durkheim, *The Elementary Forms of Religious Life,* trans. Karen E. Fields (New York: Free Press, 1995).

11. "The Ways We Celebrate: Holidays and Rituals as Seedbeds of Social Values," a conference organized by Elizabeth Tulis and the Institute for Communitarian Policy Studies, was held at the George Washington University, April 11–12, 2003.

12. Steven Lukes, *Émile Durkheim: His Life and Work* (New York: Harper and Row, 1972). Lukes, "Political Ritual and Social Integration," 289–308. Watts Miller, *Durkheim, Morals, and Modernity* (Montreal: McGill-Queen's University Press, 1996). Talcott Parsons, *The Structure of Social Action* (Glencoe, IL: Free Press, 1937).

13. Eviatar Zerubavel argues that time is utilized by societies as a means to draw a clear distinction between the sacred (a realm in which commitments are reinforced) and the profane (in which they wane). In expanding this notion of "temporal segregation," Zerubavel examines the role of the Sabbath in Judaism, and in particular, how the Jewish calendar has been conceptualized in a way that sets the Sabbath apart from other, "profane" days. Eviatar Zerubavel, "Sacred and Profane Time," in *Hidden Rhythms: Schedules and Calendars in Social Life* (Berkeley: University of California Press, 1985), 101–137.

14. Lukes, "Political Ritual and Social Integration," 292. Reviewers of a previous draft of this essay pointed out, quite correctly, that Durkheim is subject to different interpretations on the points discussed here. Given that the purpose of the essay is not to sort out the differences among these interpretations but merely to use one of them as a starting point, I will not delve into the question of what is the correct interpretation of Durkheim.

15. Edward Lehman, *Political Society: A Macrosociology of Politics* (New York: Columbia University Press, 1977).

16. Amitai Etzioni and Edward Lehman, "Some Dangers in 'Valid' Social Measurements: Preliminary Notes," *Annals of the American Academy of Political and Social Science* 373 (1967): 1–15.

17. See Danforth, *Firewalking and Ritual Healing*; Rosman and Rubel, *Tapestry of Culture*; and Kottack, *Cultural Anthropology.*

18. Edward Shils, "Dreams of Plentitude, Nightmares of Scarcity," in *Students in Revolt,* Seymour Martin Lipset and Philip Altbach, eds. (Boston: Houghton Mifflin, 1969).

19. See Elihu Katz and Tamar Liebes, *The Export of Meaning: Cross-Cultural Readings of "Dallas"* (New York: Oxford University Press, 1990); and JoEllen Shively, "Cowboys and Indians: Perceptions of Western Films among American Indians and Anglos," *American Sociological Review* 57 (1992): 725–734.

20. Durkheim, *Elementary Forms of Religious Life*.

21. See Jack Santino, *All around the Year: Holidays and Celebrations in American Life* (Urbana: University of Illinois Press, 1994); and Robert Bellah, "Civic Religion in America," *Daedalus* 96 (1967): 1–21.

22. Talcott Parsons, Robert F. Bales, and Edward A. Shils, *Working Papers in the Theory of Action* (New York: Free Press, 1953), 180–181.

23. For an exploration of the difficulty in trying to measure religious commitment (or "religious involvement") see Harold S. Himmelfarb, "Measuring Religious Involvement," *Social Forces* 53, no. 4 (1975): 606–618.

24. On this matter, see Joel Best, "The Myth of the Halloween Sadist," *Psychology Today* 19 (1985): 14; Joel Best and Gerald T. Horiuchi, "The Razor Blade in the Apple: The Social Construction of Urban Legends," *Social Problems* 32 (1985): 488–499; and Theodore Caplow, Howard M. Bahr, Bruce A. Chadwick, Reuben Hill, and Margaret Holmes Williamson, "Family Symbolism in Festivals," in *Middletown Families: Fifty Years of Change and Continuity* (Minneapolis: University of Minnesota Press, 1982).

25. Sigmund Freud, *Civilization and Its Discontents,* trans. and ed. James Strachey (New York: W. W. Norton, 1989); Dennis Wrong, *The Problem of Order: What Unites and Divides Society* (New York: Free Press, 1994).

26. Santino, *All around the Year,* 49.

27. Donald R. Winkler, "The Effects of Sick-Leave Policy on Teacher Absenteeism," *Industrial and Labor Relations Review* 33, no. 2 (1980): 232–240.

28. See Mary Ann Glendon and David Blankenhorn, eds., *Seedbeds of Virtue: Sources of Competence, Character, and Citizenship in American Society* (Lanham, MD: Madison Books, 1995); and Robert N. Bellah et al., *Habits of the Heart: Individualism and Commitment in American Life* (Berkeley: University of California Press, 1985).

29. Elizabeth Pleck, *Celebrating the Family: Ethnicity, Consumer Culture, and Family Rituals* (Cambridge, MA: Harvard University Press, 2000), 233.

30. Ibid., 236–238.

31. For a largely ethnographic study of rituals performed within various American ethnic and religious groups, see Pamela R. Frese, ed., *Celebrations of Identity: Multiple Voices in American Ritual Performance* (Westport, CT: Bergin and Garvey, 1993).

32. On this concept, see Daniel Yankelovich, *Coming to Public Judgment: Making Democracy Work in a Complex World* (Syracuse, NY: Syracuse University Press, 1991).

33. See Theodore Caplow, "Christmas Gifts and Kin Networks," *American*

Sociological Review 47 (1982): 383–392; William B. Waits, *The Modern Christmas in America: A Cultural History of Gift-Giving* (New York: New York University Press, 1993); and Anna Day Wilde, "Mainstreaming Kwanzaa," *Public Interest* 119 (1995): 68–79.

34. On layered loyalties, see Amitai Etzioni, *The New Golden Rule: Community and Morality in a Democratic Society* (New York: Basic Books, 1996), 202–203; and Ellen Litwicki, "Our Hearts Burn with Ardent Love for Two Countries: Ethnicity and Assimilation at Chicago Holiday Celebrations, 1876–1918," *Journal of American Ethnic History* 19, no. 3 (2000): 3–34.

35. Laurie Sommers, "Symbol and Style in Cinco de Mayo," *Journal of American Folklore* 390 (1985): 478.

36. Ibid., 479.

37. Alvar W. Carlson, "America's Growing Observance of Cinco de Mayo," *Journal of American Culture* 13 (summer 1998).

38. Mary Jordan, "Cinco de Mayo Isn't Just for Mexicans Anymore," *New York Times*, May 4, 2003, A26.

39. Eve Epstein and Frank James, "The Native American Perspective of Thanksgiving," interview by Bob Edwards, *Morning Edition*, National Public Radio, November 24, 1993. See also Diana Karter Appelbaum, *Thanksgiving: An American Holiday, an American History* (New York: Facts on File, 1984).

40. Pam Belluck, "Pilgrims Wear Different Hats in Recast Thanksgiving Tales," *New York Times*, November 23, 1995; and Tara Mack, "Listen Up, Pilgrims: Teachers Modernize Thanksgiving Message," *Washington Post*, November 27, 1996.

41. Joyce Price, "After Falling Off PC Calendars, Columbus Is Back," *Washington Times*, October 15, 1996, A1.

42. Wilde, "Mainstreaming Kwanzaa," 70–72.

43. Ibid., 70–72.

44. Ibid., 76.

45. Matthew Dennis, *Red, White, and Blue Letter Days* (Ithaca, NY: Cornell University Press, 2002), 262.

46. Ibid., 262.

47. Ibid., 262–263.

48. Ibid., 267.

49. Jack Estes, "The Graying of Bitterness and Pain," *Los Angeles Times*, May 30, 1994.

50. Michelle Locke, "City with a Radical History Makes Peace with Vietnam Vets," *Los Angeles Times*, November 12, 1995, 4.

51. Mark Caro and Bernie Mixon, "Veterans Get a Big Salute as Holiday Is Commemorated amid Pomp, Protest," *Chicago Tribune*, November 24, 1994.

52. Locke, "City with a Radical History," 4.

53. In a study of the Church's initial effort to schedule Easter apart from Passover, Eviatar Zerubavel argues that groups use "calendrical means" to separate

themselves from other groups. Eviatar Zerubavel, "Easter and Passover: On Calendars and Group Identity," *American Sociological Review* 47 (1982): 284–289.

54. Diana Karter Appelbaum, *The Glorious Fourth: An American Holiday, an American Tradition* (New York: Facts on File, 1989).

55. Stephen Nissenbaum, *The Battle for Christmas* (New York: Alfred A. Knopf, 1996). Theodore Caplow et al., *Middletown Families.*

56. Parsons, *Structure of Social Action,* 438–441.

57. In his discussion of rituals, Turner used the term *communitas* to describe the fellowship created by the generic bonds that exist between members of a group that lacks structure and, accordingly, hierarchy, social statuses, etc. Victor Turner, *The Ritual Process: Structure and Anti-Structure* (Ithaca, NY: Cornell University Press, 1969).

58. William Jankowiak and C. Todd White, "Carnival on the Clipboard: An Ethnological Study of New Orleans Mardi Gras," *Ethnology* 38, no. 4 (1999): 336. For another study on the importance of rituals during Mardi Gras, see Wesley Shrum and John Kilburn, "Ritual Disrobement at Mardi Gras: Ceremonial Exchange and Moral Order," *Social Forces* 75, no. 2 (1996): 423–458.

59. Jankowiak and White, "Carnival on the Clipboard," 337–338.

60. Ibid., 338.

61. Ibid., 340–342.

62. Robert Putnam, *Bowling Alone: The Collapse and Revival of American Community* (New York: Simon and Schuster, 2000), 19.

63. See Penne L. Restad, *Christmas in America: A History* (New York: Oxford University Press, 1995); Waits, *Modern Christmas in America*; and Leigh Eric Schmidt, *Consumer Rites: The Buying and Selling of American Holidays* (Princeton, NJ: Princeton University Press, 1995), 30.

64. See Bellah et al., *Habits of the Heart,* and discussions of individualism in Etzioni, *New Golden Rule.*

65. Ontario, California, Chamber of Commerce, interview with David Carney of the Communitarian Network, July 2, 1996.

66. Amy Adams Squire Stronghart, "Developing Your Own Holiday Traditions," *St. Louis Post-Dispatch,* December 27, 1994.

67. See, among others, Pleck, *Celebrating the Family*; Schmidt, *Consumer Rites*; and James H. Barnett, "The Easter Festival—A Study in Cultural Change," *American Sociological Review* 14, no. 1 (1949): 62–70. And for a short novel that draws out the costs and benefits of commercialization, see John Grisham, *Skipping Christmas* (New York: Doubleday, 2001).

68. To conduct the informal survey, I queried six anthropologists about all the cultures with which they are familiar and, additionally, scanned the literature regarding the cultures with which I am familiar.

69. See Mircea Eliade, *Cosmos and History: The Myth of the Eternal Return,* trans. Willard R. Trask (New York: Harper, 1959).

70. Caplow et al., "Family Symbolism in Festivals," in *Middletown Families*, 235.

71. See Laura Adams, "Celebrating Independence: Holidays and Cultural Renewal after the Soviet Union," paper presented at "The Ways We Celebrate" conference, 2003.

72. See Schmidt, *Consumer Rites*; and Leslie Bella, *The Christmas Imperative: Leisure, Family and Women's Work* (Halifax, Nova Scotia: Fernwood, 1992).

73. Ralph Linton and Adelin Linton, *We Gather Together: The Story of Thanksgiving* (London: Abelard-Schumann, 1949).

74. See Pleck, "Family Symbolism in Festivals," in *Celebrating the Family*, 39–41. John P. Robinson and Melissa A. Milkie, "Back to the Basics: Trends in and Role Determinants of Women's Attitudes toward Housework," *Journal of Marriage and the Family* 60 (1998): 205–218.

75. Nicholas Kulish, "Turning the Tables: Bachelorette Parties Are Getting Risqué," *Wall Street Journal*, September 3, 2002, A1.

76. On the implications of this difference, see Amitai Etzioni, *The Active Society: A Theory of Societal and Political Process* (New York: Free Press, 1968).

77. William Lloyd Warner, *The Living and the Dead: A Study of the Symbolic Life of Americans* (New Haven, CT: Yale University Press, 1959).

78. Durkheim, *Elementary Forms of Religious Life*. For additional discussion, see Matthew Schoffeleers and Daniel Meijers, *Religion, Nationalism, and Economic Action: Critical Questions on Durkheim and Weber* (Assen, The Netherlands: Van Gorcum, 1978), 35–39.

79. Alessandra Stanley, "December 25 in Russia: The Adoration of the Monetary," *New York Times*, December 24, 1996, A4.

80. "Reintroduction of Christmas Hailed," Daily Report/Soviet Union, Foreign Broadcast Information Service Database, New Canaan, CT: DataNews, Inc., January 7, 1991.

81. Eric Convey, "Spirituality: Passover by the Book," *Boston Herald*, March 26, 1999, 2.

82. Personal observation, 2001.

83. Diana Karter Appelbaum, *Thanksgiving*.

84. John R. Gillis, *A World of Their Own Making: Myth, Ritual, and the Quest for Family Values* (New York: Basic Books, 1996).

85. See discussions of "pluralism within unity" in Etzioni, *New Golden Rule*, 189–216; and Amitai Etzioni, "Diversity within Unity: A New Approach to Immigrants and Minorities," *Responsive Community* 13, no. 1 (winter 2002/2003): 24–40, also available at http://www.gwu.edu/~ccps/DWU_Platform.pdf.

Part II

Family Building

Chapter 2

Who Are We and Where Do We Come From?

Rituals, Families, and Identities

Elizabeth H. Pleck

When the public laments the loss of tradition, they do not have in mind gander pulling on Shrove Tuesday or Easter Monday, or blackface on Christmas, New Year's, Thanksgiving, and the Fourth of July. Nor are they thinking of children begging at Thanksgiving, sexual orgies on Pinkster, or shooting matches on Christmas Day.[1] These examples of the carnivalesque style of celebration are gone, although vestiges of the style can be found at Halloween, Mardi Gras, April Fools' Day, New Year's Eve, and during the Christmas season. Americans still enjoy some of the pleasures of masking, costuming, and excess, and children take pleasure from costumed begging for candy at Halloween.[2]

Despite these traces of an earlier style of holiday celebration, the carnivalesque diminished as two other approaches to family ritual were added, the first in the nineteenth century and the second in the twentieth, particularly in the second half of the twentieth century. Momentous change took place as domestic ritual, reconceptualized and matched to a new age, took hold. The carnival approach receded because the middle class no longer was willing to tolerate routine rowdiness as a form of cathartic release among the lower orders, especially lower-class men. They sought to defend and protect their own family's privacy, and they wanted a more orderly and humanitarian society, one devoid of blood sports, dueling, and public hangings. Such an orderly world, it was believed, could reinforce the time and work discipline an industrial society needed. Seeking a more domestic festive life and special times for far-flung kin to gather, middle-class Victorians fused religious piety, familialism, and spending. Impelled by these varied motives, and responding to complaints about sexual license, noise, drunkenness, child begging, and destruction of property, politicians and reformers, particularly in the nineteenth century and the first third of the twentieth century, tried to eliminate misrule at Christmas, Easter, and Thanksgiving.[3] To a great extent the centers of change were the centers of wealth—the Northeast and the Mid-Atlantic states—but Southern planters and urbanites also began to celebrate in this more subdued manner. Although the domestic occasion was intended to replace carnivalesque festivals, the two continued to coexist for many decades.

The Protestant middle class was not the first social group to hold family feasts, but they were the first to see the family occasion as a solution to the social changes created by the industrial revolution. The middle and upper classes of the mid-nineteenth century were made anxious by the growth of commerce and industry and by their fear that greed and the pursuit of self-interest were being put ahead of community and religious piety. Experiencing economic dislocations as a decline in morality, they worried about the loss of the national religious mission and about young people leaving the family farm to move to the city or the frontier. Sentimental domestic occasions provided an orderly way of celebrating and made people feel more comfortable with modernity by reassuring them that they were engaged in something truly old-fashioned.

Once created, the family rituals of the Victorians functioned as active agents of social change, helping to shape middle-class and national identity, sideline distinctive regional or ethnic customs, and disseminate the ideal of domesticity. The ultimate irony was that middle-class Victorians had conceptualized the family as a private world separate from and purer than the marketplace. Yet luxury goods purchased in the marketplace came to symbolize the idea of family affection. Thus, the middle-class family was not so private after all but was instead a ready market for family Bibles and baubles. While in reality there was no real barrier between the market and the home, the idea of family privacy did reinforce class distinctions. The elite, then the middle class, began to favor private family events.

Because of the emphasis on family privacy in the ideology of domesticity, some events shut out the public and were by invitation only. In excluding the uninvited guest and the larger community, the middle-class domestic occasion reinforced the social distance between one's own kin and the rest of the community. But the peer-culture birthday party, a development begun in the 1870s, also recognized that the parent could no longer exercise complete control over the child's world. Because children were educated with age peers and were entering a world in which they would have to depend on friends as well as relatives, parents in the last third of the nineteenth century began to accept the child's peer culture—his or her own chosen friends—as a necessary adjunct to the private family.

Victorian writers and editors, from Sarah Josepha Hale to Charles Dickens, created the ideology of domesticity and wrote poems, stories, and songs enshrining it. The new kind of family envisaged in this ideal seemed to require rituals that symbolically affirmed its values—domestic warmth, intimacy, romantic love, special affection for children and grandparents, and a familial and feminized view of religion. Relatives made pilgrimages to the secular shrine of the grandparent's house in the country to partake of a form of spiritual renewal before returning to a more hectic life in a town or city. Even heaven was fashioned as a family environment, where kin would be reunited. The domestication of festival increased Protestant religiosity, since many Calvinists had taken a dim view of ritual and sought to limit its scope. While this "home religion" was initially Protestant and middle class, it also developed similarly, though at later times, among middle-class Catholics and Jews.

Department store owners, florists, sellers of greeting cards, confectioners, and coffin makers had much to gain from making domestic occasions more elaborate and getting people to celebrate more often. But they were neither especially manipulative or acute in recognizing social trends and exploiting them. However inept at anticipating public demand for celebration, merchants nonetheless responded to festivals already popular by offering a cornucopia of goods and services to enhance them. Candy and desserts, presents, flowers, photographs, and fancy family table settings made domestic events more beautiful, emotional, luxurious, memorable, and satisfying for the sweet tooth. Greeting cards helped family members maintain kin contact; gifts symbolized the donor's affection for the recipient. After about 1910 it was difficult to name a holiday or rite of passage that was devoid of all four of the most common elements—presents, flowers, cards, and candy. At the same time, many critics then—as now—saw the abundance of goods and the emphasis on buying them as profaning the sacred meaning of the occasion. It was this debate about the merits of commercialized festivity that drained some of the enthusiasm from the domestic occasion.

The idea of binding local, regional, and particularistic ties into love of nation through commemoration of its founding events also contributed to the growth of family ritual in the nineteenth century. (I have not discussed the major national holidays, such as the Fourth of July, at length, because these were largely public festivals and secondarily or incidentally times for family gathering.) Thanksgiving became a historical commemoration like the Fourth of July, but one that was a family gathering as much as a national celebration. A regional holiday until the Civil War, Thanksgiving became truly national in the Progressive era. In that period of greater centralization, educated professionals and Americanizers became more aware than ever before of the conflicting allegiances of the masses and the need to make them into loyal citizens. As a huge influx of foreigners disembarked at U.S. ports, reformers turned to the calendar and the flag as a means of including new immigrants and the rural poor in the polity and socializing them as citizens. Through celebrating the family, the symbol of national unity became reality.

Schools began to use Thanksgiving and other holidays as instructional tools during this period, when the socialization of immigrant children acquired special urgency. Most teachers believed that newcomers learning about the dominant culture's holidays helped produce a sense of patriotism. This view of the calendar as a form of education in citizenship has become a prevailing educational principle. Schools succeeded quite well in their attempts at Americanization, since the agent of change in many immigrant families was the child, who wanted the ritual learned about in school to be observed at home. Later, spectator sports have also served a nationalist function. Even the football game, an entirely secular event, when listened to or viewed on Thanksgiving, New Year's Day, or (since the mid-1960s) on Super Bowl Sunday, imparted feelings of national unity and loyalty. Nonetheless, on national days some Americans protested their exclusion, while others felt they simply did not belong.

Love of the nation also came to mean celebrating in the manner of the middle class, with birthday candles, gift wrap, bows, plastic Easter eggs, and Coca-Cola, which even had its own version of Santa. It also meant acquiring middle-class etiquette and table manners—individually greeting one's guests and sending thank-you notes. Gift giving and shopping became elements of this way of life. Late-nineteenth-century immigrants wrote home that true Americans bought presents on Christmas and birthdays and married for love in church weddings. Gradually, new consumer items were added to the list, from custom photography to printed invitations.

Ever since the early nineteenth century, middle-class women put the idea of the domestic occasion into practice. They cleaned and cooked, shopped, mailed cards, decorated the home and the church, and acted as the family's chief mourner. By teaching the rules of etiquette and table manners, they trained children to take their proper place as members of a privileged class. Men became increasingly marginal figures in many sentimental occasions, even as they seated themselves at the head of the table (and took on a new role in the twentieth century, that of family photographer). Their main role, however, was as family breadwinner. The outside world regarded the man who could pay for a Thanksgiving turkey and provide his wife with a generous allowance for Easter finery and Christmas gifts as a good provider; a prosperous father spent generously on his daughter's wedding.

The work of women tested their worth as homemaker and mother. Occasions varied greatly as to the level of exertion required, with Thanksgiving, Christmas, Easter, Passover, and weddings being among the most demanding. At all these events, women derived satisfaction and even power in the family for their efforts. For every woman who complained about the crush of holiday shoppers were two or three who enjoyed leaving the house to browse in department stores or to take children to visit Santa. Women's shopping combined leisure and work and gradually came to give them increasing power over the family purse. One of the many pleasures of the domestic occasion for women was that it convened a female community. At feasts in the home, women cooked with other women and girls, displayed their creativity, artistry, and skills, received praise for their efforts, and basked in their self-image as being caring, nurturing, and charitable. Ritual can survive without women, but it cannot be very elaborate. When holidays were celebrated by mostly male groups, as in festivals of the Chinese New Year among nineteenth-century immigrants, the feast would be held at the headquarters of group associations or at restaurants.

The domestic occasion not only sanctified the middle-class woman as the queen of the home but also underscored the importance of displaying status and wealth in making an occasion memorable. Rituals that celebrated the home also made visible a system of social ranking. People of higher status had always used ritual as a way of distinguishing themselves from everyone else. In consumer rituals, positive judgments were based on the ability to use purchased goods and services creatively, while negative judgments were made if one were unable to provide a necessary show of beauty and wealth. Thus, marriage in the judge's chambers, burial in a pine box, or Christmas with a single orange in the stocking were seen as second rate.

The need for fresh symbols and rituals not seen in English culture led the American middle class between 1830 and 1870 to copy the birthday parties, Easter-egg hunts, and Christmas customs of the Germans. Searching for new customs with which to create child-oriented festivals, American writers and travelers reported on German customs that made holidays familial and festive rather than drunken and that allowed children to be indulged without being spoiled. Native-born Americans adopted some features of German ritual and ignored the rest. So successful was the cultural transfer that by the late nineteenth century the German origins of many holiday customs were forgotten. Similarly, in the twentieth century, immigrants and blacks—Israel Baline (Irving Berlin) and Frank Capra, Bing Crosby and Nat King Cole—have spun out modern secular hymns and visual paeans to holiday sentimentality. Just as the German contributions to American festivals were invisible, the ethnic and racial backgrounds of these modern cultural creators went unnoticed.

Ethnicity and Ritual

Who are we and where do we come from? Ritual seemed to provide Americans with the answer to this question. It helped to define one's identity but also indicated changes in identity. The relationship between ritual and identity was multifaceted.

The prevailing social climate affected the way people chose to define and express their ethnic identity. The restriction of the flow of immigrants in the mid-1920s (and earlier for Asian immigrants), for example, encouraged a steady dissolution of ethnic identity along generational lines. The first generation adhered more closely to tradition, while the second often wanted to do things more the way it was done here. Many ethnic groups, even Hispanics and Chinese-Americans, were trying to blend into American culture from the 1920s through the 1950s. They wanted to be Americans, not hyphenated ones. In the 1950s, the conformity imposed by Cold War fears, the crusades to root out communism, the mass marketing of consumer goods, and the new medium of television encouraged many Americans to minimize, or even conceal, their ethnic roots.

Many rituals disappeared as immigrants resided for longer periods of time in the United States and as they raised a new generation. Acculturation was evident for every group and every ritual. In examining U.S. ethnic groups in the course of the twentieth century, such signs of ethnicity as knowledge of a foreign language or dialect, residence in an ethnic enclave, and membership in a group association have fallen away. Many rituals disappeared entirely or were practiced only in a few towns or cities with unusually large ethnic populations. If a church did not encourage a practice, that practice was less likely to survive. In general, religious institutions, especially ones that combined ethnicity and religion, were important in preserving traditions. Ritual was especially likely to vanish among immigrants or their children who did not live in an ethnic enclave but instead resided in multiethnic neighborhoods and attended multinationality parishes or had changed their religious affiliation.

For every group, the acculturation process was accompanied by a streamlining of the religious and agricultural calendar once observed. For example, in 1870s Galicia, thirty-four districts had 100 to 120 nonworking days per year, twenty-two districts had 120 to 150 nonworking days, and sixteen districts had 150 to 200. In the United States, legal holidays varied from state to state. Nonetheless, in 1900 it was common for there to be only four: Christmas, New Year's Day, the Fourth of July, and Thanksgiving.[4] Most groups found it difficult to clear space for their own holidays within this public calendar. Feast days and celebrations that occurred on a day that did not coincide with an American legal holiday tended to fade away. Immigrants selected a few holidays to observe, either the ones considered most important or those that fell at the same time as an American holiday. They thus preserved a few rituals while abandoning the wider range of rituals that had once been theirs.[5] More important, celebration of the holidays of the Old Country acquired the added meaning of being a rear-guard action to preserve one's culture against the onslaught of American influences. Immigrant mothers especially took this view and redefined their role to include instructing children in their religious and ethnic heritage.

Who are we and where do we come from? This question became even more puzzling as a family rose in status and entered the middle class. Such families began to adopt more American rituals and dress up their ethnic occasions. The simple repast—a party in the backyard—no longer sufficed. Many of these events followed the Protestant middle-class pattern of excluding the public, reserving the event for family and friends. The middle-class family could have very large parties, but it made a distinction between its own social circle and a wider community. Middle-class women in these groups took on a new role as updaters of tradition, crafting not the authentic and homey but the aesthetic and fancy. (A notable exception to this class rule was among Hispanics, where the working class was more likely than the middle class to have quinceañeras.) The timing of the emergence of a fancier occasion varied for each holiday and each ethnic group. Nonetheless, the late 1940s and 1950s saw a great homogenizing of the ritual for weddings and funerals and a decline in distinctive deathways and wedding rituals.

Race was another important factor in how celebrations were handled. Nonwhite races developed their rituals in such a way as to solve some of the problems caused by inequality and racial prejudice. The lack of interest until recently in black, Chinese, and Hispanic consumers provided a protected market for ethnic entrepreneurs, including minority-group funeral directors, grocery owners, and manufacturers of religious objects and ethnic foods. Racial restrictions also led to the invention of the clan banquet for the many bachelors in the Chinese immigrant population. Black families were more likely to spend freely on a funeral than on a grave marker or family tomb. Burial grounds discriminated against blacks, and those open to them were not well maintained. Meanwhile, black funeral directors and ministers encouraged urban black families around the beginning of the twentieth century to think of embalming and a padded casket as prestigious.

One feature of ethnic adaptation was the invention of entirely new rituals that arose not from the storehouse of tradition but from the perceptions and needs of people living in the United States. The actual creation of a new ethnic tradition was relatively rare and, thus, especially noteworthy: the bat mitzvah, St. Lucia Day, and Kwanzaa are some examples. The egalitarian impulse was behind the development of the bat mitzvah, as well as more-practical considerations about the religious instruction of girls. A small number of nationalist leaders interested in increasing their group's allegiance to their homeland helped introduce St. Lucia Day and create Kwanzaa. Ethnic businesses became important in the growth of these holidays, which appealed mainly to the ethnic middle class. Creation of such new rituals appears to have been especially common at the Christmas season, where the ethnic ceremony served as a supplement or an alternative to the Christmas of the dominant culture.

Initiation rites for adolescents, once minor ceremonies, became family extravaganzas as early as the 1920s for the Jewish middle class and in the

1960s for the Hispanic working class. These initiation rites were used to allay parental anxieties about the approach of adolescence and to bridge the gap between participation in American consumer culture and allegiance to a distinct ethnic and religious identity.

Syncretization, a blending of cultures to produce a new result, was more common than the invention of wholly new rituals or the fancifying of minor ones. It allowed immigrants to inject some elements of ethnic life into the rituals of the dominant culture and thus symbolized their desire to forge a dual identity, ethnic and mainstream. Ethnic music, food, and dancing—features evoking the earliest and most positive memories of childhood—were fused with the dominant culture. Ethnic food, for example, was added to American cuisine at Thanksgiving, sometimes as side dishes. At birthday parties, ethnic food, costumes, and adult sociality were combined with the mainstream American (originally German) cake and candles.

Domestic rituals also crossed into the public sphere, as in the clan banquet or third seder. Chinese immigrants at Chinese New Year were the first to use their holidays as a means of extending hospitality to otherwise hostile Americans, in order to increase mutual understanding and to develop businesses and tourist attractions. A taste for the exotic close to home has been characteristic of Americans at least since white tourists in the late nineteenth century flocked to Chinatown for Chinese New Year. Despite the social discrimination many groups faced (or, in the case of minority-group funeral preparations, because of it), each ethnic and racial group has been able to use its rituals for commercial gain. In the twentieth century, national firms as well as ethnic entrepreneurs sought to profit from ethnic rituals, prepared foods, and tourism.

The fancy funeral falls in a special category, since it did not grow out of the status striving of the middle class. At least since the late nineteenth century, Greeks, Italians, Irish, blacks, and the poor in general have usually scraped together the money and passed the hat in order to pay for a lavish funeral. Those interested in such funerals were not concerned about rising in status so much as about not falling into ignominy. They dreaded the anonymity and lack of respect for the dead the pauper's burial conveyed. The fancy funeral gave the deceased the kind of dignity that was denied in life. If the fancy wedding symbolized economic and social success, the fancy funeral showed that survivors, even poor ones, respected their dead. Spending on a funeral served not to signal family status but to preserve family honor.

Between the 1910s and the 1940s, children of immigrants learned the values of individualism, romantic love, and consumerism through their participation in mass culture. They attended baseball games and boxing matches. They developed a fondness for the rhythms of ragtime, jazz, and the songs of Tin Pan Alley. Working girls bought the latest fashions and went on dates unchaperoned. American-born Chinese in San Francisco frequented Chinatown's nightclubs in the 1940s. Immigrant parents, especially immigrant mothers, often shrugged their shoulders. The immigrant mother came to be seen as the preserver of tradition, the bulwark against assimilation. Nonetheless, she was also an active consumer, who joined a Christmas club and saved to give her children new clothes for Easter or first communion. It is an oversimplification to conclude that consumer culture, with its emphasis on luxury, novelty, and an altered and improved self, simply overpowered ethnic, racial, or even class identity. In some cases, it served to enhance these identities. Moreover, having wishes, fantasies, and daydreams did not preclude having multiple definitions of the self.

The Postsentimental Approach to Family Ritual

It is best to think of the postsentimental approach to ritual as a third layer, added on top of the carnivalesque and the sentimental approaches, and as a stance in a debate, which presumes that others will argue and make visible the merits of sentimentality. Postsentimentalism is both a way of talking about ritual and a style of practicing it. Cynical and critical, postsentimentalism uses sentimentality as a foil. It requires the persistence, not the total disappearance, of sentimental occasions.

Funerals during and after World War I were the first rituals to show evidence of postsentimentalism. The simpler funeral was an explicit rejection of the sentimental view of death, burial, and mourning. World War I shattered the elaborate mourning customs of the Victorians. Influential Americans no longer believed that the funeral should be the grandest occasion of all. Americans, especially the middle class and liberal Protestants, wanted them to be brief, simple, and emotionally sparse, as they sought to push death aside. In addition, as increasing life expectancy led to the concentration of deaths among the elderly, deaths of kin older than seventy came to be defined as "low-grief losses."

Increasingly in the second half of the twentieth century, rituals were celebrated outside the home.[6] This change mainly occurred when a service industry took over women's unpaid work, which had usually been performed in the home. Again, funerals set the pattern. Even in the late nineteenth century, funerals were increasingly held outside the home, at a church or funeral home, and were arranged by a funeral director. Gradually, other ceremonies were moved outside the home. This new location did not necessarily lead to a decline in women's work. In hiring a wedding caterer, for example, a woman and her neighbors no longer had to cook for the wedding feast; but it was equally time consuming to engage and supervise the work of others, from florists and photographers to musicians and party planners.

Postsentimentalism was also a result of major changes that affected the family during three decades, beginning in the 1960s. The social and sexual revolutions of that time spurred sweeping family changes: an increase in divorce, a growth in cohabitation as an alternative to marriage, and a greater willingness of women to bear and rear children as single parents. Forced to confront a growing diversity of marital and family patterns, some responded with understanding, others with regret or disgruntlement. There was nothing new in the postmodern condition of discontinuity and doubt, instability and uncertainty. That had been the experience of families living through the Black Death, the slave trade, or the Great Depression. What was different about the decades between 1960 and 1990 was that dramatic social changes were accompanied by the steady march toward women's independence from lifelong marriage and a renegotiation of gender roles for couples along egalitarian lines.

Women's wage earning had been rising throughout the twentieth century, but by the 1970s it caused a loud crash in the kitchen. Many women were beginning to recognize that they suffered from double duty, attending to both the work of the family and the demands of their paid job. To be sure, married women's employment brought increased money for presents and party goods as well as for more practical items. But it also contributed to women's discontent, since paid work fueled the resurgence of feminism and contributed to a surging divorce rate. Women, better educated than ever before and more committed to paid work throughout their lifetimes, pared down family size and complained about the holiday blues. Their response to the blues was often to reduce the amount of ritual work. Many women began to encourage husband and children to help cook or clean for family feasts, or to ask guests to bring dishes for a potluck buffet. Another solution was to substitute services for women's unpaid labor—to purchase birthday cakes at a bakery or to dine at a restaurant on Easter Sunday.

Equally important in shaping postsentimental ritual was the changing attitude toward racial integration and the issue of minority groups' participation in the American mainstream. Disenchantment as a result of stalled progress in civil rights in the mid-1960s led to a resurgence of black nationalism. Initially, blacks who celebrated Kwanzaa intended to symbolically demonstrate their support of black nationalism. Maulana Karenga, the creator of Kwanzaa, believed that American blacks needed to celebrate the holiday to learn and affirm their African identity. Christmas, he contended, confirming the suspicions that many American blacks had long held, was a white people's holiday. Many blacks began to wear the Afro hairstyle, take an African first and last name, and give their children African names. Much black invented tradition, from Kwanzaa to African drumming at weddings to initiation rites for youth at black churches, sprang from a desire on the part of American blacks to recover an African heritage.

Black nationalism had as much influence on nonblacks as on people of African descent. The growth of racial identity among Asians, Hispanics, Native Americans, and many other ethnic groups owes much to black power. Families were encouraged to recapture lost customs or add ethnic elements to their celebrations; they rediscovered rarely practiced traditions and invented new ones. Local chambers of commerce and businesses developed ethnic parades and festivals. Some festivals, such as the New Year celebration in San Francisco's Chinatown, which had an assimilationist slant in the 1950s, took on a more "authentic" Chinese flavor in the 1970s.[7]

In the decades since the 1960s, more Americans than ever before were intermarrying and associating with neighbors and workmates from other groups. Even many recent immigrants were living in the suburbs and intermarrying. People no longer recognized taboos on marrying someone from a different ethnic, religious, or racial background. Families increasingly invited members from other groups to their ethnic feasts. Wedding rituals were often used to send a signal that the two families would accommodate the different cultures of the bride and groom.

Instead of affirming an ideal of the family, celebrations in postsentimental times upheld a set of values that can best be described as individualist, pluralist, therapeutic, and consumerist. With the exception of the therapeutic, these values had long flourished on American soil. By the end of the nineteenth century, urban workers had come to believe that purchased goods and services brought magic to one's life. The growth of real wages for ordinary working families, boosted by World War II wartime industry and American postwar prosperity, made consumer dreams a reality for ordinary folk, not just the urban middle class. Rising farm incomes during the postwar years closed the urban-rural gap, except for pockets of regional and racial poverty. It became possible for rural people to consume in the manner of their city cousins.[8] In an abundant twentieth-century America, chocolate candy became an everyday treat, birthday parties an expected rite, and sending a greeting card an assumed obligation.

Twentieth-century American popular culture was mainly optimistic and happy, upholding the belief that it was more important to celebrate happiness than to wallow in death. In an increasingly abundant society, many thought that in spending freely they could find happiness, express love, and make a joyous occasion perfect. Some came to this conclusion because of the influence of advertising and the mass media, which portrayed spending as the way to achieve happy holidays. Encouraging dreams of fulfillment through purchased goods was an aim of advertising as early as the nineteenth century, which even then depicted children asleep, dreaming of the toys Santa was going to bring them. Irving Berlin was simply adding to this image of Christmas as a time of reverie when he wrote about "dreaming of a white Christmas." Spending for certain rituals was one particular kind of dream, that of self-transformation. The making of a fantasy world was particularly suited to rites of passage, since these rituals had always been concerned with how individuals might transform themselves from one stage in life to another. By hosting a big reception for relatives from out of town at a bar or bat mitzvah, a Jewish family could help a child make the passage into adolescence truly memorable. Similarly, an expensive quinceañera offered a way for young adolescent Hispanic girls to realize their dream of being a fairy princess. The lavish wedding was intended to achieve the greatest transformation of all, waving a magic wand over a plain girl and making her into a radiant queen for a day. The honeymoon that followed, often at a tropical resort, the desired honeymoon location of couples since the 1980s, brought to life fantasies of two beautiful people experiencing romance and sensual pleasure on a white-sand beach.

Anthropologist Mary Douglas has argued that with increased individualism and the disappearance of many tightly knit communities, the amount of ritual in a society would decline.[9] Contrary to her prediction, the opposite appeared to be the case in the United States in the 1970s. Ritual was seen as a creative solution to personal and social problems. It became one of several means to achieve the dominant ethos of the decade, self-realization through therapeutic self-help. The kind of ritual then in vogue was supposed to be personally meaningful, experimental, derived from some "authentic" ancient tradition, and perhaps non- or even anti-institutional. Since the 1970s, Americans have invented a number of new rituals—initiation rites for black youths at black churches or social service organizations, home childbirth ceremonies, gay coming-out and commitment ceremonies, child-naming events, ceremonies for menstruation and menopause, even for divorce and miscarriage.[10] Feminism, New Age spirituality, black nationalism, gay and men's liberation, divorce, intermarriage—all of these developments have led to the creation of new rituals and provided a rationale for the need for new ceremonial events. The language of psychology, especially the often-repeated metaphor of "healing" a wound, provided another important rationale. Funeral directors defended the funeral as a form of grief work. Therapists endorsed the view that many family rituals had become static and obligatory and called for new, more meaningful ones that would reflect the many changes in modern American families. Many people were searching for new rituals with which they could express transcendent meaning. In the secular language of therapy, people were looking for a way to "maintain and alter important relationships, to facilitate complicated life-cycle changes, to heal losses, to express [their] deepest beliefs, and to celebrate life."[11]

Yet if the therapists are correct that the older rituals lack meaning for today's Americans, how do we explain the growth of that anachronism, the white wedding? What do we make of a couple who have a wedding reception at a hotel for two hundred guests, complete with a vocalist and a seven-piece band, and two years later hold a "dedication ceremony" for their infant, written by themselves, with a Protestant minister and a Buddhist priest officiating? Ethnic intermarriage and contact between cultures, even the popularity of ethnic food and music, have promoted experimentation and liberal cultural borrowing from religious or ethnic traditions not one's own. Great anxiety, insecurity, and nostalgia have coexisted with the quest for meaning and the desire to create new rituals. The work of blending the traditional and the new continues, as the technologically proficient construct webpages with photos of their child's birthday party, their own wedding, and their family Christmas tree with presents under it, and the cosmically oriented have their ashes sent into space.

These new practices follow the patterns of the rituals of the past, but what of the future? Do we need a larger and more varied set of rituals, ones that do not impose an unfair burden on women or exclude and alienate minorities who do not share the faith or values of the dominant culture? John R. Gillis defined a new standard for a just cultural life. He wrote, "We must strive toward new family cultures that will not unduly burden or privilege either sex or any age group, or ignore the creativity of any class or ethnic group. Men must be willing finally to pick up their share of the cultural work involved, but women must be prepared to make a place for them in this endeavor."[12] Philosopher Nancy Fraser proposes that cultural justice would consist of "the wholesale transformation of so- cietal patterns of representation, interpretation, and communication in ways that would change *everybody's* sense of self."[13] The political theory of Michael Walzer implies that the freedom *not* to go home for Thanksgiv- ing—not to feel you must go there (what he calls the "freedom to leave the groups and sometimes the identities behind")—constitutes the "liberal idea of voluntary association."[14]

If we took any of these utopian standards seriously, we would have to eliminate most of the ways we currently celebrate the life cycle and orga- nize the calendar! Gillis, Fraser, and Walzer offer quite different standards of fairness. None of their proposals is workable, let alone acceptable, for the majority of families. What is significant is that they raise questions of cultural justice. Gillis calls for gender equity and sees ethnicity and class as a matter of pluralist tolerance and inclusion. Fraser wants to democratize American popular culture. Walzer openly questions the fiction of ethnic identity, even suggesting that the freedom to escape from its burdens and demands is a fundamental liberty.

Meanwhile, women continue to be the main consumers of advice about etiquette and party planning. Martha Stewart was the most important ex- pert on ritual in the United States in the 1980s and 1990s. The transforma- tion of Martha Stewart, née Martha Kostyra, from Nutley, New Jersey, the daughter of Polish-American parents, whose father was a pharmaceutical salesman and whose mother was a housewife, to modern America's Sarah Josepha Hale—a triumph of self-reinvention as well as business acumen—showed that one did not have to come from the dominant cul- ture to become an expert on how to create it. Bursting on the national scene in 1982, not long after the defeat of the Equal Rights Amendment, she seemed almost single-handedly to stimulate a revival of domestic crafts and reinvigorate the cultural quest to make the home a sanctuary. As part of the turn toward social conservatism, women's magazines of the 1980s heralded a "new traditionalism" among women.

Through marriage, Martha Kostyra became Martha Stewart and took on the identity of a WASP. (Her father-in-law was in fact Jewish, having changed his name to Stewart in the 1930s as a way of avoiding anti-Semitism on Wall Street.) A scathing unauthorized biography suggested that Stewart's evocation of her happy family in her magazines, cookbooks, videos, housewares advertisements, mail-order catalog, website, TV shows, and radio programs is an illusion developed to cover up the reality of a stern parental home and a conflict-filled marriage, which eventually ended in divorce. Stewart, however, never sought to conceal her Polish-American background and even sentimentalized it in some of her books.[15]

Stewart combined a celebration of female (commercialized) craft skill with concepts of display (defining what good taste was) and consumption. Like Currier and Ives or Irving Berlin, she understood that nostalgia for the simple country life—for fresh vegetables from the garden, home-cooked food, domestic crafts, and a loving family set in a country kitchen in rural Connecticut—sells. Seeking to convey information about how to celebrate in an upper-class manner, she offered instruction to Americans who lacked confidence in their own taste and style. Her frequent use of the word "perfect" made Martha Stewart an exemplar of the modern approach to entertaining and domestic occasions. Martha Stewart—as iconic figure, celebrity, media personality, and name brand—inspires praise, respect, and parody. Gift stores offer wall plaques that read "Martha Stewart doesn't live here." That one can both love and laugh at Martha Stewart reveals how we Americans continue simultaneously to shape and reshape the dominant culture and to critique it. To parody Martha Stewart reveals the cynicism so characteristic of postsentimental discourse. To notice that the form of parody is a consumer object for sale in a party-goods store shows the continuing significance of consumer culture in a postsentimental age.

NOTES

This chapter first appeared in Elizabeth Pleck, *Celebrating the Family: Ethnicity, Consumer Culture, and Family Rituals* (Cambridge, MA: Harvard University Press, 2000), ch. 11.

1. Stephen Nissenbaum, *The Battle for Christmas* (New York: Knopf, 1996), 311.
2. Mrs. C. A. Halbert, "Festivals and Presents," *The Ladies' Repository: A Monthly Periodical, Devoted to Literature, Arts, and Religion* 7 (January 1871): 43.
3. Leigh Eric Schmidt calls for giving the middle-class domestic occasion and the carnivalesque equal respect; see his *Consumer Rites: The Buying and Selling of American Holidays* (Princeton, NJ: Princeton University Press, 1995), 307.
4. John J. Bukowzcyk, "Polish Rural Culture and Immigrant Working Class Formation, 1880–1914," *Polish American Studies* 41 (autumn 1984): 23–44. New Year's Day was not a legal holiday in Massachusetts until 1920. Roy Rosenzweig, *Eight Hours for What We Will: Workers and Leisure in an Industrial City, 1870–1920* (Cambridge: Cambridge University Press, 1983), 69.
5. Marshall Sklare and Joseph Greenbaum, *Jewish Identity on the Suburban Frontier: A Study of Group Survival in the Open Society* (New York: Basic Books, 1967), 50–55.
6. The trend of moving celebrations outside the home contributed to, but was not solely responsible for, the development of the postsentimental approach to ritual. To some extent, the rise of service industries enhanced family celebrations. But some out-of-home services threatened to overwhelm the idea of the family celebration and thus rejected and threatened the idea of the domestic occasion.
7. Anna Day Wilde, "Mainstreaming Kwanzaa," *Public Interest* 119 (spring 1995): 68–79.
8. Katherine Jellison, "Getting Married in the Heartland: The Commercialization of Weddings in the Rural Midwest," *Ohio University College of Arts and Sciences Forum* 12 (fall 1995): 46–50.
9. Mary Douglas, *Natural Symbols: Explorations in Cosmology* (New York: Vintage Books, 1993), 32–38.
10. Robbie E. Davis-Floyd, *Birth as an American Rite of Passage* (Berkeley: University of California Press, 1992), 2, 67, 294.
11. Evan Imber-Black and Janine Roberts, *Rituals for Our Times: Celebrating, Healing, and Changing Our Lives and Our Relationships* (New York: HarperPerennial, 1992), xvi–xvii. See also Evan Imber-Black, Janine Roberts, and Richard Whiting, eds., *Rituals in Families and Family Therapy* (New York: W. W. Norton, 1988). Religious liberals likewise called for meaningful and egalitarian rituals. See

Tom F. Driver, *The Magic of Ritual: Our Need for Liberating Rites That Transform Our Lives and Communities* (San Francisco: Harper San Francisco, 1991). For a gay affirmation of ritual, see Richard D. Mohr, "Blueberry Pancakes: Rituals and Relations," *Octopus* (December 27, 1996): 9.

12. John R. Gillis, *A World of Their Own Making: Myth, Ritual, and the Quest for Family Values* (New York: Basic Books, 1996), 239. See also Driver, *Magic of Ritual*, 46.

13. Nancy Fraser, *Justice Interruptus: Critical Reflections on the "Postsocialist" Condition* (New York: Routledge, 1997), 15.

14. Michael Walzer, "The Communitarian Critique of Liberalism," *Political Theory* 19 (February 1990): 15, 22.

15. Jerry Oppenheimer, *Martha Stewart: The Unauthorized Biography* (New York: William Morrow, 1997); Alexandra Peers, "But Martha Made It Look So Easy," *Wall Street Journal*, December 12, 1991, B10; Michelle Moravec, posting to H-Net listing for Women's History, December 5, 1997, http://h-net.msu.edu/cgi-bin/logbrowse.pl?trx=vx&list=H-Women&month=9712&week=a&msg=ojSSJHrj6nmN1mroZVq/Kg&user=&pw=; Kyle Pope, "Here's One Show Martha Stewart Might Not Find So Entertaining," *Wall Street Journal*, December 16, 1997, B1.

Chapter 3

Just for Kids
How Holidays Became Child Centered

Gary Cross

The anticipation of Christmas morning; the excitement of dashing down that dark and cool street trick-or-treating; being the birthday girl seated at a table surrounded by family, mounds of presents, and a candle-lit cake; or sharing an afternoon with a seldom-seen father at Disney's Magic Kingdom—these are all fond memories shared by many modern American children. They are also rituals invented by adults to evoke in their offspring the wonder of childhood innocence, very often expressed through gift giving. Without too much exaggeration, we could say that holidays and pilgrimages, manifestations of deep communal needs, were metamorphosed into celebrations of wondrous innocence in the last 150 years. This transformation coincided with both new attitudes toward the young and the rise of consumerism. Christmas and Halloween became the quintessential festivals of wondrous innocence, while vacations and tourist sites were transformed into children's times and places.

This occurred during the nineteenth-century reform of the "traditional" holiday cycle inherited from Christian Europe and its agrarian seasonal ebbs in work. These holidays included the post-harvest All Soul's Day (and Halloween) and midwinter Christmastide and Mardi Gras. Additional short holiday periods, including May Day, Midsummer or St. John's Eve (June 23–24), and a variable and local summer wakes week, also broke the daily grind of rural life. Each featured special customs: dancing around a bonfire at Midsummer or decorating church floors with rushes during wakes week, rites often heavily laden with religious imagery and tradition. Holiday periods often extended for days, effectively combining religious, communal, and commercial elements in anarchic profusion.[1]

Archaic encounters with the extraordinary, the supernatural, and even the bizarre survived in American freak shows and circuses.[2] Even ancient Saturnalia persisted in festival excess (sex, food, and drink) and in the social inversions of mumming and other acts of "turning the world upside down." These traditional holiday celebrations established bonds between unequals through shared rituals and feasts, as well as through an exchange of gifts. Giving to inferiors was a display of power, while presenting tribute to the superior person was a concession of subordination, but also a promise of protection. Gift exchanges reinforced dependency and power, but also harmony between unequals. These transactions were usually peaceful, but in mumming rites meandering youths and laborers apparently forced the rich into "gifts" of food and drink on holidays. "Christmas boxes" of candy or fruit, for example, had long been an obligation of superiors to subordinates (servants, apprentices, and, which is to say the same thing, children).[3]

Historians generally argue that the modern American holiday has its origins in the middle decades of the nineteenth century, years when rapid migration and sectional and social conflict seemed to demand the creation and refinement of national celebrations in the hope of creating communal bonds and new ideals of genteel and uplifting engagement. It is easy today to look back nostalgically on those Victorian goals and practices and condemn the divisive, materialistic, and hyperindividualistic holiday celebrations that seem to prevail today. The problem with this manner of thinking is not merely that it may falsely glorify celebrations based on outdated cultural models (patriarchal, northern European) or even wed to problematic values of the early nation-state and nineteenth-century capitalism, but that those invented holiday traditions contain the roots of the very materialism and individualism that many find frustrating today. This is to say more than that the sentimental values of Christmas, Easter, Thanksgiving, and other holidays were, by their very nature, amenable to commercialization. Rather, the thread running through the Victorian nationalization of holidays and the present commercialized holiday is the celebration of the "wondrous child" in the modern holiday.

The history of the modern holiday is, in large part, the history of the challenge to and decline of these classic elements of the traditional festival: wonder in the bizarre and in saturnalia and exchanges between unequals in the community. Key to this challenge has been the displacement of wonder and giving to the child. The best example of this transformation is in the modern history of Christmas.

This often-told story can be quickly summarized. Christmas was a holiday that had divided early Americans between celebrants of the traditional holiday pattern and Puritan opponents of those rituals. For many colonists in the South and middle regions where Puritans did not dominate, Christmas was a post-harvest season of eating, drinking, and frolicking, often lasting from mid-December until the first Monday after New Year's Day. Festivities included mumming (or in its Christmas form, wassailing), as groups of youths "begged" door to door for food and drink and sang and toasted their benefactors. Others intruded into the homes of colonists with masks, shouts, and swords. Even slaves were allowed to mum in North Carolina and elsewhere. The powerful and wealthy were expected to share in their bounty. They recognized that drinking and even temporary assaults on authority were necessary "safety valves." Christmas was, as historian Elizabeth Pleck notes, "a masculine, outdoor holiday rather than a feminine, domestic one." It was also definitely a holiday for adults, not children.[4] Puritan colonists were suspicious of these pagan (and unbiblical) celebrations, banning them briefly in 1659. Despite the Puritans' more accommodating attitude in the eighteenth century, tolerating feasting and even singing some Christmas hymns, the story of the nativity was not even taught in most New England Sunday schools until the 1850s. It was only between 1837 and 1890 that individual states recognized Christmas as a legal holiday in the United States.[5]

In the end, neither the traditional festival nor Puritan restraint prevailed. As historians Stephen Nissenbaum and Penne Restad argue, in the early nineteenth century, Christmas revelries became more confrontational and disruptive when youth and the poor became alien to and alienated from the rich in the large towns. In response, elites called for a new holiday tradition that unified classes and the nation. In the 1810s and 1820s, John Pintard, Washington Irving, and members of the New-York Historical Society looked for several alternatives to both the Puritan Protestant denials of holidays and the boisterous, increasingly unacceptable Christmas mummers. One idea was the restoration of the "traditional" English country Christmas in the vision of "Bracebridge Hall" stories by Irving. Another was the creation of a family-oriented exchange of gifts on New Year's Day.[6]

The more abiding solution, however, was to build a sentimental holiday around the celebration of family rather than community, ultimately shifting "patron-client exchange" to a parent-child bond. This transformation is often seen in the contrast between Dickens's *Pickwick Papers* (1837), with its scene of a rural wedding on Christmas Eve (with no children present and Christmas Day itself unimportant), and Dickens's celebration of family and the redeeming influence of innocent childhood in *A Christmas Carol*, six years later (1843). Ebenezer Scrooge may have lost the traditional fellowship of his youth, the bonding of fellow workers with the benevolent old master Fezziwig at Christmas, but he found again a loving community in old age in the scene of the Crachit family's joyous celebration centered on the innocent wonder of Tiny Tim. This signaled the transformation of Christmas from a saturnalian public festival to a sentimental celebration of family and childhood innocence. Protestants (and others) accepted this "compromise" as family became a substitute for the religious community. As historian John R. Gillis notes, "Middle-class Victorians turned the family into an object of worshipful contemplation. As a result of the crisis of faith that had caused so many to have serious doubts about the existence of God and his transcendent order, the family became proof of the existence of the divine."[7]

In new rites centering on family, and especially on the wonder of childhood, a benevolent deity could be experienced. The sentimental family Christmas in the United States required new rituals and symbols to give it substance. Often spread by popular middle-class magazines, these rituals and symbols included German Christmas trees in the 1830s, English Christmas cards in the 1840s, Dutch cookies and new carols published in the 1870s, and especially the exchange of gifts between family members.[8] Americans and many Europeans turned Christmas into a family holiday, centered on the divine baby, surrounded by loving parents. This image of the holy family was not new, but it reflected real middle-class domestic ideas as it had never done before. No longer were children seen as servants upon whom Christmas boxes were obligingly bestowed, but rather as unique individuals, upon whom parents happily showered presents. The offspring represented the family and helped confirm it as a harmonious unit set apart from the public world of class differences. In contrast to the old holiday time spent mumming, snowball throwing, or attending cheap theater, Christmas became ideally a time for subdued family activities in the parlor, especially playing moralistic board games. These domestic pleasures of Christmas directly challenged and ultimately prevailed over the old rites of mumming and revelry.[9]

As rituals became domesticated, so also the "gift economy," anthropologist Dan Miller notes, shifted from building communal bonds to reinforcing family ties. Gifts were "tamed" as they became expressions of love and personal relationship rather than of power and wealth. The refocus on family and children helped to eliminate godless ribaldry, but it did not lead to sublimity or solemnity. Spending on gifts within the home and family suggested a new kind of "liberality," no longer a joyful protest against scarcity, but a domestic inversion of the pinched calculation and competition of the business culture that Victorian Anglo-Saxon industrialism had created.[10] This process also eliminated the giving across social classes and replaced it with a "potlatch of magnification," where exchanges between family members and indulgence toward children concentrated, rather than spread, bounty. Still, the sort of carefree spending that had characterized the old saturnalia continued to be suspect in the calm and prudent domestic Christmas festival. Especially problematic were the questions: Did Christmas giving threaten the spiritual and moral development of children? How could manufactured gifts, the products of the impersonal world of machines and commerce, express love between unique family members?[11]

Of course, Victorian Americans avoided these tensions by presenting gifts of devotion (especially Bibles) or edification (parlor board games, for example). And it took decades for Christmas shopping to extend beyond Christmas Eve. Some families exchanged homemade gifts. Even when the advantages of commercial presents became obvious (saving time and offering better quality), gift givers still sought to add personal touches (complementary craftwork, fancy wrapping, or, by the twentieth century, the time and care of extra hours of shopping).[12]

Perhaps the greatest filter or decontaminator, shielding the gifting process from "materialism" and commercialism, was Santa Claus himself. This figure evolved in the nineteenth century into the "stand in" for the parental gift giver. Santa, in effect, disguised the indulgence of parents from children and to some extent from the parents themselves. It was Santa, after all, not the parents, who heaped box upon box under the tree. He also removed the ambivalence parents felt about the connection between the worlds of home and market by disguising the commercial origins of Christmas toys, masking them in the mystery and magic of their North Pole origins in the old-fashioned workshop of master toymaker Santa himself. When parents encouraged children to write to Santa with a list of wants, parents obtained vital information about what children themselves wanted. This was a concession to children's choice without inviting them to badger or beg the parent. Even more, the child's imaginative relationship with Santa made the child's longing, and even greed, charming.[13]

Repeatedly, commentators have complained that the "spirit" of Christmas has been corrupted by the materialistic appeal of Santa. Yet, as Russell Belk notes, modern Christmas and commercialization appeared simultaneously. Never was there a pure Christmas of charity and simple family traditions. Spending has always been a part of the modern sentimental holiday, and yesterday's tawdry commercialization of Christmas eventually became today's venerated traditions. Showy department store windows, the Coca-Cola Santa, ornate Christmas cards, Bing Crosby's "White Christmas," all once crass commercial exploitations of Christmas, were transformed into the hallowed tradition of nostalgia. As Belk puts the point, "With the secularization of society, we have relegated the sacred to the material world. In so doing, the control of transcendence has shifted from the central authority of the church to the diffuse authority of the media and merchant."[14]

Moreover, wonder has shifted from the world of religious and community ritual to the focal point of family life—the child. Involuntarily, the child became the priest of this transcendence through rituals of wondrous innocence that were almost seamlessly wed to the "diffuse authority" of the market. The transformation of Santa illustrates this trend. The new Santa represented abundance, from his bottomless bag of gifts to his cheery cheeks and plump belly. As Belk observes, he recalled the ancient god of pleasure, Bacchus, not a Christian Saint. Santa became a secular god, all-knowing and prayed to, a miracle worker on Christmas Eve, filling stockings with sweets and trinkets and bringing heaps of toys for which no one had to sacrifice or pay.

This shift of the gift from the community to the family and ultimately to Santa romanticized materialism and thus contributed to individualistic and market society,[15] but the appeal of Santa went further. It was a delight in the naive, innocent desire of children, whose, in Clement Clarke Moore's words, "visions of sugar plums danced in their heads" and whose fantasy of a "sleigh and eight tiny reindeer" could be relived by adults' "wondering eyes." It is, historian Leigh Eric Schmidt notes, "the romantic longing for enchantment in the face of the disenchanting forces of the Enlightenment and a market economy" that is realized through consumption, especially for children.[16] Christmas spending also restored "wonder" in adults through children, even if it was increasingly confined to the wonders of commercialism.

Late Victorians were, of course, still capable of feeling guilt about this shift of Christmas from an affirmation of community to an indulgence of their own offspring. Louisa May Alcott's characters in *Little Women* bring Christmas presents to the poor in the neighborhood after receiving their gifts at home. This gesture was in harmony with the training of middle-class girls for personalized charity. But the lesson went further. When the rich insisted that their children contribute to Christmas clubs for the poor, they understood also that they should take care of their possessions and not take them for granted. This lesson was the adults' shield against the spoiled child that they were in danger of engendering.[17] Wonder and delight would appear in the unsullied eyes of poor children, for, like rich parents' own *once*-unsuspecting child, the poor children were not yet jaded. The contrast between the longing for and the possession of the gift was always key to the meaning of wondrous innocence.[18] Santa could not take away all the ambiguity of adult longings for wonder.

The problem with the child's "faith" in a Santa who gives and gives went deeper than equating the spiritual with stuff. In the modern child-centered family, the suspension of restraint common in all festivals took on a new meaning. In sharp contrast to the excesses of the traditional saturnalia, the child was not a temporary "king for a day" but the enduring center of family attention. Thus, the "innocent" child became the indulged child, for whom Christmas was not the exception but the rule. Delight in children's youthful wonder turned into disgust with their greed and superficiality. The simple fact was that the Christmas ritual of wondrous innocence accelerated the loss of innocence and wonder.[19]

The passing of Halloween customs to children followed very much the same pattern as Christmas despite its unique and distant origins in the Celtic New Year's celebration, known as Samhain. October 31 was the day when Druids propitiated and warded off the hostile ghosts of the recently dead. They opened their doors, offering bonfires and even gifts of food to these returning ghosts, and later dressed as spirits themselves to shield themselves from ghosts' mischief. In 834 AD, the Church attempted to co-opt this ancient festival of harvest and darkening days of autumn by declaring November 1 All Saints Day. Nevertheless, Samhain traditions survived through medieval times as All-Hallows Eve or Halloween.[20]

Irish immigrants imported to the United States these and other Celtic customs in the 1840s, but it was only a century later that Halloween became truly a child-centered holiday. One set of Halloween customs was female and domestic (parties with costumes, apple bobbing, nut roasting, and divination games that had once assuaged fears of death and the future). A second set of Halloween customs centered on pranks and mumming committed by older boys and young men, in effect, attacking the domestic order. This second group of Halloween customs was part of a broad tradition of disorderly festivities: ridiculing tradition and authority as well as masquerading and begging for treats as commonly practiced on New Year's and even Thanksgiving.[21]

It is only in the 1930s and 1940s that Halloween was "infantilized." Increasing urbanization and the social tensions caused by the Depression ultimately made the traditional rowdyism of Halloween unacceptable to elites. These traditions gradually were bowdlerized when adults passed them on to young children in gentle, "cute" forms. Beginning in the early 1930s, voluntary organizations (such as American Legion, Rotary, and Lions' Clubs) and municipal recreation departments sought to persuade pranksters to join in Halloween fairs and parades. Some even sponsored window art (with washable paint) on store windows. The result was a holiday, as Tad Tuleja notes, that "has become simultaneously commercialized and infantilized."[22] Tuleja stresses how trick-or-treating became bowdlerized as well. In the 1940s and early 1950s, Halloween costumes featured spiritual or social outcasts (ghosts and witches, as well as hobos and pirates), reminding householders both of traditional fears of the unknown and recent social upheavals during the Depression. However, these gave way to costumes depicting Disney characters and other hallmarks of popular media. The tradition of inviting trick-or-treaters into the home was replaced by the quick delivery of goodies at the door with practically no exchange between adult and child.[23]

There is much truth in this characterization, but it misses the reason Halloween was passed on to children in the first place. What was the appeal to parents in dressing their children in costumes that seemed to be anything but innocent and encouraging them to do what was normally unacceptable, that is, knocking on neighbors' doors and begging for far more candy than they would be given in a year of pestering parents at the grocery store checkout line? Trick-or-treating was a classic case of the ritual's "descent" from an ancient tradition of magical propitiation to mock fear and violence, ending in complete domestication in the delightful look of the charming child at the doorstep. As important, it was also a way of letting children toy with the scary and with power within a safe and playful context. Children had their way in selecting costumes and masks, in imposing themselves on neighbors, and even in stuffing their faces with tasty but unhealthy sweets. Halloween became part of the cult of the cute, the naughty but nice, the infantilization of saturnalia.

Of course, the child-centered holiday has not gone unchallenged. While many condemned the commercialized sentimentalism of Christmas, if anything, the rites of gift giving to children became ever more elaborate by the end of the twentieth century. Other sites of wondrous innocence, however, were far more vulnerable, especially Halloween and the Disney vacation. Halloween was always the most suspect ritual of wondrous innocence because its archaic qualities had never been entirely suppressed and it remained a community celebration. Halloween did not use children to force adults to withdraw into domesticity. Instead, it invited children to go out and trick-or-treat. Halloween also retained associations with the violent and irrational traditions of mumming and the pagan occult that could not be as easily tamed and disguised as they had been for Christmas. Within a generation of its invention, trick-or-treating was condemned as too dangerous or as leading children into pagan and satanic beliefs. In 1982, widespread publicity surrounding an incident in which an individual laced Tylenol pain medicine with cyanide induced fears that led communities to ban trick-or-treating and create "safer" alternatives. The scare abated by the end of the 1980s but left many parents with lingering doubts. It is at least a little strange that parents would feel safer taking their children to the mall for trick-or-treating than letting them visit their neighbors. Little could be more telling about the decline of community trust than this.[24]

Another threat to the wonder of trick-or-treating came from the religious right. Rejecting the long-established practice of passing on to children sanitized versions of old community and even pagan traditions, these new "Puritans" wanted to shelter children from anything that could potentially threaten their Christian values. For some, this led to the belief that, because of the pagan origins of Halloween, trick-or-treating was a form of devil worship. In the 1970s, some fundamentalist Protestant churches tried to turn Halloween into an opportunity to evangelize at Christian haunted houses. By 1997, some 225 churches bought a "packaged" haunted house that displayed abortions, satanic murder, teen suicide, and the funeral of a homosexual victim of AIDS. Although all this was certainly a minority view, pressures from religious conservatives led school districts to substitute Halloween crafts and costume parades with "neutral" activities: In Frederick County, near Washington, D.C., the public schools tried to make "National Book Week" an acceptable alternative. Some schools even banned Halloween. All this, emerging only in the 1980s, was part of a broader conservative religious response to non-Christian customs and growing belief in the coming of the Antichrist. Yet it also was an assault on modern Halloween, the passing of pagan and saturnalian traditions on to children.[25]

Finally, the child-focused Halloween was threatened when adults attempted to take it over again. By the 1980s, adult Halloween costume parties had become common. In 1987, the *Washington Post* reported that Halloween had become a "paean to the powers of the imagination," an opportunity for adults to "upend etiquette." They could attend one of the many costumed balls throughout Washington, D.C., or join the crowd of one hundred thousand who rushed into the streets of Georgetown for Halloween fun. Adults wanted their saturnalia back. By 1999, an estimated 44 percent of 25–34-year-olds attended Halloween parties (with 62 percent of 18–24-year-olds dressing up in Halloween costumes).[26] The classic moment of wondrous innocence when the neighbor happily greets the naughty-looking six-year-old dressed as the devil and stuffs candy into her outstretched bag remains, of course. Yet Halloween is no longer so innocent, nor is childish wonder so central to its celebration.

The child-focused holiday has served many historically significant social and cultural needs: It created a counter to the class-based exchanges and conflicts of the traditional saturnalian celebrations and provided an alternative to pre-Enlightenment experiences of wonder in the delight of the child. It has been the occasion for the modern emotion of nostalgia and the release of tensions, no longer through saturnalian "excess" but through the "innocent" indulgence of childhood. At the same time, the child-focused holiday has been expressed primarily through consumers' wonder, the child's delightful response to the gifts of adults, a ritual relationship that, because of its one-sidedness and the fact that it leads to satiation and to desires not controlled by adults, has become perpetually problematic. It is perhaps inevitable that modern holidays are often child centered, but this phenomenon hardly provides a path toward establishing the holiday as a vehicle for community building.

NOTES

1. Fascinating details can be found in A. R. Wright, *British Calendar Customs* (London: W. Glaisher, 1936–40), 3 vols.; Robert Muchembled, *Popular Culture and Elite Culture in France, 1400–1750*, trans. Lydia Cochrane (Baton Rouge: Louisiana State University Press, 1985), 49–61; and George Homans, *English Villagers of the Thirteenth Century* (New York: Russell and Russell, 1960), 353–81.

2. Robert W. Malcolmson, *Popular Recreations in English Society, 1700–1850* (Cambridge: Cambridge University Press, 1973), 21; and William Addison, *English Fairs and Markets* (London: B. T. Batsford, 1953), 95–225.

3. Christopher Gregory, *Gifts and Commodities* (London: Academic Press, 1982), 41; Lisett Josephides, *The Product of Inequality: Gender and Exchanges among the Kewa* (London: Lavistock, 1985); and the classics, M. Maus, *The Gift* (New York: Norton, 1967), 37, 69, 76; Bronislaw Malinowski, *Crime and Custom in Savage Society* (London: Kegan Paul, 1926), 39–45; and Leigh Eric Schmidt, *Consumer Rites: The Buying and Selling of American Holidays* (Princeton, NJ: Princeton University Press, 1995), 108.

4. Elizabeth Pleck, *Celebrating the Family: Ethnicity, Consumer Culture, and Family Rituals* (Cambridge, MA: Harvard University Press, 1999), 45; Penne Restad, *Christmas in America: A History* (New York: Oxford University Press, 1995), 4–5, 84; Frederick Douglass, *The Life of Frederick Douglass* (New York: New American Library, 1968), 84–85; Stephen Nissenbaum, *The Battle for Christmas* (New York: Knopf, 1996), 5–11.

5. William Waits, *The Modern Christmas in America: A Cultural History of Gift Giving* (New York: New York University Press, 1993), ch. 2; Restad, *Christmas in America*, 17–41, 91–104; Nissenbaum, *Battle for Christmas*, 14–45.

6. Schmidt, *Consumer Rites*, 113–120; Nissenbaum, *Battle for Christmas*, 49–65; Karal Ann Marling, *Merry Christmas: Celebrating America's Greatest Holiday* (Cambridge, MA: Harvard University Press, 2000), 122–30; Restad, *Christmas in America*, 30–35, 137; and Adam Juper, "English Christmas and the Family," and James Carrier, "The Rituals of Christmas Giving," in Daniel Miller, ed., *Unwrapping Christmas* (Oxford: Clarendon Press, 1993), 65–68, 160. Note also Russell Belk, "Materialism and the Making of Modern American Christmas," in Miller, *Unwrapping Christmas*, 75–104; and R. Belk, "Materialism and the Modern U.S. Christmas," in Elizabeth Hirschman, ed., *Interpretive Consumer Research* (Provo, UT: Association for Consumer Research, 1989), 115–35.

7. John Pimlott, *The Englishman's Christmas: A Social History* (Atlantic Heights, NJ: Humanities Press, 1978), 23–29, 120–24; James Barnett, *The American Christmas: A Study in National Culture* (New York: Macmillan, 1954), ch. 1; Katherine Richards, *How Christmas Came to Sunday Schools* (New York: Dodd, Mead, 1934); J. Golby and A. Purdue, *The Making of the Modern Christmas* (London:

Batsford, 1986); and John Gillis, *A World of Their Own Making: Myth, Ritual, and the Quest for Family Values* (New York: Basic Books, 1996), 71.

8. Restad, *Christmas in America,* 58–68, 96; Pimlott, *Englishman's Christmas,* 94, 110.

9. Nissenbaum, *Battle for Christmas,* ch. 3 is especially insightful on these themes.

10. Daniel Miller, "A Theory of Christmas," in Miller, *Unwrapping Christmas,* 18–22.

11. Nissenbaum finds an ad for children's Christmas books in an 1806 Salem, Massachusetts, newspaper, though by the 1840s candies became common, even caramelized sugar and chocolate molds in the shape of beetles, spiders, and cockroaches (clearly appealing to boys). *Battle for Christmas,* 136, 138.

12. Restad, *Christmas in America,* 70; James Carrier, "Gifts in a World of Commodities: The Ideology of the Perfect Gift in American Society," *Social Analysis* 29 (1990): 19–37; David Cheal, "'Showing Them You Love Them': Gift Giving and the Dialectic of Intimacy," *Sociological Review* 35 (1987): 150–69; Belk, "Materialism," 86–87, 94–95; Schmidt, *Consumer Rites,* 127; Waits, *Modern Christmas,* ch. 2.

13. Restad, *Christmas in America,* 143, 151; Belk, "Materialism," 92–93; and Michael Barton, "The Victorian Jeremiad: Critics of Accumulation and Display," in Simon Bronner, ed., *Consuming Visions: Accumulation and Display of Goods in America, 1880–1920* (New York: Norton, 1989), 55.

14. Belk, "Materialism," 89.

15. Ibid., 95.

16. Schmidt, *Consumer Rites,* 173.

17. Susan Warner's *Carl Krinken: His Christmas Stocking* (New York, 1854), 14, cited in Nissenbaum, *Battle for Christmas,* 245–46.

18. Sophie Swett, "The Crust of the Christmas Pie," *Harper's Young People,* January 8, 1884, 149; and Marling, *Merry Christmas,* 140–50.

19. Nissenbaum, *Battle for Christmas,* 209–11.

20. Ralph Linton and Adelin Linton, *Halloween through Twenty Centuries* (New York: Schuman, 1950); Christina Hole, *British Folk Customs* (London: Hutchinson, 1976), 91; Peter Opie and Iona Opie, *Language and Lore of Schoolchildren* (Oxford: Clarendon, 1959), 269–83; Tom Sinclair-Faulkner, "How the Pumpkin Lost Its Teeth," *Christian Century,* October 29, 1980, 1033. Good sources can be found in Tad Tuleja, "Trick or Treat: Pre-Texts and Contexts," in Jack Santino, ed., *Halloween and Other Festivals of Death and Life* (Knoxville: University of Tennessee Press, 1994), 95–102.

21. For contemporary accounts, note, for example, Ruth Kelley, *The Book of Halloween* (Boston: Lothrop, 1919); Bellamy Patridge and Otto Bettman, *As We Were: Family Life in America 1850–1900* (New York: McGraw-Hill, 1946), 24; George William Douglas, *American Book of Days* (New York: H. W. Wilson, 1943), 53; "Halloween Pranks and Pumpkins Are Traditional," *Life,* November 3, 1941, 68–

70; and Alvin Schwartz, ed., *When I Grew Up Long Ago* (Philadelphia: Lippincott, 1978), 127–30.

22. Margaret Mead, "Halloween, Where Has All the Mischief Gone," *Redbook*, December 1975, 31–32; "A Victim of the Window Soaping Brigade," *American Home*, November 1939, 48; "New Tricks and Treats for Halloween," *American Home*, November 1940, 95–96. Other articles illustrating Halloween reform include *Recreation*, October 1941, 420; *American City*, October 1941, 99; *Recreation*, September 1946, 297; *Parents' Magazine*, October 1946, 60; *Rotarian*, October 1949, 34; and Tuleja, "Trick or Treat," 89.

23. Tuleja, "Trick or Treat," 91–95. See also Brian Sutton-Smith, "What Happened to Halloween?" *Parents' Magazine*, October 1983, 64; Gregory Stone, "Halloween and the Mass Child," *American Quarterly* 11, no. 3 (fall 1959): 372–79; and Ervin Beck, "Tricker on the Threshold: An Interpretation of Children's Autumn Traditions," *Folk-Lore* 96, no. 1 (1985): 24–28.

24. "Halloween Safety Guide," *Parents' Magazine*, October 1971, 20; *Newsweek*, November 11, 1982, 33; *New York Times*, October 31, 1982, 45; *Omaha World Herald*, October 6, 1983, 23; *Seattle Times*, November 11, 1984, B3; *Omaha World Herald*, October 31, 1984, 34; *Dallas Morning News*, October 31, 1989; *Seattle Times*, November 1, 1984, B2; *Los Angeles Times*, October 28,1985, C3; *Washington Post*, October 31, 1985, A21; *New York Times*, October 27, 1985, 34; Jan Brunvand, *Curses! Broiled Again: The Hottest Urban Legends Going* (New York: Norton, 1989); and *Seattle Times*, October 30, 1990, B3.

25. *Washington Post*, October 18, 1990, M1, and October 31, 1994, M1; *Los Angeles Times*, October 30, 1995, 1; and *Palm Beach Post*, October 31, 1998, 1.

26. "Halloween, an Adult Treat," *Time*, October 31, 1983, 110; *Washington Post*, October 30, 1987; 1; *Wall Street Journal*, October 22, 1999, 1; PR Newswire, October 13, 1999, Lexis-Nexis; *St. Petersburg Times*, October 31, 1986, 1; and *Houston Chronicle*, October 30, 1988, 2.

Chapter 4

This Is Our Family

Stepfamilies, Rituals, and Kinship Connections

Mary F. Whiteside

Holidays are generally seen as times of celebration and reaffirmations of family belonging. Old, familiar rituals can make the world feel orderly and natural, reminding us of who we are and where we come from. For stepfamilies, however, holiday celebrations do not come so easily. Particularly in the years immediately following a remarriage, the need to develop a vision of a "normal," societally acceptable family identity may clash with the unique structural characteristics of stepfamilies. There are strongly held traditions from first marriages which resist and compete with attempts to establish new, more inclusive celebrations. The tasks facing the family include developing a vision of family identity with connectedness and familiarity, honoring the different histories and traditions of various family members, dealing with a complicated extended family network, and being patient with the very slow process of family reorganization.

Because family celebrations are such a visible and dramatic marker of family definition and change, they represent a rich opportunity to observe and to understand processes of stepfamily formation. In the rituals enacted during these critical times, we can observe families deciding who belongs. We can also hear messages about the family's beliefs about themselves, what is "normal," what is to be celebrated, and what has been lost.

Steven Wolin and Linda Bennett have described the ritual process in nuclear families as a key area for the creation and maintenance of family cohesion. They define ritual in this context as "a symbolic form of communication that, owing to the satisfaction that family members experience through its repetition, is acted out in a systematic fashion over time.

Through their special meaning and their repetitive nature, rituals contribute significantly to the establishment and preservation of a family's collective sense of itself, which we have termed the 'family identity.'"[1]

Wolin and Bennett have categorized family rituals into three areas: everyday patterned interactions, family traditions, and family celebrations. Each area of ritual involves a different subgroup of family members and a different degree of abstraction of family identity. For the remarried family, each of these areas requires a new model of family organization in which roles from old family traditions do not fit and new ones are only beginning to emerge. As each special occasion occurs during the early years of a remarriage, a complex process occurs in which decisions are made about who plays which roles in the family, who is "in" and who is "out," and how close various family members will be to one another. Over time, a stable organization will evolve that may be more or less functional for the needs of individual members.

Kinship in Remarried Families

The kinship system that emerges from a second marriage is complex and confusing.[2] It includes the wide network of people and relationships created through the divorce and remarriage. These ties include blood, in-law, former in-law, and step relationships. The smallest subgroup is the family membership of the household of the remarried couple. This family includes the couple and their biological (or adopted) children, whether or not the children reside with the couple full-time. For the purposes of this article, this unit will be referred to as the stepfamily. (The psychological "immediate family" of each of these individuals will most likely vary from this definition.) At the second level we have the binuclear family (or families).[3] The binuclear family includes the households of both of a child's biological parents. If both parents have remarried, and/or if stepparents have been formerly married, the chain of interconnecting binuclear households can be quite complex. The third level of family membership includes grandparents, former in-laws, step-in-laws, aunts, uncles, and so on; this level will be referred to as the remarried family "suprasystem."[4]

Every family has its own rules and traditions that regulate relationships within the family. These continuing patterns of relationship establish a sense of family identity that is stable over time and differentiated from the outside world. During the divorce period, these everyday patterns are disrupted and the old rules break down. A new family identity is gradually developed, as a "one-parent unit" or a "family with two separated households." Feelings of belonging and of stability are gradually restored during this period, only to be disrupted anew with the introduction of additional family members from the remarriage. The experience of disorganization, the clash of competing patterns of living, the sense of loss, and the uncertainty about belonging trigger strong emotional responses in all family members. All stepfamilies face the task of developing family rules that stabilize their relationships. In addition, some have the extra baggage of conflictual relationships with former spouses or in-laws, insufficient preparation time for being together, and/or children only too ready to protest and express their disapproval.

The patterns of everyday routines—mealtimes, bedtime, discipline, recreation, and the transitions of children between homes—define the nature of the remarried couple's "immediate family." The movement from competing family cultures defined along biological lines to the comfortable exchanges on common ground of a well-established family group can take years of painful, awkward, and discouraging negotiations.[5] Many families do not make it. Sally Cunningham Clark and Barbara Foley Wilson report that 60 percent of remarriages end in divorce within five years.[6]

Holidays in Remarried Families

Holiday celebrations have the potential and power to either create a family disaster, leaving everyone alienated and wondering if the marriage will work, or provide an opportunity to engender feelings of closeness and common experience which can create an emotional cushion for weathering difficult times. Holiday celebrations are times of family tradition that are idiosyncratic for each family and say, "This is the way we are, this is our family."[7] Psychologists commonly advise stepfamilies to approach holidays with flexibility and creativity. Stepfamilies are encouraged to create new rituals that will begin to define the stepfamily unit as unique, different, and special. The development of rituals creates a solemn and/or exuberant atmosphere set apart from everyday life. Even a family member who does not wholeheartedly participate in a ritual is nonetheless included in the family's membership and its evolving history. As these experiments with family "special times" succeed enough to recur and to emerge as customs, the stepfamily unit begins to feel that it has a life of its own.

Unlike celebrations within nuclear families, however, many of the traditional occasions for remarried families inevitably involve the binuclear family. Thus, an occasion that is or was traditionally celebrated with all immediate family members may include only a subgroup of the family because of the children's schedules. This introduces into the warmth of celebration the additional theme of loss. One man, whose three-year-old son resided primarily with the child's mother, described his visits to his parents' home without his son as follows: "Everyone knew it was hard for me, therefore no one mentioned him—it was as if he were dead." A woman whose new husband was struggling to establish a relationship with her nine-year-old daughter said, "It was at Christmas time that I realized most clearly how much I missed the close times as a single parent with my daughter." A couple in their first year of marriage had coordinated their children's schedules with the other household so that major holidays would alternate during the year. They had anticipated that celebrating this first Thanksgiving alone would feel like a small honeymoon. Unexpectedly experiencing painful feelings of the loss of family, they found themselves in a bitter argument. Even when all stepfamily members are together, the other household's presence is felt, as each person brings an allegiance to the traditions developed in the first marriages. There may be strong resistance to celebrating in a new way with new family members, and children in particular may eloquently voice their reluctance.

Alternatively, the remarried family can develop traditions that stretch across households and acknowledge that children have primary relationships in at least two places. For some families, the symbolic statement becomes, "We are a 'binuclear family' rather than a 'nuclear family.'" In other families, a tight boundary is drawn around the stepfamily, with the message, "We are a 'normal family' again with two parents in the same household." Yet this message contradicts the reality of a difference in quality of relationship between step and biological dyads—a difference that often becomes more marked as the child grows older. This message denies the past life in the first marriage and devalues the importance to the child of maintaining contact with the parent in the other household.

On the other hand, while acknowledging the reality of cross-household ties, the stepfamily must develop traditions that reinforce a boundary around its stepfamily subgroup and integrate the husband's and wife's family subsystems. These traditions may need to flexibly accommodate the comings and goings of varying numbers of household members. In early remarriage, many of these traditions are in flux and experimental, even though the developmental stage of the family may be well advanced.

When one follows a remarried family through the process of dealing with celebrations, several critical times are observed. First, there is the extended period of anticipation and negotiation preceding the event. During this time, most family members actively consider both the view of the remarried family to be presented and the statements made about their relationship to others in the potential kin network (e.g., Will the former spouse be included in the Thanksgiving dinner celebration? Will we insist that all the children from both families be together for some point in the Christmas celebration? Will we go to the Seder dinner with my former in-laws? Should I ask my mother to have birthday gifts for the step-grand-children?). Because it is a time of change and reorganization, even small considerations that are normally assumed, routine, and automatic need to be made explicit and consciously discussed. This process makes all the family members feel anxious and uncomfortable. They may feel that if all family unity and connection is discussable, then it can be dissolved. Family members feel separate, isolated, and burdened by this "new family" outside of themselves.

On the other hand, once a pattern has been made explicit, there is the potential for creating an openness to trial solutions and input from each family member. Unintended exclusions can be foreseen; grandparents can be reminded ahead of time to include stepchildren in the gift exchange; and parents can realize that the child who has been the youngest at the Seder for years now has a younger step-sibling and that they need to develop a plan beforehand to avoid the child's feeling displaced.

During the event itself, family members acknowledge the tension, anxiety, and awkwardness of performing new and different roles, yet they also express pleasure in their ability to carry out their aims and surprise in the creative possibilities that can emerge. If the event is successful, afterward there can be a marked decrease in family tension and an increase in the feeling of "normality."

New Stepfamily Traditions

Throughout the first few years of the remarriage, family traditions are constructed from several different sources. Some traditions emerge from the successful navigation of novel and/or distressing situations, some are carried over from one side of the family or the other, and others represent a creative solution to the clash of competing heritages.

Mastery of the Novel Experience

Many families see vacations spent together, in a new place, as important consolidating experiences.[8] Time spent away from usual routines offers a wealth of opportunities for negotiating and defining new relationships. Thus, there are discussions about who sits where in the car, who rides with whom if there are too many for one car, how it is decided who sleeps on the floor, and so on. The fishermen debate with the jet-skiers and the snorkelers ally with the swimmers. When a solution is reached by pooling everyone's ideas and cracking a few jokes, all members of the group feel closer and more trusting. In the process of making these decisions, new family values become evident. For example, "There will be no favorites— we'll draw straws for the comfortable bed"; "We'll rent a van for vacation so there will be room for everyone"; "There are new groupings in this family by interest: swimmers in one car and jet-skiers in the other"; "When you are injured and your mother is far away, your stepmother can care for you."

Direct Incorporation of Old Rituals

One way of handling a holiday event is to continue one family's tradition without challenging the old ways and without creating serious tension in the stepfamily unit. This solution is likely to occur when one spouse carries highly organized and ritualized traditions and the new spouse does not.

For example, in one family the stepmother has learned to cook certain dishes in her mother-in-law's style and now reads the Seder service from a book in which her name is written over the crossed-out name of the previous spouse. Since her own family placed very little importance on the Passover celebration, she has enjoyed the opportunity to adopt traditions she felt her family had neglected. The basic pattern of the Passover ritual has not been altered by the remarriage. The old structure continues with replaceable actors.

The Integration of New and Old

Some household celebrations evolve into a mixture of small traditions from both households in a blend of new and old. One family practiced the tradition of lighting a candle in the Advent wreath before Sunday dinner. In the remarried family, they added to the candle lighting a time when each person speaks a few words about something personally important. In this way, the form of an old ritual was used to enable the new family members to know one another more intimately.

Common Patterns of Remarried Kinship Networks

If one takes a cross-sectional view of a remarried family as it participates in family traditions and celebrations, a measure can be taken of the pattern of kinship connection. Although much work has been done on the coparental relationship following divorce and remarriage, only a handful of studies have addressed the nature of extended family kinship connections. Constance R. Aprons and Roy H. Rodgers, as well as the author, suggest that when parents are able to be relatively cooperative, they are more able to coordinate both everyday routines and planning for celebrations.[9] When the relationship is highly conflictual, or when spousal issues are not separated from parenting issues, planning is disrupted, competition over the child permeates special family events, and relationships with extended family members are affected.

Generally, grandparents and step-grandparents are seen as potential resources who can add emotional and other kinds of support to parents and grandchildren during the transitions of divorce and remarriage. However, Marilyn Ihinger-Tallman and Kay Pasley report that contact with grandparents is diminished after remarriage.[10] Similarly, Gretchen Lussier and colleagues have found that children in stepfamilies have the most contact and feel closest with the grandparents related to their residential parent and stepparent. Therefore, for example, children in father-stepmother homes had more contact with their paternal grandparents and their stepmother's parents than they did with their maternal grandparents.[11] And Lawrence H. Ganong and Marilyn Coleman argue that even when relationships are good, former in-laws are likely to lose family ties and family-based obligations after remarriage.[12]

These studies look primarily at North American or British families and report frequency of contact and feelings of closeness among family members, generally finding a positive correlation between the two. A study conducted by Caroline Henry and Sandra Lovelace is one of the few that look at the connection among family routines, frequency of family celebrations, and family satisfaction. The researchers found that adolescents in remarried households who perceived their families to be more flexible and who perceived regularity in family time and routines reported significantly greater satisfaction with the overall remarried family households than did adolescents who reported greater rigidity and less regularity.[13] The researchers did not, however, find a significant correlation between frequency of family celebrations and satisfaction.

Reorganizing Remarried Families through Celebration

Drawing on the findings from the studies discussed above and from exploratory clinical studies by the author,[14] we can describe three basic processes of family reorganization for American remarried families: expansion, contraction, and substitution. With each family reorganization there is a choice to expand or to contract the kinship network. If connections are maintained following divorce, in the positive sense of the binuclear family, remarriage organization can provide an opportunity for a greatly expanded network.[15] Alternatively, it may provoke a contraction in contacts with former spouses and in-laws. Decisions to cut off family ties after divorce can either make it more difficult to incorporate stepfamily kin, for the children in particular, or create a vacuum, leading to the drawing in of stepkin as a substitute for biological kin.

The Expanded Kinship Network

Expanded or inclusive families retain as family the relatives from previous marriages and also include stepkin as relatives. These families celebrate both within the remarried household and with extended families. Some children in these families have as many as six holiday celebrations during the winter holiday season. The expanded network is the pattern that reflects the most flexibility, the most access to resources, and the least interference of unresolved conflict. This is the pattern that is cited as the most beneficial to the families who are able to accomplish it. As stated by Frank Furstenberg and Graham Spanier, "It is generally in the interests of everyone to retain as many relatives as possible."[16] Colleen Leahy Johnson and Barbara Barer found that grandmothers in expanding kinship systems have more permissive and flexible values on divorce, are less disapproving of their children's lifestyles, and are more satisfied with their relationships with their children and grandchildren.[17] Children in divorced families whose parents are cooperative, who have a positive relationship with the nonresidential parent, and see that parent frequently are better adjusted emotionally and cognitively than children whose parents continue in conflict or are cut off from each other.[18]

Work by Constance R. Aprons and Roy H. Rodgers suggests that within an expanded kinship network there are differences across families in the level of inclusion of both households in everyday routines and in family traditions. In one group of former spouses, which Aprons refers to as "Perfect Pals," both adults and children define former in-laws as family. In a second group, called "Cooperative Colleagues," the adults are less close to former spouses and former in-laws. In both of these functional coparenting styles, major life events are planned jointly between households and contact is maintained with former in-laws. However, Perfect Pals are more likely to celebrate together as a family unit, while Cooperative Colleagues maintain a more distinct boundary between households, need more explicit negotiating of plans, and are more formally defined. Both styles are functional and maintain access to an expanded network, but they vary in their degree of inclusion.[19]

The major thrust of this research is the formulation of a kinship model for divorced/remarried families that is different from the stereotype of divorced families as broken and fragmented. However, the task of maintaining connections with former in-laws and forging connections within the new stepfamily at the same time is not an easy one. In thinking about adaptive patterns, it is useful to think of different degrees of inclusion on a continuum of kinship networks. In families interviewed by the author, the vision of family identity varied greatly within the subgroup of inclusive families.[20] For example, one family viewed its remarried extended family as a series of concentric circles (the couple with their biological child, this group plus stepchildren, the former spouse and in-law relatives, and so on). The family's holiday plans included a variety of events, with varying membership, all seen as integral parts of a complicated whole. Another family, less inclusive, conscientiously supported the children's participation in celebrations of extended family for each household, accommodating schedules and providing transportation as needed, but kept careful distance between the households. The children moved between two separately organized, minimally overlapping household organizations. Additionally, different patterns of inclusion of relatives are seen in different areas of ritual performance. In particular, interactions on the level of daily routines are critical in the development of stepfamily cohesion and are limited to household membership, while rite-of-passage celebrations usually are planned to cast as wide a net as possible.

The Contracted Kinship Network

In the contracted kinship network, major portions of the potential kinship connections are cut off and considered to be outside of the family. This can arise from ongoing difficulties with families of origin, which can result in families making attempts to create a cohesive stepfamily unit that is in isolation from extended families but is not cut off from the children's other parent. In these families, children have celebrations with their other household but not with grandparents or step-grandparents. Clinically, the lack of support or contact with extended families during holidays is frequently accompanied by an upsurge of conflict between spouses, with children, or with the other household as the family members struggled with their feelings of isolation, anger, and/or disappointment.

A second type of fault line can be seen when the "cut off" results from the inability of parents to establish a workable coparenting relationship with the other household. In these families, children have less contact with their nonresidential parent and that parent's family. Although the relationship between high conflict in the coparental unit and children's adjustment difficulties is well established, the relationships between coparental relationship style, the connections with former in-laws, and the stepparenting adjustment have been explored less vigorously. The expectation is that children would have more difficulties connecting with a stepparent when faced with the ongoing tension, sense of loss, and loyalty demands that accompany dysfunctional coparenting. James Bray found this to be true in the early years of a remarriage, but when the remarriage was well established (after six or seven years) the quality of the step-relationships was less influenced by the other household and more influenced by the success of the remarried family in developing its own culture.[21]

Furstenberg and Spanier make the important point that it may be easier for children to feel like part of an expanded family network following a divorce and remarriage than it is for adults. The researchers state that 85 percent of respondents to their survey reported that their children regarded their noncustodial parent's family as relatives, while only 32 percent of parents thought of former in-laws as relatives. Psychologically, children appear to have a wider kin network than their parents do. However, the adults continue to control the children's access to this network.[22]

The nature of the relationship between households in dysfunctional coparenting relationships can range from rigid boundaries with parallel, uncoordinated celebrations, as described by Aprons and Rodgers's "Angry Associates," to ongoing active exclusion with continual violation of household and personal boundaries and disintegration of effective rituals, as described by their "Fiery Foes" couple.[23] Both categories of families do not continue positive relationships with former in-laws. For Angry Associates, important life events represent major stress. Often there are two parallel processes of parenting; for these families, household traditions may be maintained but held rigidly separate and, perhaps, duplicated. Children participate in the traditions of both households as long as contact with the other parent is maintained. However, the necessity to keep households separate takes its toll. One sixteen-year-old girl, both of whose parents have remarried and have angrily continued to refuse to speak directly to each other, reported, "My father will not allow me to speak of anything which goes on in my mother's house since she remarried. How can he care about me if 90 percent of what is important in my life cannot be shared?" For this young woman, parallel holiday celebrations may be manageable, but planning for her high school graduation ceremony becomes difficult and stressful. She worries, "What will happen when they ask the parents of the honor students to come on stage? Maybe I should get a few bad grades and avoid the whole mess."

For the Fiery Foes, Aprons and Rodgers state "the highlights of children's lives—birthdays, weddings, holidays, and other ceremonial occasions—often lose their celebratory character in the struggle for control and/or exclusion of one of the parents."[24] For these families, the conflict between former spouses intrudes into the stepfamily's life, disrupting special occasions that might otherwise provide opportunities for positive connection. The rituals that are repeated are those that David Reiss terms the "rituals of degradation."[25] Ceremonial occasions become opportunities to symbolize the undying bitterness of the former marriage. They provide yet another chance to demonstrate the other parent's deficiencies and to externalize blame for the children's difficulties and the parent's pain.

For dysfunctional families, the period leading up to holiday times is accompanied by an increase in tension, which can precipitate a crisis. Planning is disrupted by the interference of old, unresolved conflicts. Discussions about holiday celebrations become lost in dealing with acute family crises. Whereas functional families may also have unresolved issues, they are able to keep them from interfering significantly in the establishment of a new family structure. These families have lively, highly emotional debates about "the right way" to celebrate, but they also have the ability to develop a workable plan. The more-dysfunctional families would likely express more denial about the importance of ritual events and about the effects of exclusion. They would be less able to deliberate in their construction of new traditions and would be less able to develop a flexible vision of family identity that accommodated to the realities of the complex stepfamily connections.

A contraction pattern in ritual observances can also signal difficulties in stepfamily integration. When there is a conflicted relationship between stepparent and child, particularly when the child is an adolescent, parents may decide to allow the child to avoid participation in occasions involving the stepparent's extended family. In this way, the child is defined as "not family," and the split between the child and the stepparent is reinforced. The results of this pattern show up in families in which remarried couples make little attempt to create a home-based celebration and each adult goes separately to his or her family of origin, taking along biological children and not including stepchildren.

In sum, the families most vulnerable to serious dysfunction in the contracted kinship network would probably be those unable to maintain or to develop successful family traditions and for whom conflict actively interferes with family celebrations. Those able to continue family traditions by maintaining rigid boundaries provide a greater degree of continuity and positive connection for their members, yet they may lack the flexibility to accommodate to the more complex levels of the remarried suprasystem.

Substitution

Many couples who remarry want their second marriage to quickly approximate that of a nuclear family, with the new spouse better than the old one and the stepparent smoothly stepping into the nonresidential parent's shoes. This myth is usually quickly dispelled in the early stages of the remarriage. However, there is an important subgroup of stepfamilies in which the biological parent (usually the mother) and child lived as a true single-parent family before the marriage. In these cases, the other biological parent has been absent since the child was very young, and that parent's family has been defined out of the system. The task of the stepfamily becomes the integration of the spouse's kin into the resident biological parent's family. For those families that successfully substitute stepkin for the nonresident biological parent's kin, kinship patterns and family rituals could be expected to more closely resemble patterns of nuclear families at all levels of ritual. It would be important to explore here the ways in which stepchildren become defined as members of the stepparent's extended family. This pattern is less likely for remarriage following the death of a parent because, in these cases, contact with the former in-laws is usually maintained. Although the remarried family does not have to coordinate with parents in other households, patterns from the "old family" and the memories of the deceased parent remain strongly influential. Somehow the losses and the memories have to be acknowledged at the same time as the family moves ahead.

Conclusion

Inquiry and observation about details and patterns of family ritual development provide a rich portrait of family structure and role relationships. There are several configurations of family identity that can be functional for stepfamilies, most of them quite different from that of nuclear families. Family traditions and celebrations must be handled by each stepfamily, and the traditions and celebrations provide particularly compelling, naturally occurring problem-solving situations. As the family identity evolves, the shape of the celebration changes. As the celebrations are navigated, successes strengthen the sense of family "normality" and failures add even more obstacles to family integration. The results of these experiments in inclusion or exclusion of potential kin help sharpen our understanding of the factors that make a difference in the everyday lives of stepfamilies as they struggle to define a vision of normality for themselves without a great deal of assistance from larger social institutions.

NOTES

1. Steven J. Wolin and Linda A. Bennett, "Family Rituals," *Family Process* 23 (1984): 401.

2. See Emily B. Visher and John S. Visher, *Old loyalties, New Ties: Therapeutic Strategies with Stepfamilies* (New York: Brunner/Mazel, 1988); Mary F. Whiteside, "Remarriage: A Family Developmental Process," *Journal of Marital and Family Therapy* 8 (1982): 59–68.

3. See Constance R. Aprons and Roy H. Rodgers, *Divorced Families* (New York: W. W. Norton, 1987).

4. Clifford Sager et al., *Treating the Remarried Family* (New York: Brunner/Mazel, 1983).

5. See James H. Bray, "From Marriage to Remarriage and Beyond: Findings from the Developmental Issues in StepFamilies Research Project," in *Coping with Divorce, Single Parenting, and Remarriage: A Risk and Resilience Perspective*, E. Mavis Hetherington, ed. (Mahwah, NJ: Lawrence Erlbaum, 1999): 253–271; Patricia Papernow, *Becoming a Stepfamily: Patterns of Development in Remarried Families* (Cambridge, MA: GIC Press, 1998); Whiteside, "Remarriage."

6. Sally Cunningham Clarke and Barbara Foley Wilson, "The Relative Stability of Remarriages: A Cohort Approach Using Vital Statistics," *Family Relations* 43 (1994): 305–310.

7. Wolin and Bennett, "Family Rituals," 405.

8. A. Cochran, "Vacation Victories: The Simple and Complex Versions," *Your Stepfamily* (July–August 2003): 36–39.

9. Aprons and Rodgers, *Divorced Families*; Mary F. Whiteside, "The Parental Alliance following Divorce: An Overview," *Journal of Marital and Family Therapy* 24 (1998): 3–24.

10. Marilyn Ihinger-Tallman and Kay Pasley, "Stepfamilies in 1984 and Today: A Scholarly Perspective," *Marriage and Family Review* 26 (1997): 19–40.

11. Gretchen Lussier, Kirby Deater-Deckard, Judy Dunn, and Lisa Davies, "Support across Two Generations: Children's Closeness to Grandparents following Parental Divorce and Remarriage," *Journal of Family Psychology* 16 (2002): 363–376.

12. Lawrence H. Ganong and Marilyn Coleman, *Changing Families, Changing Responsibilities: Family Obligations following Divorce and Remarriage* (Mahwah, NJ: Lawrence Erlbaum, 1999).

13. Caroline S. Henry and Sandra G. Lovelace, "Family Resources and Adolescent Family Life Satisfaction in Remarried Family Households," *Journal of Family Issues* 16 (1995): 765–786.

14. Mary F. Whiteside, "Consolidation of Family Identity through Ritual Performance in Early Remarriage," in *Rituals in Families and Family Therapy*, Evan Imber-Black, Janine Roberts, and Richard A. Whiting, eds., rev. ed. (New York: W. W. Norton, 2003), 300–329.

15. Constance R. Aprons, *The Good Divorce: Keeping Your Family Together When Your Marriage Comes Apart* (New York: HarperCollins, 1994).

16. Frank F. Furstenberg Jr. and Graham B. Spanier, *Recycling the Family* (Beverly Hills, CA: Sage, 1984), 137.

17. Colleen Leahy Johnson and Barbara M. Barer, "Marital Instability and the Changing Kinship Networks of Grandparents," *Gerontologist* 27 (1987): 330.

18. Mary F. Whiteside and Betsy Jane Becker, "Parental Factors and the Young Child's Postdivorce Adjustment: A Meta-Analysis with Implications for Parenting Arrangements," *Journal of Family Psychology* 14 (2000): 1–22.

19. Aprons and Rodgers, *Divorced Families*.

20. See Mary F. Whiteside, "Family Rituals as a Key to Kinship Connections in Remarried Families," *Family Relations* 38 (1989): 34–39.

21. Bray, "From Marriage to Remarriage and Beyond."

22. Furstenberg and Spanier, *Recycling the Family*.

23. Aprons and Rodgers, *Divorced Families*.

24. Ibid., 128.

25. David Reiss, *The Family's Construction of Reality* (Cambridge, MA: Harvard University Press, 1981).

Chapter 5

Gathering Together
Remembering Memory through Ritual

John R. Gillis

There is a tendency for those who remember memory to see it as perpetually fading, uniquely subject to the erosions of time. Frances Yates, the great historian of ancient and early modern memory, was convinced that "we moderns have no memories at all."[1] In our own time, fears of forgetting have reached unprecedented levels. In America, if there is one thing left and right agree on, it is national amnesia. "A refusal to remember . . . is a primary characteristic of our nation," writes the conservative critic Lynn Cheney. Responding for the liberals, Michael Wallace declares, "Ours is a historicidal culture."[2] Edward Casey tells us that "we have turned over responsibility for remembering to the cult of the computers, which serve as our modern mnemonic idols."[3] He regrets what he sees as an end of the social practice of reminiscing, once a "frequent feature of family gatherings and social settings. It is now . . . an increasingly uncommon phenomenon—doubtless due to the disintegration of the extended family structure and to the concomitant lack of veneration for the elderly in our culture."[4]

There is no question that certain kinds of memory are in eclipse in Western Europe as well as in North America. People are less engaged with national histories than they were a generation ago. In their recent survey of Americans' understandings of the past, Roy Rosenzweig and David Thelen write that history as it is taught in schools does not engage most Americans.[5] But this is not to say that Americans are not deeply involved with other dimensions of the past, most notably their family pasts. Rosenzweig and Thelen found that 91 percent had looked at family photos in the

previous year and that 36 percent had worked on family history or geneal-
ogy in the same period. When asked what past mattered most to them, 66
percent mentioned family, 22 percent national history, and only 4 percent
community, leading the authors to conclude that "almost every American
deeply and regularly engages the past and the past that engages them most
deeply is that of their families."[6]

Americans are not alone in this respect. David Lowenthal has recently
written that "in recovering from grievous loss or fending off a fearsome
future, people the world over revert to ancestral legacies."[7] The recent
growth of the "heritage industry" is well documented; and there is no
denying that memory occupies an expanding place in the public and economic life of both Europe and America. Every year sees the creation of
new sites of memory—museums, historic restorations, preserves of every
description—and the expansion of the calendar of anniversaries, commemorations, and reenactments. We are kept so busy remembering to remember that we have little time to do anything memorable.[8]

Evidence of private memory practices are more difficult to come by.
Rosenzweig and Thelen are the first to survey them on the national level,
and their study leaves no doubt that we are in the midst of an explosion of
domestic commemorative practices. In this essay, I will argue that memory has become essential to whatever sense of togetherness the modern
nuclear family manages to generate. Memory is not just a matter of re-
trieval of family pasts but is rather a *re*-membering in the creative sense of
the term. Memory as an imaginative, constitutive act is one of the things
that distinguishes modern family life, setting it apart from private life in
previous centuries.

Most of the familial memory practices we take for granted today do not
predate the mid-nineteenth century. Apart from aristocratic and patrician
elites, few Europeans or Americans bothered about ancestors or origins
before 1850. When the seventeenth-century English cleric Ralph Josselin
imagined his family tree, it had branches but no roots. Most of his con-
temporaries would not have known where or when their forebears were
born or buried. Anniversaries were rare and family reunions unknown.
When family members came together, it was for practical purposes. Time
spent together was dedicated to either work or play and was devoid of ceremony. Baptisms, weddings, and funerals were not family but communal
occasions; and notions of "family time" and "family place," so central in
our day, had no meaning whatsoever.

To understand the indifference to family past, one must understand that until the mid-nineteenth century family was identical to household, and it included persons unrelated as well as those related to one another. High mortality and fertility, accompanied by scarcity of resources, meant that the nuclear family was unable to sustain a viable household without the addition of strangers. Fatherhood, motherhood, and childhood were all socially rather than biologically defined. Most people spent a large part of their childhoods and adolescence in households other than those of their natural parents. It was a person's place in the household rather than chronological age that determined whether he would be considered a boy or a man, or she a girl or a woman.

The timing of leaving home, getting married, having children, and retirement varied widely; and there was no sense of a normative life course as we know it today.[9] As a result, familial relationships—parent/child, husband/wife—were understood differently than they are now. Neither aging nor death affected families of that time in quite the same way as today, because household members were, like the members of any socially or economically constituted institution, seen as replaceable. The nest was never empty for long. When a child grew up and left the pre-industrial household, he was replaced by another through apprenticeship or informal adoption. Widows and widowers remarried with a haste that we would find unseemly, but this was necessary to the survival of the family-cum-household.

Defined by its economic, social, and cultural functions, the household as family was, like any other institution, a thing of the moment. The typical household had a profound sense of being but little sense of becoming. Its past did not run deep; and its future did not extend much beyond tomorrow. In an era when a sense of place was far more important to identity than a sense of time, memory was not an asset but an obstacle to a household's successful functioning. It is little wonder that before the middle of the nineteenth century, forgetting was regarded with greater favor than remembering. "The things and relationships of this life are like prints in the Sand, there is not the least appearance of remembrance of them," wrote Thomas Hooker. "The King remembers not his Crown, the Husband the Wife, the Father the Child."[10]

But all this was to change with the onset of the industrial revolution, which not only separated family from household but also made time itself the basic constitutive element of familial identities. Families ceased to be things of the moment and acquired both a past and a future. From this point onward, remembering replaced forgetting as the central cultural practice of family life.

We can see this happening first among the Protestant middle classes of northwestern Europe and North America in the mid-nineteenth century. They were the first to see themselves as part and product of a linear time, of processes that came to be called "development." Like the nation, the family was now understood in terms of becoming, constituted through time rather than, as the household had been, through place. As such, these families were undergoing what Martin Kohli has called "chronologization." They became subject to ever more rigid temporal norms that dictated the time to marry, to have children, to retire, even to die.[11] In turn, these rigidly calibrated age markers separated generations.

Middle-class families acquired both a future and a past, but in doing so they found themselves exposed to what David Harvey has called modernity's "time-space compression," an experience of vastly accelerated rates of change and radically shrinking distances "so that the world sometimes seems to collapse inward upon us."[12] The effect of the political and industrial revolutions of the late eighteenth and early nineteenth centuries had been to sever perceived connections with the past and create a nostalgia that no longer focused on place but on time.

Nowhere was this more evident than in family life, where all kinds of new commemorative practices emerged to bridge the distance between the present and a past that now seemed lost and gone forever.[13] The imposition of standards of mechanical time and abstract space had been both disruptive and alienating, but it also had its constructive side. "The experience of time-space compression is challenging, exciting, stressful, and sometimes deeply troubling, capable of sparking therefore a diversity of social, cultural, and political responses," notes Harvey.[14]

Anthony Giddens is pursuing the same line of thought when he writes that, while the separation of time and space is the essential characteristic of modernity, effectively terminating the ancient sense of place that had previously united them, "the severing of time from space provides a basis for their recombination in relation to social activity."[15] Against those who see nothing but the terrors of modern linear time compounded by the agoraphobia associated with "empty" modern space, both Harvey and Giddens urge us to look more closely at the dialectical process that has produced a host of new times and new places.

And on close inspection, we find that it was from the mid-nineteenth century onward that families began to construct new family time(s) to cope with the sense of loss associated with the workings of irreversible linear time.[16] It was also then that memory was first deployed domestically as defense against the centrifugal forces of modern time and space. The great scholar of collective memory Maurice Halbwachs assumed that strong memories were an expression of strong group solidarity, weakening or disappearing as that solidarity eroded. But memory can just as well create as reflect a sense of togetherness; and this has been the case with the nuclear family, whose commemorative activity has increased even as the day-to-day interaction of its members has decreased. Today, the times that families live *by* need not be the same as those they live *with*. Today's families live by what they like to call "quality time," which is by no means the same as the time that divides them. Understanding this distinction is crucial to understanding the way memory functions in contemporary family life.

Modern family life, like modern society more generally, operates in two quite different time zones. In one of these zones families live *with* a monochronic time, perceived as external and objective, which is relentlessly linear and discontinuous, separating men's and women's time, adults' and children's time, the time of the young from that of the old. The families we live with today are small in size and short in duration, and especially prone to fragmentation. They are also voluntary, consciously planned, and (with modern divorce) consciously terminated, with much more sharply defined beginnings and endings than was the case in earlier forms of family life. Supposed to proceed by developmental "stages," nuclear family life has discontinuity built into it from the very beginning. A nuclear family is said to begin when children arrive and is understood to end when they leave home, something quite different from families in the past, when the family, defined as household, existed prior to birth and endured beyond death.[17] As a prime example of planned obsolescence, the nuclear family is uniquely vulnerable among the institutions of modern society to discontinuity and sense of loss, accounting for the perpetual sense of crisis attached to it.

Ironically, parents work very hard at inculcating a time and age consciousness that will ultimately produce distance and separation between themselves and their children. They teach them that the date of their birth is destiny, ensuring that childhood, then adolescence and youth, are ultimately things to be left behind, "lost" as it were. "The family relationships through which most of us emerge as selves . . . are inherently vulnerable to the passage of time," note Andrew Weigert and Ross Hastings. "Within the family, time is 'normally' experienced as aging, and aging ends in death." The ultimate sense of loss is produced by death, but modern family life is a series of little losses or little deaths. At the heart of the modern family is a paradox: "to succeed as a parent is eventually to lose the present identity as parent; to succeed as child is inevitably to lose the identity of child."[18] Modern families produce the very notions of generational difference that are the cause of so much discomfort to themselves. While other modern institutions manage to survive the aging and death of their members, the nuclear family is unique in its unwillingness to find substitutes for missing members. Institutions survive by forgetting; only the family relies so heavily on remembering. It is where that other time zone—cyclical and memorial—enters in.

We usually think of family as passive, responding to change, not as a creative force in its own right. Yet modern families have taken up the challenge presented by the alienating powers of modern time and space and turned both to their own purposes. Mechanical linear time and empty abstract space undermined preexisting communal and religious understandings of place and occasion but in doing so opened up new possibilities for the creative use of both space and time to restore that sense of being that had been so rudely disrupted. The same means of rapid communications that tore the household asunder made it possible for people to remain in touch with and to visit relations who in earlier periods would have been out of sight and therefore out of mind. The modern triumph of time over space has made it possible for us to think of ourselves as "close" to persons not only at ever greater spatial but also temporal distances.[19]

One of the novel features of modernity is the possibility of combining presence with absence, bringing the distant near and drawing the past and future into the present. Modern technology, beginning with the telegraph and culminating in the Internet, allows persons to be intimate at a distance. Photography and now video erase barriers of time as well as space, so that contemporary family life depends no more on propinquity than it does on contemporaneity. Family has long since ceased to mean the same thing as the household, even though the official census continues to act on the assumption that persons present in a certain place at a certain time constitute a family. But this is not what most of us mean by family, a set of relationships that have undergone what Giddens calls a disembedding process, "the 'lifting out' of social relations from local contexts of social interaction and their restructuring across indefinite spans of time-space."[20]

A world mapped by a single set of abstract universal coordinates empties all places of their original meaning, but this modern mental feat also makes available to us places we have never seen and may never visit, opening up to the imagination places beyond the horizons of our ancestors. "In conditions of modernity, place becomes increasingly *phantasmagoric*," Giddens notes.[21] And for almost two centuries Americans and Europeans have been in the process of creating a whole new set of imagined places that now constitute their mental, if not their physical, destinations. Nowhere is this more evident than in the changing meaning of "home," which is now less a physical location than a mental construct, a thing of dreams as well as memories, present even in its absence, no less real even if it is rarely, sometimes never, actually inhabited.[22]

Having thus been disembedded, we have gained a much larger measure of freedom to place ourselves in the world. Our families are no longer confined to those we live with. Our potential circle of kin has been vastly expanded to the point that we can begin to imagine ourselves a part of a "family of man."[23] In reality, the circle of those with whom we are on familiar terms is much more constricted, yet the boundaries of family are no longer limited by physical place. Because family can now take place virtually anywhere, it has become incumbent on families to make their own sense of place, another one of the peculiar features of our modern age.

Modernity has also disembedded us from older meanings of occasion, with the result that it too has become phantasmagoric. However much we may be subject to the dictates of the modern clock and calendar, modernity's separation of time from space has allowed us a greater opportunity to create new modes of temporality that serve to calm the terrors of linear time through the restoration of cycles of events (such as birthdays and anniversaries) that provide for us a sense of continuity and permanence. Even as those who live together feel they have less and less time for one another, the number and variety of special occasions set aside for family continues to grow at an astonishing rate. Just as our mental maps are filled with family places, so our mental calendars are crowded with the anticipations and memories of family occasions.

In fact, most of the time we spend on family gatherings is in anticipation and remembrance rather than on the actual moment itself. When it comes to family, the modern imagination works overtime, producing a plethora of dreams and memories, compensating for the short supply of time with which to experience other family members as complex human beings. Unfortunately, in our contemporary family times we are more apt to encounter parents, children, and kin in their most stereotypical roles, thus producing a terrible yearning for an intimacy that cannot be.

Memory first entered into family life among the European and American middle classes in the mid-nineteenth century as a compensatory device to counter the centrifugal effects of linear time.[24] It was among this group that the living began to haunt the dead. Family graves, previously largely neglected, were now visited regularly as the Victorian cemetery was redesigned to make room for weekly and annual pilgrimages.[25] Never before had mourning been so extended and the memory of the dead kept alive for so long, a task assigned mainly to women.[26] Women were also favored mediums in the spiritualist movements which were to become so much a part of middle-class family life from the middle of the century onward.[27]

Among the Victorians, every little loss also required the appropriate commemorative ritual. They were the ones to make of the birthday the memorable occasion it is today. The christening became for the first time a major familial gathering; and children's birthdays began to be celebrated with regularity. Rites of passage, which had not been strongly accentuated prior to the late nineteenth century, now took on huge significance. Confirmation, Bar Mitzvahs, and graduations became major family occasions. But the most memorial event of all was the wedding, which grew even more elaborate at all class levels in the nineteenth century.[28]

Inseparable from all these events was the photograph.[29] "Photography becomes a rite of family life just when, in the industrializing countries of Europe and America, the very institution of the family starts undergoing radical surgery," writes Susan Sontag, whose insight into the role of images in family life is worth quoting at greater length:

> As that claustrophobic unit, the nuclear family, was being carved out of a much larger family aggregate, photography came along to memorialize, to restate symbolically, the imperiled continuity and vanishing extendedness of family life. Those ghostly traces, photographs, supply the token presence of the dispersed relatives. A family's photograph album is generally about the extended family—and, often, is all that remains of it.[30]

In previous ages, public places were people's *aide de memoire*.[31] In the course of the nineteenth century, public spaces progressively lost the "placeness" that had allowed them to serve as sites of memory. But Victorians found a substitute in the home, that "especially architecturally modeled domestic space [which became] a privileged domain of memorability."[32] Memories abhor empty spaces, and Victorian architecture served memory particularly well, for, in the words of Gaston Bachelard, if a house "has a cellar and a garret, nooks and corridors, our memories have refuges that are all the more clearly delineated."[33]

Closed domestic spaces would henceforth bear the weight of memory. By the late nineteenth century, the parlor had become "a kind of museum or sanctum—the repository of things which have, or which once had, an emotional significance: wedding dresses and other old clothes, some belonging to the departed."[34] The parlor was where the dead were laid out, but it was also the place for all those events—courtships, weddings, christenings, and, of course, Christmas—that were meant to be memorable, when the past was invoked as "tradition" and when ritual brought the past imaginatively into the present.

In the twentieth century, every bourgeois couple's home became their castle, but also their palace of memory. Today, every home has become a museum and an archive filled with things that speak to that which is absent. As Eugene Rochberg-Halton puts it, homes and homey things "are the repositories of personal and collective memories, they embody kinship ties, they are valued as tangible evidence of friendship and family bonds, they are signs of our presence in a paradoxically material yet evanescent world."[35] Recently, as modern domestic architecture has taken on some of the empty functionalism characteristic of modern space more generally, memory has tended to migrate to summer or weekend houses, places that have come to feel more like home than our regular residences because they seem to offer safer storage for the shared dreams and memories of generations geographically dispersed and constantly on the move from one nondescript domicile to another.[36]

Today most of us fasten on the home as the one place we feel we can animate meaningful, habitable worlds. There we gather our significant others, or, in their absence, their photos, mementos, and other cherished objects that connect us to them on the symbolic level. They speak to us, and we to them. As Rochberg-Halton has shown, "transactions with cherished objects are communicative dialogues with ourselves."[37] As more and more of us live alone, we fill our empty nests with things that allow us to connect with more people than our ancestors ever knew existed. It is even common for those who are wholly bereft to turn pets and stuffed animals into surrogate families.[38] Our fondness for things should not be mistaken for materialism, however, for without objects to symbolize ourselves and our significant others our world would lose all meaning.[39]

From the mid-nineteenth century onward, homecoming became a regular part of the family calendar. What had previously been a public communal event, located in the summer months, was repositioned and domesticated in the form of the modern Christmas.[40] In England and North America, if not in Scotland, the modern Yule included a return not just to a place but to a past. Even as it was being invented in the 1840s and 1850s, the new family Christmas was constructed as an endangered tradition that put all generations in symbolic if not actual touch with the past and thus with one another.[41] Each successive version of Yuletide invariably presents itself as "old," "customary," and "traditional," regardless of how many innovations it incorporates.

The annual, weekly, even daily cycles of modern life provide people who usually have precious little with real time to share a common past and a common future. Drawn together in anticipation and remembrance, families find in this symbolic interaction what they do not find in daily life. Often enough, the actual family meals, vacations, and reunions prove disappointing, resulting in what some have called modern "holiday trauma."[42] Yet this only seems to intensify the cycle, for what is experienced as painful and divisive is often remembered as joyful and comforting.

Weddings, funerals, and birthdays are so much more than the mere datable and locatable "facts of life" that modern social science has managed to reduce them to. At those moments, actual behavior is far less important than the accompanying symbolic activity. These are the precious moments we seize from fleeting linear time to break out of our present preoccupations to imagine a past that will see us through into our imagined future. "The novelty of the very future demands a novel past," George Herbert Mead noted in 1902; and recently social psychologists have found that people whose pasts run deepest have the greatest faith in their futures.[43] It turns out that our ability to imagine the future depends very heavily on our capacity to create "images of absent events and believe in their validity."[44] We require the presence of things past to ensure the presence of things future, but, of course, when remembering becomes an end in itself, it becomes "mere nostalgia, it degenerates into a terminal bubble of past that both closes one off from the living spontaneity of the present and denies the possibility of a future."[45]

Nuclear families are prone to nostalgia, but they have no choice but to seize upon the ineffable passing moment, turning this into a symbol of duration and extension, defying time and space, even death, to create sufficient hope in order to be able to move on. In so-called future-oriented societies, ritual is supposed to disappear, yet it is through ritual that we make the future probable and possible. Ritual time differs from linear time not just in its repetitiveness but also in the way it erases the perceived distance between past, present, and future. As Barbara Myerhoff put it, "Ritual inevitably carries a basic message of order, continuity, and predictability. . . . By stating enduring and underlying patterns, ritual connects past, present, and future, abrogating history and time. Ritual always links participants to one another and often to wider collectivities that may be absent, even to the ancestors and those yet unborn."[46]

Even as we speak, new rituals for coping with losses, big and little, proliferate. For example, in this age of the "hurried child," when children are not allowed to linger even in their infancy, the image of the "unborn child" has appeared as if to satisfy our craving for proof of the immortality of family relations. Viewing ultrasound images, existing outside real time and space, and thus exempt from the imperfections that birth itself may bring, has become the latest rite of family.[47]

A more religious age could comfort itself by telling itself, "Men forget, God remembers."[48] Once divine memory ceased to be believable in the nineteenth century, the burdens of memory were brought down to earth and transferred to the persons and things of this world.[49] On the public level, the history profession was invested with the duty of remembrance, a role it found very difficult to sustain in the final quarter of the twentieth century. In contrast, the memory work of families has been left largely to amateurs, most of whom have been women. Today, this gendered division of labor is changing as women enter the history profession, insisting that it pay attention to the history of private as well as public life, while men begin (very gradually) to share the responsibility for the domestic ritual and memory work they have so long neglected. The boundaries between history and memory have become more permeable, though it is too early to tell what new forms of relating to the past will emerge in the twenty-first century.[50]

"Time's arrow is the intelligibility of distinct and irreversible events, while time's cycle is the intelligibility of timeless order, the law-like structure. We must have both," writes Stephen J. Gould.[51] In this new millennium, more and more cultural critics have pointed to our need for a polychronic sense of time that will resolve the cultural contradictions that our commitment to notions of linear development have heaped upon us.

Nowhere is this more evident than in the realm of the family. "Our ideology of what family time is leaves us in an unhappy present," notes Kerry Daly. "The past and the future maintain the dream of family time, but the present is the site of our disillusionment."[52]

As T. S. Eliot observed, "only through time, time is conquered."[53] We dwell so much on other times and other places because we feel we have so little time and space left. Even the affluent fear time, famine, and homelessness. And so we live vicariously by our "ghostly traces," relying more and more on imagination. Every day we move between zones of linear and cyclical time, using dream and memory as compensation for the losses experienced through time and history.[54] It is when we stop moving between past, present, and future, when the past becomes an end in itself, that memory ceases to be a creative resource and becomes the paralytic condition diagnosed as nostalgia. It is important therefore that we always remind ourselves that, as Edmund Bolles has put it, "remembering and imagining are of one piece,"[55] for we must learn to live with multiple temporalities—history and heritage, linear and cyclical time, rationalism and ritual—if we are to make for ourselves a world that is sustainable and at the same time meaningful.

NOTES

1. Quoted in Edward Casey, *Remembering: A Phenomenological Study* (Bloomington: Indiana University Press, 1987), 1.

2. Quoted in Roy Rosenzweig and David Thelen, *The Presence of the Past: Popular Uses of History in American Life* (New York: Columbia University Press, 1998), 3.

3. Casey, *Remembering*, 1.

4. Ibid., 7.

5. Rosenzweig and Thelen, *Presence of the Past*, 5–18.

6. Ibid., 19–36.

7. David Lowenthal, *Possessed by the Past: The Heritage Crusade and the Spoils of History* (New York: Free Press, 1996), ix.

8. John Gillis, "Remembering Memory: A Challenge for Public Historians in a Post-National Era," *Public Historian* 14, no. 4 (fall 1992): 83–93; also Lowenthal, *Possessed by the Past*, 194. The role of memory in American history is discussed at length by Michael Kammen, *Mystic Chords of Memory: The Transformation of Tradition in America* (New York: Knopf, 1992); John Bodner, *Remaking America: Public Memory, Commemoration, and Patriotism in the Twentieth Century* (Princeton, NJ: Princeton University Press, 1992); David Glassberg, *American Historical*

Pageantry: The Use of Tradition in the Early Twentieth Century (Chapel Hill: University of North Carolina Press, 1990). On Europe, see William M. Johnston, *The Cult of Anniversaries in Europe and the United States* (New Brunswick, NJ: Transaction Press, 1991); also see Eric Hobsbawm and Terence Ranger, eds., *The Invention of Tradition* (Cambridge: Cambridge University Press, 1982).

9. Thomas Cole, *The Journey of Life: A Cultural History of Aging in America* (Cambridge: Cambridge University Press, 1992); Howard Chudacoff, *How Old Are You? Age Consciousness in American Culture* (Princeton, NJ: Princeton University Press, 1989).

10. Quoted in John Gillis, *A World of Their Own Making: Myth, Ritual, and the Quest for Family Values* (New York: Basic Books, 1996), 18.

11. Martin Kohli, "The World We Forgot: An Historical Review of the Life Course," in *Late Life: The Social Psychology of Aging*, Victor Marshall, ed. (Beverly Hills, CA: Sage, 1985).

12. David Harvey, *The Condition of Postmodernity: An Enquiry into the Origins of Cultural Change* (Oxford: Blackwell, 1989), 2.;0.

13. Peter Fritschke, "Specters of History: On Nostalgia, Exile, and Modernity," *American Historical Review* 106, no. 5 (December 2001): 1587–1619.

14. Harvey, *Condition of Postmodernity*, 240.

15. Anthony Giddens, *The Consequences of Modernity* (Stanford, CA: Stanford University Press, 1990), 19.

16. Juliet Shor, *The Overworked American: The Unexpected Decline of Leisure* (New York: Basic Books, 1991), 30.

17. Surprisingly little attention has been given to the ways we construct beginnings and endings. See Joan Busfield and Michael Padden, *Thinking about Children: Sociology and Fertility in Post-War Britain* (Cambridge: Cambridge University Press, 1977); Margaret Mead, "The Contemporary American Family as an Anthropologist Sees It," *American Journal of Sociology* 53, no. 6 (May 1948): 453–59. On beginnings more generally, see Eviatar Zerubavel, "In the Beginning: Notes on the Social Construction of Historical Discontinuity," *Sociological Inquiry* 63, no. 4 (November 1993): 457–59; on endings, see Michael Kearl, *Endings: A Sociology of Death and Dying* (New York: Oxford University Press, 1989).

18. Andrew J. Weigert and Ross Hastings, "Identity, Loss, Family, and Social Change," *American Journal of Sociology* 82, no. 4 (May 1977): 1175–76.

19. Giddens, *Consequences of Modernity*, 42.

20. Ibid., 21.

21. Ibid., 18–19; emphasis in the original.

22. Yi-Fu Tuan, *Space and Place: The Perspective of Experience* (Minneapolis: University of Minnesota Press, 1977), chap. 10; Gillis, *A World of Their Own Making*, chap. 6.

23. Alex Shoumatoff, *The Mountain of Names: A History of the Human Family* (New York: Simon and Schuster, 1985).

24. There is a prior memorial practice of the European aristocracies. See Philippe Aries and George Duby, eds., *A History of Private Life* (Cambridge: Cambridge University Press, 1989).

25. On pilgrimages and family reunions, see Gwen Neville, *Kinship and Pilgrimage: Rituals of Reunion in American Protestant Culture* (New York: Oxford University Press, 1987), chaps. 3 and 4.

26. John Gillis, "The Cultural Production of Family Identities," unpublished paper, Rutgers Center for Historical Analysis, 1989, 18–22; Philippe Aries, *The Hour of Our Death* (New York: Vintage, 1981), 510–43.

27. Ann Braudy, *Radical Spirits: Spiritualism and Women's Rights in Nineteenth-Century America* (Boston: Beacon Press, 1989), 41–54.

28. For Germany, see Ingeborg Weber-Kellerman, *Saure Wochen, Frohe Feste: Fest und Alltag in der Sprache der Brauche* (Munich: Bucher, 1985); for France, see Anne Martin-Fugier, "Bourgeois Rituals," in *A History of Private Life*, Michelle Perrot, ed. (Cambridge: Harvard University Press, 1990).

29. On this development, see Bjarne Kildegaard, "Unlimited Memory: Photography and the Differentiation of Familial Intimacy," *Ethnologica Scandiavica* (1985): 71–89.

30. Susan Sontag, *On Photography* (New York: Delta, 1972), 9; see also Eugene Rochberg-Halton, *Meaning and Modernity: Social Theory in the Pragmatic Attitude* (Chicago: University of Chicago Press, 1986), 166–67, 170.

31. Peter Burke, "History as Social Memory," in *Memory: History, Culture, and the Mind*, Thomas Butler, ed. (Oxford: Blackwell, 1989), 101–4.

32. Casey, *Remembering*, 210.

33. Quoted in Casey, *Remembering*, 211.

34. Alywn Rees, *Life in a Welsh Countryside* (Cardiff: University of Wales Press, 1975), 46.

35. Rochberg-Halton, *Meaning and Modernity*, 169.

36. Asa Boholm, *Swedish Kinship: An Exploration into the Cultural Processes of Belonging and Continuity* (Gateborg, Sweden: Gateborg University Press, 1983), 222–24; Michael Ann Williams, *Homeplace: The Social Use and Meaning of the Folk Dwellings in Southwestern North Carolina* (Athens: Georgia University Press, 1991).

37. Rochberg-Halton, *Meaning and Modernity*, 155.

38. Ibid., 161, 178.

39. Ibid., 180.

40. John Gillis, "Ritualization of Middle-Class Life in Nineteenth-Century Britain," *International Journal of Politics, Culture, and Society* 3, no. 2 (1989): 213–36.

41. Clement A. Miles, *Christmas in Ritual and Tradition: Christian and Pagan* (London: T. Fisher Unwin, 1912), 18.

42. Nils Arvid Bringeus, "Bitte, keine Feier, order Das Fest als Trauma," *Hessische Blatter fur Volksund Kulturforschung* 7/8 (1978): 39.

43. Mead, quoted in Thomas J. Cottle and Stephen L. Kleinberg, *Present of Things Future: Explorations of Time in Human Experience* (New York: Free Press, 1973), 12. A similar argument for the centrality of memory in modern life is made by Michael Young, *The Metronomic Society: Natural Rhythms and Human Timetables* (Cambridge: Harvard University Press, 1988); and Paul Fraisse, *The Psychology of Time* (New York: Harper and Row, 1963), 291ff.

44. Cottle and Kleinberg, *Present of Things Future,* 16.

45. Rochberg-Halton, *Meaning and Modernity,* 188.

46. Barbara Myerhoff, "Rites and Signs of Ripening: The Intertwining of Ritual, Time, and Growing Older," in *Age and Anthropological Theory,* David Kertzer and Jennie Keith, eds. (Ithaca, NY: Cornell University Press, 1984), 306.

47. Gillis, *A World of Their Own Making,* 158–62.

48. Arab proverb, quoted in Peter Berger, *The Sacred Canopy: Elements of a Sociological Theory of Religion* (New York: Anchor, 1967), 37.

49. On the role that the ideology of romantic love played in this process, see Karen Lystra, *Searching the Heart: Women, Men, and Romantic Love in Nineteenth-Century America* (New York: Oxford, 1989). On the contemporary importance of family relations to identity formation, see Anthony Giddens, *Modernity and Self-Identity: Self and Society in the Late Modern Age* (Stanford, CA: Stanford University Press), 1991.

50. John Gillis, "Memory and Identity: The History of a Relationship," in *Commemorations: Politics of National Identity,* John Gillis, ed. (Princeton, NJ: Princeton University Press, 1994), 3–24.

51. Stephen J. Gould, *Time's Arrow, Time's Cycle: Myth and Metaphor in the Discovery of Geological Time* (Cambridge, MA: Harvard University Press, 1987), 15–16.

52. Kerry J. Daly, *Families and Time: Keeping Pace in a Hurried Culture* (Thousand Oaks, CA: Sage, 1996), 205.

53. Quoted in Harvey, *Condition of Postmodernity,* 206.

54. Fraisse, *Psychology of Time,* 292.

55. Edmund Bolles, *Remembering and Forgetting: Inquiries into the Nature of Memory* (New York: Walker, 1988), xvii.

Part III

Community Building

Chapter 6

The Festival Cycle
Halloween to Easter in the Community of Middletown

Theodore Caplow

In 1924 Robert and Helen Lynd immersed themselves in a small industrial town in Indiana, which they called Middletown, in order to study the culture and values of its residents. After publishing their findings in 1929, the Lynds returned to Middletown six years later to perform the first replicated community study of its kind. In 1978, Theodore Caplow and a team of sociologists returned to Middletown, now identified as Muncie, Indiana, for a second restudy of the Middletown community. The following is taken from their essay about the community's festival cycle.[1]

We assume for purposes of the following analysis that in each festival the emblems[2] convey one kind of message repeatedly, that each festival produces a different message by being contrasted with the others, and that these messages express different aspects of the same themes: the importance of family and social ties and of women in maintaining both. Since Middletown's festival cycle begins with Halloween, we can usefully begin our analysis here.

Halloween is clearly an antifestival; it is also an antefestival, and this is not just a pun.[3] Following Edmund Leach and Alfonso Ortiz, we assume that the inversion marks the importance of what follows by making a mockery of the serious.[4] The mockery increases the seriousness: for one thing, the mockery suggests what could occur if the serious were no longer taken seriously. At one and the same time, we are allowed to escape normal social bonds and to see, or to infer, the consequences of habitual escape (that is, of not obeying the rules).

Let us start by considering the Halloween witch, a kind of person always described in anthropological writings as a social inversion.[5] The witches of any culture do contrary things, such as walking on their hands, flying, going out at night, killing close relatives, eating babies, trafficking with undesirables, et cetera. Middletown's Halloween witch has been relieved of most of her antecedents' nasty attributes, but a few still remain. She is old, ugly, skinny, warty, hook-nosed, snaggle-toothed, and wild-haired; she dresses in black clothes and a tall, pointy hat; she rides a broomstick; and she has a black spitfire cat for a pet. She lives alone, unmarried and childless, and she emerges on Halloween with malevolent intentions and powers (although no actual harm is ever attributed to her). She is an inversion of several things at once. First, the witch inverts the American Mom, who is usually represented as young, attractive, and cheerfully dressed; who uses a broomstick for sweeping; who lives very much en famille; and who has the most benevolent intentions and powers. The only similarity between Mom and the witch is their sex. But the witch also inverts other festival emblems: Santa Claus (with whom she shares age and aerial navigation) by being female, ugly, sexless, and malevolent; the Cupid of Valentine's Day (with whom she shares supernaturality and flight) by being malevolent, female, aged, and heartless; the Easter Bunny (equally asocial) by being among other things human, aged, childless, female, specific, nocturnal, and mean. She demonstrates an evil, selfish femininity; a soured, ungenerous old age; and an aversion to society prompted by hatred rather than shyness. Note that the cat, like the broomstick, is a feminine attribute. The dominant color black is not shared by any of the emblems of the serious holidays following Halloween. The witch thus combines in herself the opposites of characters that will, during the holidays to come (and even to some extent at Halloween itself), be venerated and celebrated.

Inversion explains the jack-o'-lantern, today a less important emblem, as well. An important part of the Thanksgiving meal is the pumpkin pie. The pumpkin, together with cornstalks and gourds, symbolizes the fall harvest. The jack-o'-lantern makes horrific this otherwise innocuous vegetable. The tastiness of the Thanksgiving dessert is emphasized by this perversion of the raw pumpkin.

The newspaper accounts of Halloween parties in Middletown did not mention the witch as an emblem until the mid-1950s. At the beginning of the twentieth century, the major emblem was the jack-o'-lantern. The addition of the witch supports the empirical finding mentioned earlier that family and family life have become more important to Middletown since the beginning of the twentieth century. Halloween used to be a celebration of harvest and of civic pride. Middletown was famous in the region for its unique Halloween celebration, in which the adults dressed in costume and paraded for two or three hours before going to one of the many private Halloween parties.[6]

The other emblems of Halloween are ghosts, skeletons, and haunted houses. The haunted house is cold, dark, and comfortless, and it is inhabited by dreadful beings. These inhabitants, the ghosts and skeletons, prefigure the resurrection celebrated at Easter, the end of the familial phase of the festival cycle.[7] Halloween burlesques Thanksgiving by making commensality impossible; and it burlesques Christmas by mocking the importance of widespread gift exchanges and the benevolence of mothers and Santa Claus. Because Halloween and Easter stand at ends of the festival cycle, however, the most important aspect of Halloween is its mockery of the resurrection. Easter celebrates the resurrection of body and soul; Halloween displays the horror of either body or soul resurrected without the other.

The practices of Halloween are as revealing as the emblems, and they bear out the hypothesis that Halloween is an antifestival. Since the practices are familiar to us all, I need not describe them in detail. They can be summarized for our purposes: at Halloween, nonpersons imitating nonbeings demand and receive nonmeals from nonrelatives in a nonneighborly way.

Children are not yet persons or social actors. They have no roles beyond being children since they are not tinker, tailor, soldier, sailor, or any other kind of social actor. The costumes they put on represent characters in fiction (Peter Pan), characters no longer in existence (Pocahontas, Robin Hood), characters of the imagination (witches and ghosts), abstractions of persons (a queen, but not Elizabeth II), or nonhuman characters (animals, toys, et cetera). Transvestism is permissible with no stigma attached. A few costumes are not permissible: Santa Claus, the Easter Bunny, and such supernatural beings as God, Christ, the Virgin Mary, and the saints.[8]

The standard treat demanded is candy, but even if it takes another form, it must always be something that could never be part of a meal: pretzels, gum, cookies, and so on. (Apples are a partial exception.) The food is usually in small packets—that is, not part of a whole. It would never be proper to hand out pieces of cake or pie at Halloween; these items are sweet, but they are parts of a whole and they are archetypal desserts, parts of a meal. The small packets emphasize a lack of sharing which is, of course, contrary to the spirit of the feasts to follow, beginning with Thanksgiving. The food is presented by unobligated neighbors, rather than by one's own family. The anonymity of the visitors increases the social distance. The treats are given in response to a type of demand that would ordinarily be considered outrageous in Middletown. Hospitality must not be solicited and should appear to be spontaneous. Demands with a threat of violence are contrary to the gift ethos. Here also Halloween is an inversion of the normal order of things.

The two festivals following closely on this antifestival emphasize family solidarity in different ways. Thanksgiving celebrates the family alone, and Christmas celebrates the family within its social network.

The major emblem of Thanksgiving is the turkey, and once again the emblem provides the key for understanding the festival. A roast turkey is an entire undivided animal. Roast beef, ham, and leg of lamb are only parts of animals, the rest being shared by persons unknown; such meats are less suitable for a gathering that denotes unity. Another bird could do as well as the turkey if it were to symbolize unity only, but the bird to be eaten must also suggest abundance by providing more food than even a large family gathering could consume. Among commonly eaten fowl, only the turkey is large enough. The turkey also suggests the mythologized first Thanksgiving in Massachusetts.

Christmas is unquestionably Middletown's most important holiday. Its great variety of activities and symbols conveys two important messages: maintain social ties and nurture the children. These are, as we have seen, the major responsibilities of women in Middletown.

Social ties and gift giving go hand in hand: neither exists without the other.[9] The gift affirms the relationship and symbolizes the kind of relationship it is. Each gift must also be "fitting to the character of the recipient."[10] Gifts are given on many occasions in Middletown, but only at Christmas is it obligatory to give one to nearly every close relative, friend, and associate. Ideally, each gift given should differ from all the others given by that person. This unwritten (indeed, generally unstated) rule is burdensome, but Middletown people obey it remarkably well. The Christmas present not only reaffirms each relationship, it also specifies what that relationship is, while it flatters, if possible, the recipient's taste and personality. That each gift must convey so much and that overt speculation about the motives for choosing any gift is taboo explain why Christmas shopping is such a problem. Yet it must be done. Social cohesion depends on this annual reaffirmation of relationships.

Within most families, children receive more presents than adults do. This brings us to the other major theme of Christmas: the nurture of children. In this, Christmas stands opposed both to Halloween (when children demand a kind of nurture—not very wholesome—from nonparents) and Easter (when children are urged to be independent). The iconography of Christmas is full of protective images such as firelit interiors, large meals, and warm clothing in agreeable contrast to snowy outdoor scenes.

Santa Claus, the principal emblem of the secular Christmas, symbolizes these same themes. Santa Claus is foremost a gift giver, and a specific gift giver. Each of his gifts is designated for an individual person. Most of his presents are given to children. But while children do give presents to their parents, Santa Claus, a grandparental figure, receives nothing for his generosity (unless the improved behavior of the children is considered a recompense). This relationship exaggerates the predominantly one-way flow of gifts from parents to children. Santa epitomizes the generosity, particularism, and nurturance of Christmas. He also exhibits nurturing in another form: although he lives at the frozen North Pole, he has a warm house full of merry elves and a cheerful, helpful wife. Like the fathers of Middletown's families, he is visualized as bringing good things into the family from the harsh outside world;[11] but, having done so, he plays no further part in the holiday celebration.

Most Christmas preparations are done by women: decorating the house, sending the cards, buying the presents, and above all fixing a lavish Christmas dinner. Christmas is also a time when a woman's involvement with housekeeping and her family is dramatized. Usually she keeps the house clean, but at Christmastime she dresses it up. She cooks meals in a relatively humdrum way the rest of the year, but she "puts the big pot in the little one" for Christmas dinner. At other times of the year, she does little things for her family, as well as routine chores; at Christmas she does lavish, showy things for them. The secular Christmas glorifies the hearth and home, and the housekeeper most of all. That the secular Christmas celebrates the nurturing of children is even more evident when the two minor festivities immediately preceding and following it are considered and when the gospel story of the first Christmas is examined. The minor festivities are the office party and New Year's Eve, the first falling roughly a week before Christmas and the other a week after. Both are aggressively adult in tone, with drinking and some loosening of sexual restraints. Neither of these activities is proper for children or for the celebration of Christmas. The child-oriented nature of Christmas stands out strongly against these two antifestivals that rigorously exclude anything to do with children.

The religious and secular Christmases are usually contrasted, to the disparagement of the secular. "Keep Christ in Christmas!" cries Middletown. "Christmas is too commercialized!" That may be, but we have seen that extensive Christmas gift giving serves an important purpose by maintaining all sorts of personal relationships. The message of secular Christmas is not really different from the message conveyed by the Christmas story. The episodes of the Nativity convey the necessity of looking after a child's, and a family's, welfare. In a sense, we can say that God the Father is caring for His creation, the human race, as parents should care for their own creations, their children. This message is repeated on a smaller scale in the story of the Holy Family itself. Again and again, the family or the Child is threatened, but each time it is rescued. At the beginning, when Joseph was disinclined to marry Mary, an angel ensured the creation of the family and the preservation of the baby by explaining what appeared to be immorality in Mary. The birth of the Christ Child is attended by many nurturing figures from different levels of creation: His own parents, the stable animals, the angels, the shepherds, and, finally, the three kings bearing gifts, each gift symbolizing the nature of the recipient as "king and god and sacrifice." (Here also there is no return made for the gifts.) The Slaughter of the Innocents presents a serious threat to the newborn child; but again, by the intervention of the divine Father and the speedy action of the human one, the Child is saved. The secular and the religious iconographies are analogous in that they use different elements to convey the same meaning: children are helpless, and their parents must help them. They convey also the related message that families must use all possible means to preserve themselves against influences tending to split them apart.

The next family-related festival in the cycle after New Year's is Valentine's Day. This day also has Christian and even older origins. It was once thought to be the day on which birds began their mating season. Today, not much is known of St. Valentine himself; certainly *he* is not celebrated on February 14. Thus Valentine's Day is similar to Halloween in having originally had a part, now only dimly remembered, in the church calendar. Today both holidays are entirely secular.

Valentine's Day, with its dominant colors of red, pink, and white and its emblems of the pierced heart and Cupid, obviously celebrates sentimental attachment. Until recently it was solely concerned with male-female relationships among adults. About three decades ago, children began to be encouraged to send valentines to their friends. In the last few years people in Middletown have been sending valentines to their parents and children of the opposite sex and increasingly even to those of the same sex. Indeed, it is now common for valentines to be sent to participants in any relationship except one between adult males.

The emblems of Valentine's Day express the theme of nonphysical love. Cupid is a small boy, a type of person judged by Middletown to be free of sexual cravings. The convention that represents Cupid in silhouette further removes him from any association with the erotic. The valentine heart is similarly abstract. It does not bleed when pierced but remains as distant from physiological function as the sentimental love it symbolizes. The valentine colors reflect this attitude also. We could say that red symbolizes heat and blood and passion, but these are cooled and rendered acceptable by the purity of white; the lover is passionate but pure minded. Valentine's Day symbolically protects the inviolable privacy of eroticism within the family circle.

The gifts given on Valentine's Day in Middletown suggest that the holiday is primarily a celebration of women. The typical valentine gift is given to a woman by a man and more particularly to a woman as an object of courtship. Flowers, candy, perfume, and jewelry are appropriate. Electric irons, gardening tools, and hair curlers, though sufficiently feminine, are not considered suitable. Women may give cards or small presents to all the members of their families, but in many families men are obligated to give presents to their wives. Again, we see the wife/mother keeping the family together while the husband supports her efforts from outside.

The nonerotic love associated with Valentine's Day, like the pseudohorrors of Halloween and the universal benevolence of Christmas, is related to the secular celebration of Easter, the last major festival of the cycle. After we have investigated Easter in detail, we should be able to see the festival cycle as a whole, with every part related to other parts in opposition or by analogy. The end, Easter, is prefigured in the beginning, Halloween; but Halloween also prefigures the other festivals, and they anticipate, in their various ways, the culmination at Easter. What, then, happens at Easter?

Like Christmas, Easter has both a secular and a religious iconography. The two parallel each other without overlapping. The Easter Bunny never appears at representations of the Crucifixion, nor are the instruments of the Passion ever included in an Easter basket. The symbols of Easter convey a sense of new life, but they also convey, more subtly, the message that the conventional categories of Middletown's culture (especially the social categories) are merely conventional. In this regard, especially, Easter is the opposite of Christmas, when Middletown identifies and reinforces each social relationship. Easter is also, in a different way, the opposite of Halloween. Behavior at Halloween recognizes categories and deliberately goes to the opposite extreme by making nonmothers into mothers, nonfood into food, and so on, in a burlesque that depends for its effect on the fact that everyone involved recognizes and accepts the normal categories so perverted. Easter, however, seems to say that particularizing these relationships is unimportant. The symbols do not invert particular categories so much as negate "category" itself. This is especially true in relations between people.

The secular emblem of Easter is the Easter Bunny. An enumeration of the traits of this animal shows him to be an inversion of the great Christmas emblem, Santa Claus.[12] The Easter Bunny is nameless, homeless, without friends or family, dumb, comparatively immature, dubiously charitable, and biologically ambiguous. Santa Claus has a personal name, a known home and family, many friends, speech and literacy, great age, boundless charity, and biological specificity. Santa Claus is specific, the Easter Bunny is general. The presents Santa brings are for individuals and are so designated on the labels, but the Easter Bunny leaves eggs in the garden for anyone who can find them. Because the emblems of these two great festivals are so opposed, we can safely assume that they celebrate opposite things; and, since Christmas emphasizes particularity in social relationships, Easter must emphasize generality, or a blurring of social categories.

The Easter Bunny is an eminently suitable emblem for this kind of celebration, because it is the most ambiguous animal Middletown recognizes.[13] There are many young animals associated with Easter; usually, though, the animals are not those kept as pets but those found in the farmyard (another blurring of conventional distinctions)—chicks, ducklings, lambs (a symbol for the crucified Christ), as well as bunnies. Such animals are consonant with the general theme of renewal of life at that time of the year. Flowers, pale colors, new clothing, and eggs express the same theme. Of such youthful animals, however, only the bunny is ambiguous. The chick, the duckling, and the lamb will grow into adult forms enough unlike the baby forms to be easily distinguishable from them; moreover, in the adult forms, males can easily be distinguished from females. (This is true of all farm animals, not just those associated with Easter.) It is possible to compare a young rabbit with an old one and decide on the basis of size that one is older than the other, but otherwise there is no great difference between them. And, in any case, sexing rabbits without close and expert scrutiny is very difficult (as many have discovered to their chagrin). In these regards, the rabbit is less easily classified than the other young animals of Easter, and, therefore, it makes a better emblem than they would. The ambiguity of rabbits lies in more than their characterless gender and maturity, however. Sheep, chickens, and other such animals are unquestionably part of a class of livestock destined to be eaten as food. As a class, they are differentiated from pets, which are considered inedible, and from wild animals, which are categorized by species as edible or inedible. The important point is that Middletown recognizes four classes of animals and so is able to place any animal into its proper class: domestic and inedible (cats), domestic and edible (cattle), wild and edible (deer), wild and inedible (foxes).[14] Only the rabbit fits all of these categories. Rabbits can be pets, they can be eaten or avoided as food, they can live in the wild, and they can be hunted. The Easter Bunny further exaggerates the ambiguity of rabbits by producing eggs. Not only does he fit into no conventional category, he makes no distinctions himself. His only gifts are eggs, and he gives them to no specific person. Gift giving at Easter provides as valuable a clue as gift giving at Christmas for the understanding of the festival. Because Christmas gifts must be appropriate to particular relationships, the range of possible gifts is nearly infinite. At Easter, by contrast, only a few kinds of things are appropriate as gifts: eggs, candy (particularly an Eastery kind such as jelly eggs, chocolate bunnies, and marshmallow chicks), and plush or live animals. These may be given by anyone to anyone. The giving recognizes that there is a relationship, but it does not specify the kind of relationship. All relationships become more or less equivalent, because complementary social roles, such as parent and child or teacher and pupil, are blurred or ignored. The theme of these activities is clearly opposed to the theme of Christmas.

Do the secular celebrations at Easter oppose the Christmas emphasis on nurturing children? As we would expect, there is an opposition here, too, and it is evident in the custom of the Easter-egg hunt. At Christmas, the presents are brought into the house, where they can be opened in cozy leisure. At Easter, the eggs are hidden outside and must be hunted competitively by the children. Children are urged to go out and do for themselves; they are deprived of overt parental aid and are forced to be independent. Again, the Easter Bunny and his eggs symbolize this idea. Eggs are, in a sense, offspring without parents. The separation from the parent bird is complete because the eggs are brought and hidden by an animal utterly incapable (in the real world) of producing an egg of any kind. Rabbits themselves are famous for the number of offspring they produce, but not much is said about the preliminary activities producing those offspring. Lapine fecundity gives us an image of many young for not much activity. Stretching this, we could say that the Easter Bunny symbolizes children produced asexually. As at Valentine's Day, the element of sexual intercourse is rigorously suppressed, and in this we have a connection between Valentine's Day and Easter. At Valentine's Day, Middletown celebrates women romantically (they are potential sexual partners and, therefore, potential mothers, but these feminine characteristics are never mentioned). Some time later, at Easter, essentially parentless children appear and are celebrated. Obviously, sexual activity of some kind must have taken place during the interval, but it is not even hinted at. The mother and the child are celebrated separately, and the umbilical cord is hidden. Familial sexuality remains intensely private.

As we would expect, the themes of the secular Middletown Easter can also be identified in the religious Easter celebration. Middletown celebrates the confounding of death and the assertion of life; the two concepts are no longer distinguished or, indeed, distinguishable. There are apostles who betray or deny their teacher. The Son gives His Mother to another "son" (St. John the Divine) and considers Himself abandoned by His Father. Conventional distinctions are ignored, and ordinary categories are confused. There is also an emphasis on the independence of children, or offspring. Jesus, the Son, is no longer cherished and protected by all the levels of creation. He is on His own, independent and almost deserted. At Easter itself, we celebrate the Resurrection. The language of the Apostles' Creed demonstrates the shift from dependence at the Nativity to independence at the Resurrection. Whereas Christ was incarnate (that is, by someone else), at Easter He arose (that is, He did this Himself). His subsequent actions—He ascended into heaven and will come again, et cetera—all display an independence in that He is not being looked after as at Christmas but is looking after Himself (and others). As Christ the helpless infant and

Christ the willing victim are opposed, so Middletown's offspring as dependent children and as (potentially) independent adults are opposed; each is celebrated at its own festival.

Middletown has difficulty balancing the irreconcilable demands of nurturing and liberating children and is afraid to go too far in either direction. The festival cycle eases some of the burden of Middletown's anxiety. Halloween, Christmas, and Easter each treat the problem in their own way. Halloween combines the themes of nurturance and independence (albeit in a topsy-turvy, joking atmosphere) by having children assert to neighboring mothers their dependence by paradoxically demanding care from them. Christmas and Easter try to reduce the conflict by separating the two and concentrating on one at a time.

Easter seems to end Middletown's festival cycle in an anticlimax. It is a celebration of negation. Social categories are ignored; ordinary definitions are made meaningless. Each of the previous festivals has celebrated some particular aspect of family life, but Easter appears to insist on the unimportance of family relationships. Even the independence of children constitutes a kind of negation in that they are represented as being isolated, without any kin or indeed any identity (the eggs, their Easter gifts, being anonymous and essentially uniform). Things can be identified only by their context, and at Easter children are symbolically removed from any context.

But the message conveyed to Middletown by the Easter symbols is not so much that categories do not exist as that things Middletown chooses to separate from other things, and to place in different categories, are ultimately parts of the same whole. The religious Easter celebration proclaims that death can be transformed into life; the secular Easter, that any kind of family relationship is much like all the others. Children, urged to be independent, are the same as adults. Easter reunites everything that the preceding celebrations separated. Without the final celebration of Easter, the festival cycle would celebrate the particulars of Middletown family life without ever relating those particulars to each other. Middletown's festival cycle first celebrates different aspects of family life separately and then suggests that the differences are illusory, since all things are parts of the same order. Once the whole is reassembled at Easter, Middletown is ready to begin the cycle of analysis and synthesis over again.

NOTES

1. Originally appeared in Theodore Caplow, Howard M. Bahr, Bruce A. Chadwick, Reuben Hill, and Margaret Holmes Williamson, *Middletown Families: Fifty Years of Change and Continuity* (Minneapolis: University of Minnesota Press, 1982).

2. "An emblem is a type of symbol that represents a complex but bounded social or cultural phenomenon by means of an easily recognized picture or design which has no more philological relationship to the thing represented." This definition is adapted from David Efron, "Gesture, Race, and Culture," in Thomas A. Sebeok, ed., *Approaches to Semiotics*, rev. ed. (The Hague: Mouton, 1972). See also Raymond Firth, *We, the Tikopia: A Sociological Study of Kinship in Primitive Polynesia* (London: Allen and Unwin, 1936), and Edmund Leach, *Culture and Communication* (Cambridge: Cambridge University Press, 1976), both of whom have supplied variant uses.

3. For an illuminating comparison of antifestivals in two other cultural settings, see Roger D. Abrahams and Richard Bauman, "Ranges of Festival Behavior," in *The Reversible World: Symbolic Inversion in Art and Society*, Barbara A. Babcock, ed. (Ithaca, NY: Cornell University Press, 1978): 193–208.

4. Edmund Leach, *Rethinking Anthropology* (London: Athlone Press, 1961), 132–136; Alfonso Ortiz, "Ritual Drama and the Pueblo World View," in Alfonso Ortiz, ed., *New Perspectives on the Pueblos* (Albuquerque: University of New Mexico Press, 1972).

5. For anthropological discussions of witches and witchcraft, see Mary Douglas, ed., *Witchcraft Confessions and Accusations*, Association of Social Anthropologists [of Great Britain] Monographs, vol. 9 (London: Tavistock Publications, 1970); Lucy Mair, *Witchcraft* (New York: McGraw-Hill, 1969); Max Marwick, ed., *Witchcraft and Sorcery* (New York: Penguin Books, 1970); and especially, E. E. Evans-Pritchard, *Witchcraft, Oracles, and Magic among the Azande* (Oxford: Clarendon Press, 1937). Compare to Rodney Needham, *Symbolic Classification* (Santa Monica, CA: Goodyear, 1979).

6. *Muncie Star,* 1907.

7. The holidays following Easter are not as intensely celebrated as those preceding Easter or as Easter itself; and, except for Mother's Day and Father's Day, they are not family oriented. Mother's Day and Father's Day are exceptional in having no emblems, no religious associations, and only minimal gift giving.

8. It is, however, perfectly proper to impersonate these beings in other contexts: the secular emblems at their proper holidays, the sacred persons at holidays or in passion plays at other times. The mockery, save by the vehicle of the witch, may not be made.

9. Marcel Mauss, *The Gift: Forms and Functions of Exchange in Archaic Societies,* trans. Ian Cunnison (London: Cohen and West, 1954).

10. Needham, *Symbolic Classification,* 34.

11. Why does Santa come down the chimney? He must enter by an unusual way because he is an unusual person; see Arnold van Gennep, *The Rites of Passage,* trans. Monika Vizedom and Gabrielle Caffee (London: Routledge and Kegan Paul, 1960), 20ff. He cannot use a window because those are portals for illicit persons—burglars and eloping daughters. What remains but the chimney, situated on top of the house and pointing toward the sky, where Santa travels, and associated with heat, or warmth, which he embodies? How mundane if he were to come in by the front door like an insurance salesman!

12. For a fuller discussion of the Christmas/Easter opposition, see Theodore Caplow and Margaret Holmes Williamson, "Decoding Middletown's Easter Bunny: A Study in American Iconography," *Semiotica* 32 (1980): 221–232.

13. For an interesting discussion of the possible significance of our "animal categories," see Edmund Leach, "Anthropological Aspects of Language: Animal Categories and Verbal Abues," in *New Directions in the Study of Language,* E. H. Lenneberg, ed. (Cambridge, MA: MIT Press, 1964); John Halverson, "Animal Categories and Terms of Abuse," *Man* (New Series) 11 (1976): 505–516.

14. It must be emphasized that only the *classes* of animals and their attributes are considered, not cases in which dogs and cats have been eaten (as during wartime) or geese, chickens, sheep, and the like have been kept as pets.

Chapter 7

Mainstreaming Kwanzaa

Anna Day Wilde

Ralph Kennedy, a manager at IBM who lives in Cambridge, Massachusetts, has celebrated the African-American holiday Kwanzaa since 1974. When he started, he says, "there was a great deal of active discussion going on about the tendency or lack of tendency of people of color to come together as extended family." It was out of a desire to bring their relatives and friends together that he and his wife initiated their Kwanzaa celebration.

In his home, the observance is a graceful and intimate one, having grown through the years to include about forty family members and friends. "How we use it is our own tradition," he says. Guests, most with small children, bring food for a communal feast. After the meal, the families gather in the living room, and adults are asked to read a poem or other work that has moved them in the past year, or tell a story they would like to share with the others in the room. Many read from authors such as Nikki Giovanni and the poet LeRoi Jones; others tell personal stories, mostly of experiences meaningful to them in terms of family or history. A "unity cup" is passed around, and celebrants are asked to pay tribute to a relative or African or African-American leader who has touched their lives. The tributes and stories "get quite poignant," Kennedy says, with people telling of their lost grandparents and other relatives.

After the tributes, the children light candles and explain the values of Kwanzaa, which revolve around community, family, and creativity. The Kennedys' Kwanzaa tradition sounds almost perfect. What could be wrong with a holiday apparently embodying so much of what Dan Quayle, certain popular television sit-coms, James Q. Wilson, and public-opinion polls seem to agree are called "American values"?

Unfortunately, not all examples of the holiday's rapidly expanding observance are so positive. Arthur Hardy, the child of an African-American father and a white mother, left crying from a Kwanzaa celebration at the Roxbury Boys and Girls Club in Boston in December 1993. His mother, along with several white journalists, had been asked to leave the event in order to preserve its "African-ness." "I don't go to Hanukkah events because they're for Jewish families to come together. I wouldn't go to Hanukkah because I wouldn't feel welcome," Sadiki Kambon, who chairs the Boston Community Kwanzaa committee, told the *Boston Globe*. "Seven days, that's all we ask for," added another organizer of the celebration, Zakiya Alake. "This is a closed event. It's a time we come together to affirm our African-ness."

Kambon was quickly repudiated by Kwanzaa organizers and authorities nationwide and, a few days later, the policy of exclusion was reversed. Yet the incident reveals tensions inherent in this holiday, whose changing nature has brought it in twenty-eight years from a fringe observance invented by a black nationalist leader to an increasingly mainstream event celebrated by between five and eighteen million blacks worldwide, a majority of them middle or upper-middle class. The question is not simply what has fueled its undoubted success but whether it is the Kennedys' Kwanzaa or Kambon's Kwanzaa that represents the essence of the holiday. In a broader context, the "question of Kwanzaa" is the same that many pose about other "multicultural" efforts and claims regarding the importance of ethnic identity: Do these initiatives, in the classroom and in popular culture, more truly represent pride or cultural chauvinism?

Anatomy of a Holiday

Since Kwanzaa is a new tradition, there has been a proliferation of books on its meaning and rituals for the prospective celebrant. The most authoritative work currently available is *The African American Holiday of Kwanzaa*, written by the holiday's inventor, Maulana Karenga. It details at length the African links of the holiday and its proper observance. Two other books aimed at adults, Cedric McClester's *Kwanzaa: Everything You Always Wanted to Know but Didn't Know Where to Ask* and *New York Times Magazine* editor Eric Copage's *Kwanzaa: An African-American Celebration of Culture and Cooking*, give variations on Karenga's material but with less academic jargon

The name "Kwanzaa" perfectly exemplifies the holiday's origins as a "product of creative cultural synthesis," or a combination of creator Karenga's imagination and ideas drawn from African and African-American traditions. It is a made-up word, from the Swahili phrase *matunda ya kwanza*, which, according to Karenga, means "first fruits"; an extra "a," he writes, "has become convention," though he does not explain precisely why. The basis for the holiday is not a single observance celebrated by any one African people or nation but an amalgam of several harvest festivals. Karenga explains that "the values and principles of Kwanzaa are selected from peoples from all parts of Africa—South and North, West and East— in a true spirit of Pan-Africanism."

The fundamental creed of Kwanzaa, the *Nguzo Saba* (seven principles), emerges from the basic values Karenga sees embodied in the harvest festivals. These are *umoja* (unity), *kujichagulia* (self-determination), *ulima* (collective work and responsibility), *ujamaa* (cooperative economics), *nia* (purpose), *kuumba* (creativity), and *imani* (faith). These values are celebrated over seven days and nights, from December 26 through January 1, with each day dedicated to one of the seven principles. Most households light a candle each night in honor of the principle of the day. The candles (called *mishumaa saba*) are black (representing the African people), red (representing their struggles), and green (representing both Africa itself and the hope for deliverance after the struggles) and are placed in a simple seven-candle holder called a *kinara*.

The rituals as explained by Karenga also require fruits and vegetables, each identified by its Swahili name and symbolizing "the rewards of collective productive labor" (*mazao*), a straw mat representing tradition or history (*mkeka*), ears of corn equaling the number of children in the family (*vibunzi*), and simple, homemade gifts emphasizing education and African culture (*zawadi*). The *kinara* is placed on the straw mat amid a display of the fruits, vegetables, and ears of corn. Gifts can be given each night or just on the final, climactic night of December 31, when family members are supposed to gather for a communal feast (*karamu*). The feast usually includes a tribute to ancestors and African-American historical figures, along with several points of "creative expression" and a speech by a guest lecturer, generally on African or African-American topics.

While these are the basic aspects of Kwanzaa, observances vary widely, from small, family gatherings to larger groups of several families to huge community Kwanzaa events, like the one in Boston in 1993, which drew four thousand. A common feature in some of the larger ceremonies is a name changing, from a "slave name" to an African one selected by the participant.

From Radical to Mainstream

Kwanzaa was launched in the aftermath of the Watts riots, by Karenga, then a graduate student and black nationalist leader allied with LeRoi Jones (who by then had changed his name to Amiri Baraka). Karenga founded the US (as opposed to "them") organization in 1965, a group dedicated to the "creation, recreation and circulation of Afro-American culture. . . . the fact that we are Black is our ultimate reality." Karenga's Afrocentric and antiwhite rhetoric was not always soothing:

> The more you learn, the more resentful you are of this white man. Then you see how he's tricking your people, emasculating your men, raping your women and using his power to keep you down. The white *boy* has been waging a race war since he has been here.

Kwanzaa was an attempt "to reaffirm African culture," Karenga explained in an interview. However, "it was at the same time a political act of self-determination. The question is how to make our own unique culture. We were talking about re-Africanization." The first celebration drew only a few hundred people, mainly members of US, and the second drew a mere two hundred. In the years after Kwanzaa's invention, Karenga spoke around the country to black groups, pushing the holiday, and Baraka brought it to thousands of activists at Congress of African Peoples' meetings. There was, however, a lull from 1971 to 1975, when Karenga's movement went underground while he served a prison term for ordering the beating of a woman, according to newspaper accounts.

The holiday has been transformed in the twenty-five years since its original conception, and many of its celebrants today bear little resemblance to the revolutionaries of the late 1960s. It is a change of which Karenga himself has been quite aware. "This book on Kwanzaa is clearly a different book than the one I wrote previously," he admits in the preface to the 1988 book *The African American Holiday of Kwanzaa*:

> It is void of the polemical style and content and is directed not toward specific segments of the African American movement as before, but rather

to a wider audience. I realize that Kwanzaa has become a vital part of the lives of millions of African Americans who may or may not be in the Movement but nevertheless are very interested in and committed to Kwanzaa.

There is little firm demographic data on who celebrates Kwanzaa. However, anecdotal evidence strongly indicates that celebrants are just as, if not more, likely to resemble *The Cosby Show*'s Huxtable family as the Black Panthers. Henry Louis Gates Jr., Harvard's W. E. B. Du Bois Professor of the Humanities, sees Kwanzaa as a largely middle-class phenomenon. His point was echoed in a *Time* magazine article on the holiday, which concluded, "No one knows precisely how many people observe Kwanzaa, but its biggest boosters are middle-class professionals seeking to give their children a sense of black pride."

The most obvious and well-documented evidence of the middle-class nature of Kwanzaa has been the holiday's widespread commercialization. Perhaps the most dramatic manifestation of the Kwanzaa marketing juggernaut is the appearance of convention-center gatherings of merchants peddling Afrocentric goods and art, known as "Kwanzaa Expos." For example, the Kwanzaa Expo in St. Louis, Missouri, draws about 220 merchants and thirty-five thousand people over a two-day period. Its founder, Malik Ahmed, has called it the perfect embodiment of *ujamaa*, or "cooperative economics." The biggest expo in 1993, in New York City, had to move into the Jacob Javits Convention Center to accommodate three hundred merchants and approximately fifty thousand visitors. The expo, which began as a small gathering in a Harlem school in 1981, now draws corporate America in force: Anheuser-Busch, Pepsi-Cola, Revlon, Chemical Bank, AT&T, and Time-Life Books all have booths.

These companies were not the only ones paying tribute to the formidable spending clout of the middle-class black community, which supports a national market for Kwanzaa goods estimated to be worth as much as $100 million. The holiday could no longer be considered a fringe phenomenon when, in 1992, Hallmark began offering Kwanzaa cards. Woolworth's has also started running Kwanzaa promotions, as have J. C. Penney, Sears, Spiegel, and Montgomery Ward. Kwanzaa even has a video, entitled *Kwanzaa: An African-American Cultural Holiday*.

To further promote the holiday, Cedric McClester created a black Santa Claus, a griot named Nia Umoja, who tells children of the seven principles. Pop musician Imhotep Gary Byrd added the official Kwanzaa song, "Kwanzaa Nguzo Saba," which has been described as a "rich, rhythmic melody supplemented by gospel vocals." Ironically enough, although many Kwanzaa celebrants observe Christmas, the reason often given for partaking in Kwanzaa is the "growing commercialism" of the Christian holiday.

Purists do not always approve of the spread and commercialization of the holiday. "These things are going to happen, just as they have with Christmas, Chinese New Year and Hanukkah," an official at Karenga's African American Cultural Center told *Time*. Those who defend the commercialism, like McClester (who is spokesperson for the New York Kwanzaa Expo), say it is justified by *ujamaa*. "There is no problem with commercializing it, but who will be the benefactors of the commercialization?" he asked, before suggesting that "it should be people of African descent, not just corporate America."

Other mainstream institutions have also embraced Kwanzaa on a large scale. Many museums, for instance, offer Kwanzaa workshops or exhibits, including the American Museum of Natural History in Washington, D.C. Joanne Rizzi, co-director of the multicultural program at the Children's Museum of Boston, says her museum has done a Kwanzaa exhibit for years as part of an exhibit called "Winter Celebrations" about Kwanzaa, Hanukkah, and Christmas. Many black churches are also offering Kwanzaa celebrations, and one specialist in African religions has gone so far as to publish a liturgy entitled "ChristKwanzaa." In Atlanta's Providence Baptist Church, Reverend Gerald Durley has used Kwanzaa as a "rite of passage" for young men in the church.

The mainstreaming of the holiday is easily traced in major newspapers and magazines. Kwanzaa has received increasingly heavy coverage in the nation's major newspapers, beginning with a small trickle of prose in the late 1980s and early 1990s, as the holiday gained wider appeal. It seems as though each December, every newspaper feels compelled to do a new "trends" article on the spread of Kwanzaa, often coupled with suggested recipes or accessories such as room decor. In 1993 in particular, Kwanzaa features—food sections, book reviews, editorials, and shopping guides— were ubiquitous around the winter holiday season. This is scarcely the treatment the press seems likely to give a phenomenon limited to a controversial "revolutionary" element of a major community.

A Middle-Class Holiday?

The changing celebration patterns of Kwanzaa reflect national patterns in America, notably the rise of the black middle class and the simultaneous popularization in the 1980s and 1990s of a "multicultural" ideal in which people reassert themselves as members of ethnic minorities instead of aspiring to integration into the "majority culture." In the late 1960s, Kwanzaa was a manifestation of the black separatism of that decade, a backlash by "revolutionaries" against what was seen as the failed integrationism of the "black bourgeoisie," or "white-oriented, schizophrenic freaks," in the words of LeRoi Jones. During this period, the black middle class was on the rise: The percentage of middle-class blacks approximately doubled between 1960 and 1970, according to one historian. The overlap between this growing middle class and the celebrants of Kwanzaa in its early days was very small, however. There was a stark contrast in the two approaches to race relations, between the integrationism of the growing middle class and the separatism of the "revolutionaries."

However, a substantial percentage of these middle-class, integrationist, "successful" blacks are today still living in segregated housing. Beginning in the late 1980s and early 1990s, it became evident that, despite the swelling of the black middle class, racism is still a problem for them. Eric Copage links the celebration of Kwanzaa partially to these difficulties faced by middle-class African Americans working in integrated environments: "It's a way of saying there are other parts of our history. Especially when you're in a white environment, it's a way of reminding yourself who you are and staying focused."

Henry Louis Gates suggests that the rise of Kwanzaa among those who once seemed unlikely to embrace it is connected to the emergence of a black middle class, which, because of its integration into white America, feels alienated from black culture. "We were the first large-scale number of black people to come to historically white institutions," he says of his own generation. "There is a resulting cultural alienation." Successful blacks can feel "the guilt of the survivor," and they do things like wear kente cloth as a way of "remaining black." K. Anthony Appiah, a professor of Afro-American studies and philosophy at Harvard, agrees with Gates:

> African American culture is so strongly identified with a culture of poverty and degradation . . . you have a greater investment, as it were, more to prove

[if you are middle class], so Kwanzaa and kente cloth are part of proving you're not running away from being black, which is what you're likely to be accused of by other blacks.

This reclaiming of, and pride in, ethnic roots is not a new phenomenon, but it is a growing one among all American ethnic groups and might well have dangerous implications. Historian Arthur Schlesinger writes,

> A cult of ethnicity has arisen both among non-Anglo whites and among nonwhite minorities to denounce the idea of a melting pot, to challenge the concept of "one people," and to protect, promote and perpetuate separate ethnic and racial communities.

That this "cult" exists among those who have succeeded economically through integration is hard to doubt, with children of the most elite of the middle-class African Americans wearing "X" hats, calling for Afro-American studies, and cheering for Nation of Islam speakers on their campuses.

Kwanzaa in the Schools

Perhaps the best place to explore Kwanzaa as part of the rise of multiculturalism is where the battle over pluralistic ideals is being fought most intensely—in the schools. Nationwide statistics for the observance of Kwanzaa in the schools are hard to find, but newspaper articles provide evidence that "progressive" districts everywhere have found the holiday a welcome addition to efforts to bring diversity to their curricula.

The schools of Cambridge, Massachusetts, provide an interesting case study of the holiday's use in the classroom, based on interviews done in 1944. According to Shelley Wortis, co-chair of the Cambridge schools' Multicultural Committee, people began to be more aware of Kwanzaa as an educational aid in the late 1980s and early 1990s. Nearly all teachers observe the holiday in conjunction with Hanukkah and Christmas, according to Wortis and Gail Sullivan, director of social studies curricula for the town of Brookline, Massachusetts.

The teachers and school officials give many reasons for bringing the African-American holiday into their classrooms. "I would say the main purpose is to make sure the black community knows about the African culture and the African-American culture," says one teacher. Another celebrates it with her students because "the values are so universal." Still another teacher explains that "it's important for all cultures to know about each other. It's everybody's culture that needs to be affirmed." Ann Bolger, who is the parent coordinator in the Gramm-Parks school, adds that the goals of these teachers are to "make every child feel . . . validated, make them feel good about who they are."

The teachers' reasons for bringing Kwanzaa into the classroom are a good example of the wider debate over multicultural education in the schools. Writing in the *American Scholar* in 1990, Diane Ravitch, a fellow at the Brookings Institution, advocated a vision of "cultural democracy," or "pluralist multiculturalism," in which children would learn the "warts and all" history of American ethnic groups and "listen to a diversity of voices in order to understand our culture, past and present." Molefi Kete Asante, professor of African-American studies at Temple University and author of the 1992 book *Afrocentricity,* responded with the "Afrocentric" (and Latinocentric and Americocentric, he clarifies) defense of a scholarship "presenting the African as subject, rather than object," and showing black children especially a vision of African culture and achievement in mathematics, science, and other fields.

The battle over the place of Kwanzaa in the public schools reflects this tension: Is Kwanzaa part of an effort to teach children about a "diversity of voices" or a vehicle for making black children feel pride in their ethnicity? According to Sandra Stotsky, editor of *Research in the Teaching of English,* the goal should not be the divisive one of "degrading or diminishing mainstream culture, by trying to elevate a so-called minority group." Regarding Kwanzaa, she explains that, "if it has no real academic value, if children are spending time on something devised by a graduate student with no more academic context," it deserves little class time.

In this sense, the Cambridge public schools' Kwanzaa celebrations appear generally to fall short. Many classrooms celebrate the holiday with parties, not history books. Several teachers and officials concede that the reason for Kwanzaa in the classroom is, indeed, to make black students feel "validated" as blacks. When one teacher says she uses Kwanzaa because "it's important for kids to know themselves as a more capable, centered person," is that a valid (or possible) pedagogical goal? Perhaps it is, but the value of such labor may be undermined by those more interested in using the holiday to emphasize exclusive Afrocentrism than to teach all children their own history and that of their fellow students.

Kwanzaa and Pluralism

Is, then, Kwanzaa a positive step for blacks, or is it simply a force for divisiveness? As Philip Gleason, in an essay in the 1992 book *Concepts of Ethnicity*, observed of ethnocentrists such as Asante and Karenga, "the approach implicitly denies that there can be a unitary American identity based upon common assent to universalist principles, an identity that makes Americans one people despite differences of ethnic derivation." Karenga himself states that Kwanzaa "speaks to the people's need for cultural and spiritual grounding from an Afrocentric perspective." He wouldn't try to celebrate Hanukkah, he says, implying that white people should not try to observe someone else's holiday. Indeed, the Black Community Information Center, which sponsored the Roxbury Kwanzaa, had on its answering machine an advertisement for a scheduled speech by the anti-Semitic Nation of Islam spokesman Khalid Muhammad. However, the holiday has gone beyond Karenga and the political forces that created it, and its middle-class celebrants cannot be assumed to endorse any such sentiments. Kwanzaa is now a part of the commercial, educational, and cultural mainstream. It is an American phenomenon—what other nation could generate what Appiah calls the "kitsch Africana" of items like authentic J. C. Penney kente cloth garments? The holiday involves people of all races, despite the efforts of some exclusionists. In fact, many of the teachers who use Kwanzaa in the classroom are white, and many celebrants echo the sentiments of Ramon Wigfell, a manager at Gallery African in Washington, D.C., who says, "We find more Europeans taking an interest in Kwanzaa. We like that. Being able to understand other cultures will help us get along with each other."

Kwanzaa is essentially an effort on the part of African Americans to create community cohesiveness, though still unfortunately coupled in some cases with antiwhite feeling. Most African Americans view Kwanzaa not as an opportunity to bash whites but as a force for oneness among blacks. Admittedly, the resulting positive effects seem to be largely limited to the middle class at this point, not necessarily the underclass which seems to need it most, but strengthening such ties at any level can be valuable.

This class orientation limits the extent to which Kwanzaa is a positive influence in the black community as a whole. However, the hope is that the positive values Kwanzaa articulates can become a force, not just to enable families like the Kennedys to see forty relatives a year but to encourage members of the underclass to do the same. There is no real evidence that it has done so in any widespread way (and certainly not the way actual inner-city jobs or effective educational opportunities would), but that does not mean that the holiday is unnecessary. It remains to be seen how widely underprivileged communities will celebrate Kwanzaa in the coming years. There are potential benefits if they do, particularly since Kwanzaa undoubtedly has a more positive ethnic message than rapper Ice-T's "Cop Killer" or Khalid Muhammad.

Kwanzaa is not just a device for hostile separatism, as it may have been when it started; it can also be seen as a force for a cooperative, "pluralist" society approaching the American ideal. As the ubiquitous slogan has it, "one, and yet many."

NOTE

This essay previously appeared as Anna Day Wilde, "Mainstreaming Kwanzaa," *Public Interest* 119 (spring 1995): 68–79.

Chapter 8

Victorian Days

Performing Community through Local Festival

David E. Procter

My wife and I walk up the limestone stairs and into Waterville's historic Weaver Hotel. We are here for an English "high tea." Inside the hotel, first built in 1905, I feel like I've stepped back in time. I am surrounded by women in Victorian dress and the delicate sounds of stringed instruments. We are directed across worn oak floors to a table covered with a white lace cloth and set with blue willow china. From our table, we notice the polished hard pine trim and numerous paintings depicting frontier life. We gaze through a large six-foot window onto Waterville's Front Street and notice a large crowd gathering. As we sit down, an elderly, genteel-looking woman serves us from a three-tiered cake plate brimming with tea sandwiches and pastries. We sip almond tea as we taste blueberry scones with clotted cream. We notice the crowd on Front Street now seems agitated. People are running around, pointing and talking excitedly. The sounds of cello and violin bring us back to our English tea. We sample quiche Lorraine and tea sandwiches of smoked salmon and cucumber watercress. We finish the tea with desserts of lemon curd, white chocolate tartlets, Madeira cakes, four cream chocolate drops, and English tea cakes. Several large blasts from a shotgun jar us from our casual conversation. Our hearts race as we notice men running down Front Street shooting pistols and shotguns. A cowboy lies face down on the dirt road. People along the street are laughing, cheering, and walking away. The "End of the Line" gang has just performed another street play depicting good and evil on the frontier.

Victorian Days is in full swing.

Community Festivals as Civic Communion

Scholars from a variety of disciplines have argued that community festivals provide a special moment in civic life when a community reflects upon, celebrates, and ultimately presents an image of itself. Cultural theorist Frank E. Manning argues that community festivals represent a "text" or a vivid aesthetic event that depicts, interprets, informs, and celebrates social truths.[1] Anthropologist Carole Farber holds that community festivals "provide ideal *entrees* into a community's symbolic, economic, social, and political life."[2] Robert H. Lavenda, a cultural anthropologist, has referred to festivals as "one of the few moments in the annual cycle when . . . a community publicly celebrates itself . . . and a public culture emerges."[3] Likewise, Michael Marsden, a professor of English, suggests that "the community festival might provide a significant window into the culture of a community. It may well provide us with a narrative about the community's cultural essence."[4] And communication professor Raymond J. Schneider contends that by examining the way people play—the way they take time out to celebrate or to tell stories during festivals—we are able to determine much about the culture and even subcultures shared by communities.[5] All of these scholars, representing a variety of academic disciplines, argue that through civic festivals communities celebrate, sanctify, and promote important local sociopolitical structures. In short, community festivals function as civic communion.

Community festivals are brief but recurring intense moments in the life of a town or city when citizens come together to celebrate some facet of their community. In this celebratory process, citizens also organize and perform important cultural, community truths. Community festivals have been labeled "authentic popular culture," highlighting important local values, histories, events, and/or individuals. Further, by highlighting or privileging certain events, issues, and people over others, community festivals also function to create and sustain certain community hierarchies. Through festival performance, communities highlight and reinforce a certain public identity that is ultimately communicated to both local citizens and external publics.

Interestingly, however, many scholars have also pointed out that festivals remain a virtually unstudied context of civic life and cultural production. Michael Marsden and Ray Browne, for example, contend that "the community festival is one of the least understood areas of celebration."[6]

Festivals are paradigmatic of civic communion. Initially, festivals are symbolically and behaviorally framed moments in the life of communities. They are generally annual events, organized around some significant community event, history, issue, or person. While festivals do occur repeatedly, they are not the normal state of community affairs. They are, as Roger Abrahams writes, "times out of the ordinary . . . when gifts are given and ties are renewed, and community of spirit becomes more important than social structure."[7] During festivals, according to Alessandro Falassi, a community's "daily time is modified by a gradual or sudden interruption that introduces 'time out of time,' a special temporal dimension devoted to special activities."[8] Festivals are a moment of both celebration and pause. Festivals offer special moments of reflection and performance of cultural truths. Lavenda argues that, through festivals, "municipalities create a *momentary, if recurrent, . . . symbology of local significance*" (emphasis mine).[9] Festival organizers take significant time out of their daily routine to produce the event. For the core organizing group, festival preparation ultimately becomes a full-time endeavor. As the event grows closer, a sense of urgency and intensity settles over the organizing group. Likewise, festival-goers take time out from their daily and practical affairs to participate in this performance of local social structures. Further, as Falassi argues, "Festival time imposes itself as an autonomous duration, not so much to be perceived and measured in days or hours, but to be divided internally by what happens within from its beginning to its end, as in the 'movements' of mythical narratives."[10] Importantly, festivals are recognized as a special community moment. It is a transitory yet significant event, bracketed by months of planning and concluded with a time of celebration and festivity that ultimately performs a text of some community ideal.

Festivals are special events generally organized by a small group of deeply committed citizens and produced by an ad hoc committee of concerned citizens. These citizens come together for the express purpose of organizing and producing the community festival. This production group often begins slowly, meeting irregularly and sporadically months in advance of the event. As the event gets closer, however, the group meets more and more frequently and the communication becomes more intensely focused on the impending festival. It is also not unusual for the organizing committee to draw in outside assistance from townspeople or public and private agencies.[11] These outside groups often function as consultants or evangelists, energizing both the organizing committee and local citizens. These evangelists may help organize and produce the festival or function as special entertainment features drawing in additional community participation. Lavenda summarizes the civic communion character of organizing community festivals when he writes, "Organization of the festival, since it takes several months of meetings and coordinated effort, creates a special sense of solidarity among organizers."[12]

In addition to participation through organizing the festival, community events such as festivals provide a moment of common experience, a reference point for interaction and reflection in which a broad range of collective participation from local citizens is invited. Frank Manning, for example, argues that "celebration is participatory. . . . Celebration actively involves its constituency; it is not simply a show put on for disengaged spectators."[13] Initially, the organizing group often tries to be as inclusive as possible. It seeks to include business leaders, civic leaders, volunteer groups, and educational groups in the creation and production of the festival. It needs to include a variety of stakeholders not only because of the variety of special knowledge and skills necessary in producing festivals, but also because involvement from a variety of community sources likely increases the civic participation in the festival. Actual festival performance exhibits a broad range of participation. From a town's children reciting poems to historical reenactments of significant events, from speeches to community-wide parades, from dances to business leaders promoting the community to outside vendors by selling wares at the festival, the shared goal is to attract and entertain a large and diverse group. Festival celebrations are also available to anyone wishing to attend. Certainly many centrifugal forces exist in the community including religion, politics, patterns of kinship, class, social networks, mutual interests, and work.[14] But festivals provide a momentary opportunity to transcend these differences and come together as a collective body to produce, reflect upon, and perform community ideals and identity. As Lavenda et al. conclude, festivals "provide a meeting place and a set of common experiences" for citizens.[15]

Also characteristic of communion is full and active participation—what Ivan Karp calls "totalizing participation."[16] Festival participation often involves the entire person. Citizens listen to and watch parades and festival performers. Participants smell and taste foods distinct to the particular area and festival. They can touch crafts, festival performers, and community monuments. Citizens become part of the festival performance, joining in parades, dances, speech events, or community skits.

In a religious community, holy communion recalls important religious texts and truths as part of the service. These texts remind and encourage the faith community to participate in a certain lifestyle, according to religious values. Likewise, community festivals are organized to dramatically enact important civic values. As Carole Farber argues, "the small-town festival is precisely [a] key dramatic performance—a performance in which official town myths and ideology are presented and re-presented in parades, talent shows, costume judging, sports competitions, masquerades, and the like."[17] By highlighting, celebrating, and performing important community symbols, histories, events, or people, the festival is a moment when citizens collectively participate in reflection and promotion of civic truths.

Victorian Days as Civic Communion

Victorian Days is a festival that highlights the prairie Victorian past of Waterville, Kansas. As a promotional brochure proclaims, "Waterville's Victorian elegance was born out of a more rough-hewn time."[18] In the late nineteenth century, Waterville briefly rivaled other cow towns like Abilene, Kansas; Kansas City, Missouri; and St. Joseph, Missouri, in terms of commerce generated from the cattle industry. Because of rail car availability and good grazing land, cattle were herded to Waterville and then transported east. The railroad was a significant presence in Waterville, and while cattle were shipped east, the railroad brought settlers west.[19] Capital flowed into the town. During this time, "the little town shed its rough image and took on a gracious air of gentility as the monied and professional people began building new homes."[20] The cattle boom, however, didn't last long, and the money, the railroad, and the capitalists soon left Waterville. Still, there are remnants of this bygone era. Large, stately Victorian homes, "replete with gables, gingerbread balconies, colonnades, turrets and towers, still stand today along the tree-shaded streets of Waterville."[21] Don Fitzgerald also writes that the Victorian homes stand as a symbol of "the financial success of early Waterville . . . a reminder of the Victorian era and the 'Gay Nineties.'"[22] A once-elegant hotel and an opera house also remain as reminders of Waterville's past. Victorian Days is a festival that performs and celebrates these former times through an English "high tea" in the historic Weaver Hotel, frontier reenactments of pioneer days gone by and street performances of good and evil, Victorian home tours and Victorian dress, an 1880s church service and a saloon, and quilt displays and tea shops created specifically to highlight the Victorian era.

Victorian Days in Waterville provides a good example of the civic communion function of community festivals. There are two moments of civic communion associated with the festival. Waterville citizens begin celebrating and sanctifying their community as they plan for the festival, and the second civic communion moment occurs during the actual festival weekend.

Civic communion begins with the genesis of the festival. As with all civic communions, this festival begins with a strong commitment from a small group of individuals. Victorian Days is actually the brainchild of LueAnn and Ruth Ann Roepke. These sisters-in-law had a strong desire to host a community high tea and saw the opportunity to use the tea as a vehicle to create a community festival that would also highlight Waterville's Victorian past. The Roepkes reached across Waterville to recruit a number of women to help them produce this community festival. They tapped other Roepke relatives, but also many unrelated women who possessed special skills in organization, communication, education, baking, and media relations. As LueAnn explained, "You ask the women that you know are capable of doing what you're wanting done . . . and try to get them in a slot that really fits their talent."[23] Waterville's festival committee is currently constituted by sixteen to twenty dedicated women who have now produced the festival for eleven years. These women have connections all across Waterville, and the breadth of this committee membership translates into a broad level of support from a variety of segments in Waterville.

This organizing committee decided that the Victorian Days festival should enhance the visibility and promote the identity of Waterville and that they would use the funds they raise to help preserve historic community buildings. Ultimately, they have decided to organize and produce a community festival that would (1) highlight the prairie Victorian past of Waterville, (2) feature a "high tea" and Victorian home tours as festival centerpieces, and (3) use the money raised to preserve Waterville's historic buildings.

Victorian Days is organized for the last weekend of April. Preliminary planning for the festival begins in September, but the significant and intense planning begins in January. Planning meetings are models of organizational efficiency. The committee chair methodically moves around the table asking each of the women present to report on their Victorian Day activities for the prior month. Unlike so many academic meetings, nearly everyone on the Victorian Days committee attends every meeting and has progress to report. Meetings last 90 to 120 minutes and are almost always on task. There are some moments of small talk, but most speech is directed at the purpose of organizing and producing Victorian Days.

Strikingly, during the planning phase of Victorian Days, this group of women transforms from the individual identities of separate women living separate lives into a cohesive committee moving toward one goal— producing Victorian Days. Cooperation and the community goal of staging Victorian Days is paramount. Weeks before the festival, most of the committee meets at Ruth Ann's house to bake pastries for the high tea. At a meeting in March 2001, Ruth Ann announced that the baking was finished and that "you girls now need to all take some of these things and put 'em in your freezers." Following the meeting, all the boxed pastries disappeared into the night and into freezers across Waterville. At an early April meeting, Gay Stewart and Ruth Ann were looking for tables for "Priscilla's Ice Cream Parlor" and for the one-hundredth-year celebration of Ruth Ann's Victorian home. Women from around the table reported whether they had tables and where in their homes they could be located. "That table is on my deck; just come by sometime and pick it up," one announced. Whether the problem is cleaning downtown buildings, baking pastries, transforming downtown businesses into tea shops and ice cream parlors, finding props for displays, or finding volunteers, this committee models cooperation and interdependence, always keeping the objective of producing Victorian Days as the preeminent goal.

The second moment of civic communion occurs the weekend of festival performance. During the festival weekend, a sociocultural text of Waterville is performed through street performances, the English high tea, home tours, and the various Victorian shops created for the weekend. Through festival performance, citizens and visitors celebrate and enact cultural symbols and values associated with Waterville.

Waterville's sociocultural text is performed through a number of symbolic rituals. Falassi argues that festival rituals valorize civic symbols through processes of symbolic intensification and symbolic inversion. He further explains that during festivals, people do things they normally do not do; "they carry to the extreme behaviors that are usually regulated by measure [and] they invert patterns of daily social life." These two symbolic processes often function in concert. For example, a symbolic reversal occurs so that an important community symbol can be valorized or intensely highlighted. The civic function of all this festive symbolism, according to Falassi, "is to renounce and then to announce culture, to renew periodically the lifestream of a community by creating new energy, and to give sanction to its institutions."[24]

Symbolic inversion, a process by which a community reverses the "normal" state of affairs and in the process highlights important cultural symbols, is performed in several ways during Victorian Days. For example, throughout the Victorian Days festival, important Waterville symbols are transformed from their standard state into spaces and symbols of civic import. Most important, the Weaver Hotel and Waterville's Victorian homes are transformed from private, mundane, and relatively unused spaces into sanctified community symbols. In 1906, the *Waterville Telegraph* called the Weaver Hotel "the pride of Waterville," and proclaimed that "we believe we can boast of having the finest hotel of any town of its size and even many times larger in the state." Today, the Weaver Hotel stands unused and vacant for much of the year. It is, in many ways, symbolic of rural America's steady decline. Still, the hotel remains an important civic symbol of Waterville's past prosperity. So, for Victorian Days, the hotel is identified as the space for the festival's most important event—the English high tea. Weeks before the festival, Waterville citizens clean, paint, and ultimately transform the hotel from a derelict building into the luxury hotel it once was. Much the same process occurs for Waterville's fine Victorian homes that are used as tour sites. For example, Alan Minge's Victorian home is frequently used as such a tour site. The *Waterville Telegraph* explains that Minge's current home is "an exquisite Queen Anne house" first built in 1895 by banker Samuel Powell. The newspaper goes on to state that Powell "had come from Buffalo, New York, and brought charm, class and plenty of money from the East to build his house."[25] Home owners, festival committee members, and even hired help converge on the houses to transform the private homes into public museums of Victorian display.

Other public spaces are also physically and symbolically inverted. They are transformed from their normal, everyday functions into spaces dedicated to articulating a sociocultural text of pioneer Victorian times. Educational and economic spaces are converted into festival performance spaces. For example, a downtown building normally used as the Valley Heights Preschool is transformed into "Priscilla's Ice Cream Parlour." A one-time produce market, now a vacant building, is converted into "The Front Street Saloon." The Waterville library becomes a display site of quilts constructed by local women in community quilting guilds. The local Masonic Hall is transformed into "Victoria's Tea Shop."

Even Commercial Avenue—home to Waterville's business district—is closed to vehicular traffic and transformed into a blacktop arena for Victorian-era performances. "Wheelmen"—Victorian-era bicyclists—ride up and down Commercial Avenue on antique bicycles, providing symbolic import to this form of transportation made popular during the Victorian era. At the east edge of the street, the Victorian Days festival performs its railroad heritage with a miniature steam engine and train that provide children with rides. Pioneer encampments were also set up at the end of Commercial, performing vignettes of life that early settlers in and around Waterville might have faced.

The people involved in Victorian Days also engage in symbolic inversion. During the festival weekend, community members assume roles unlike their everyday personas. High school girls become "can-can dancers" in a saloon. A physician's assistant becomes the proprietor of the ice cream parlor. Retired farmers' wives become elegant servers at an English high tea. Speech communication graduate students become Victorian home tour guides. Dress functions to assist with the performance of symbolic reversal as everyone wears costumes reminiscent of a pioneer Victorian era.

Not only do festivals employ symbolic inversion to highlight important sociocultural truths, but festivals also employ symbolic intensification to valorize civic structures. Symbolic intensification occurs through festival performances in which participants engage in some extreme or exaggerated behavior with the purpose of highlighting and emphasizing some valued civic structure. Falassi suggests that symbolic intensification may occur through "rites of conspicuous display" and "ritual dramas." Rites of conspicuous display "permit the most important symbolic elements of the community to be seen, touched, adored, or worshiped."[26]

Two powerful examples of rites of conspicuous display include the English high tea and the Victorian home tours. Each of these festival performances highlights artifacts and activities that most festival-goers do not possess or engage in. Most festival participants have not participated in a high tea. Most likely, festival tourists have not sampled the varieties of tea and the range of pastries provided, so the festival tea allows them to engage in a performance of high society. Likewise, the home tours are performances of conspicuous display. As Falassi argues, "Sacred shrines . . . are solemnly displayed and become the destination of visitations from within the immediate boundaries of the festival, or of pilgrimages from faraway places."[27] Private homes are constructed as public museums. Festival-goers "sign in" to gain entrance into the homes. At one home, tourists were required to don surgical booties before entering. Festival participants were directed by volunteer docents through magnificent homes restored to Victorian elegance and adorned with objects of wealth. The festival thus provides tourists a vicarious sampling of foods, activities, objects, and lifestyles that they have heard and seen but not personally experienced.

In addition to these rites of conspicuous display, Victorian Days also performs ritual dramas. According to Falassi, "By means of the drama, the community members are reminded of their Golden Age, the trials and tribulations of their founding fathers in reaching the present location of the community."[28] The Golden Age and values of Waterville are enacted through various dramatic performances. The "End of the Line Gang" displays good and evil with a street drama depicting "Waterville's early history as a rough railroad town."[29] The performance illustrates the danger of frontier Kansas and the importance of being able to take care of oneself. Depicting the clash between duly appointed lawmen and vigilante bounty hunters, the performance features outlaws riding into town, kidnaping ladies from the local saloon, only to be thwarted and killed by local sheriffs.

Ritual dramas are also performed during Victorian Days by "reenactors" who set up pioneer camps depicting prairie life during the late nineteenth century. These pioneer camps illustrate the hardships pioneers faced when cooking, washing, and maintaining cattle and horses. The pioneer camps illustrate the harsh conditions on the prairie and the values necessary for survival on the Kansas plains. Additionally, school children in period dress perform short declamations and recite Victorian-era poems in Waterville's "Game Fork Schoolhouse"—a one-room schoolhouse built in 1904.[30] A religious service honoring the frontier church is also conducted.

Ritual dramas also draw festival-goers into the dramatic performance. Citizens line the streets to watch the "End of the Line Gang" enact frontier values through their street performance. The twenty-first-century audience becomes a frontier crowd, heckling evil and cheering justice as frontier law is dispensed through saloon fights and street shootouts. Bystanders are thus transformed from festival spectators into participants in a larger drama depicting the civic values of the frontier. Likewise, festival participants touch, smell, and taste the constructed frontier in the drama of the pioneer camps. Tourists touch and smell recently tanned leather. They watch and smell as iron is molded through fire into horseshoes, hammers, and nails. They smell and taste food cooked over open camp-

fires with cast-iron kettles. In short, festival-goers become active participants in a frontier civic drama depicting appropriate behaviors and values.

Community Constructed through Victorian Days

From the Victorian Days festival, a civic image of Waterville emerges. Victorian Days casts Waterville as an affluent, God-fearing, pioneer community on the Kansas plains. Festival performances also highlight civic values
of innovation, self-reliance, and cooperation.

As mentioned earlier, the two events that highlight Victorian Days are
the English high tea and the home tours. Both events are performances of
conspicuous display. Both festival performances trade on symbols of
wealth and the elite, and both remind festival participants of Waterville's
brief moment of affluence. Just as important as these two festival performances is the prominence of the railroad at the festival. During Victorian
Days, festival participants are encouraged to tour the Depot Museum and
children are encouraged to ride a miniature version of an 1880s steam engine. "The railroad gave birth to Waterville" and in the late nineteenth
century was symbolic of community affluence.[31] Railroads were the
agency whereby significant commerce occurred and whereby goods were
transported to rural areas, and they were the most sophisticated mode of
travel. Thus, these very prominent symbols of Victorian Days function to
communicate a community of affluence.

Religion also plays a significant part of the Victorian Days.[32] The festi-
val organizing committee holds all their meetings in Waterville Methodist
Church. During the festival, this same church is open and visitors are en-
couraged to view Biblical murals that depict significant religious stories.[33]
The local Lutheran Church is also used to serve festival-goers box lunches.
Finally, a Victorian-style church service is held each Sunday of the festival.
Festival organizers report that over a hundred people attend the service,
with many attending in Victorian costume.

Besides performing religious values, Victorian Days also enacts pioneer
values of innovation, self-reliance, and cooperation. Innovation is performed in several ways during Victorian Days. For example, festival-goers
view how early Kansans cooked, made clothes, and made tools. The
"Wheelmen" and their antique bicycles also enact innovation during the
Waterville festival. Bicycling was significant during the Victorian era. During this time, bicycling was popular both nationally and internationally;

even Waterville had its own bicycling club. During the mid-to-late nineteenth century, several bicycle innovations occurred, making the bike a more affordable, attractive, and comfortable mode of transportation. The evolution of the bicycle also led to changes in styles of clothing so people could more comfortably ride and to changes in road conditions.[34]

Self-reliance is another value performed during Victorian Days. Again, the pioneer camps illustrate early Kansas life when settlers had to rely on their own resources and abilities. Likewise, the street performances dramatize frontier good and evil and depict individualism and the importance of relying on oneself. They dramatically perform being able to defend oneself and taking the law into one's own hands. Festival committee members also use Victorian Days to communicate the importance of self-reliance to one another. According to Sandy Harding, during one of the rehearsals for the children's program at the Game Fork School, a child's mother frantically exclaimed,

> "I just don't know how I'm going to get my son ready," she said, "I'm not a seamstress. I can't make him a pirate's costume." And she was just really upset and I said, "Ya' know, in the era that they're portraying," I said, "do you that think those mothers had fancy sewing machines and they could run down to Wal-Mart and get the fabric? They had to get in their closets." I said, "Just get in your closet. Tie a bandana on his head and put a patch on his eye and send him off." But, it was kind of a learning experience for some of the parents too, the mother, you know. To go back, to step back in time. I thought that was kind of neat.

But the most significant value communicated through the Victorian Days festival is cooperation. It is a value exhibited among members of the organizing committee, Waterville citizens, and various businesses in Waterville. Businesses and landlords turn their buildings over to the Victorian Days festival. A variety of citizens come together to clean and convert downtown buildings into spaces appropriate for the festival. Citizens help one another prepare for the festival by finding and offering furniture and china for the tea and ice cream parlor. They help one another find and secure volunteers for the various festival sites. The committee members do an excellent job of helping one another brainstorm and deal with problems. The entire festival, then, becomes symbolic of cooperation among the committee and community. In fact, very little anger or resentment was expressed in any of the committee meetings that I observed, as well as in our interviews or participant observation. One source of anger that did surface concerned a lack of cooperation by the city officials. When asked at the wrap-up meeting about festival problems, committee members complained that too many children were downtown on skateboards and scooters, riding on sidewalks and streets, zipping in and out of the crowds, and placing festival-goers in danger. The problem was cast as a lack of interest and enforcement by city government, as illustrated in the following exchange:

> *Sandy*: We need some crowd control. We need some cooperation from the town officials that we don't get. That's it in a nutshell. Doris actually called, and I don't know if she called Chuck or Larry. But she called and asked him to come and be on the streets Sunday. Because it was dangerous out there. I mean, in and out of the crowd. If we'd had a busy crowd, somebody would've been hurt. I think it is unfortunate that we don't have any cooperation from our city officials, which we don't have.
>
> *Gay*: Yeah, that's right.
>
> *Sandy*: And, I don't know how we get it.
>
> *Pam*: Well, is that for a lack of asking?
>
> *Sandy*: Oh no. No. It's for lack of interest on their part.[35]

This conversational exchange also illustrates how the values of self-reliance and cooperation are connected. Private citizens first generated the idea of Victorian Days, the organizing committee is completely composed of private citizens, and organizers do not rely on public support from the Waterville city government.

In addition to highlighting community values, civic communions also articulate a community hierarchy. Indeed, Victorian Days is perceived by some in the community as an elitist and restrictive festival. Comments received by both interviews and participant observation indicate that some in Waterville view Victorian Days as the property of an elite group. One committee member referred to the organizational committee as "cliquish," while another committee member indicated that her family wasn't truly accepted into Waterville because they did not have "three generations of family buried in the Waterville cemetery." During an encounter at a Waterville convenience store, citizens said they saw the festival as a way for "some folks to show off." Members of the festival committee recognize this perspective. One member stated that there are "people that just don't get excited about it. Maybe because the word Victorian is . . . intimidating to some people." Another committee member also recognized the community division and indicated how the committee responds to that division: "There are a few people in town who don't like [the festival]. They think 'so and so' is making money off of it and they wouldn't touch it with a ten-foot pole. We [on the committee] just proceed as if they didn't exist."

Another issue that creates an elitist perception is the admission cost of the festival. The most celebrated events—the high tea and the home tours—are accessible only by purchasing $20 tickets for admission. While people in most urban areas would perceive this cost as minimal, some locals view this expense as excessive. One festival-goer commented, "I've always wanted to attend Victorian Days, but it's so expensive. I never would've come, but I had a ticket given to me this year." Another visitor to Victorian Days commented, "I thought [Victorian Days] was fun. I thought it was a little spendy, but I thought they knew what they were doing."

A final source of community division comes from the focus of the festival. There is community-wide perception that Victorian Days is a festival for women. This is a widespread perception held both by those on the committee and among the townspeople. The perception is fueled in many ways. All the festival's key players are women. In all the meetings I attended over a two-year period, I saw three men. Each attended only one meeting. During one meeting where the committee was searching for volunteer help, someone suggested asking some men and another woman sarcastically responded, "finding men helpers, that's like looking for hen's teeth."[36] A local man agreed, conceding that male volunteers were "a group that hasn't previously been involved."[37]

In most ways, the festival is constructed toward female interests. The major festival events are geared toward women; for example, the high tea, the Victorian home tours, and the tea shop. As one male indicated, "you've got a group of guys who aren't interested in the tea, they're not interested in the tea shop, they're not interested in those kind of things."[38]

Additionally, all advertising for Victorian Days—from signage to brochures to publicity fliers—is printed in pink. At one committee meeting, the woman in charge of the Victorian tea shop related how she had to "take the 'man look' away" from the local Masonic Hall. Much of the talk during committee meetings is related to the costumes and the sewing of the costumes. During the festival weekend, nearly every woman working with the festival is dressed in Victorian costume.

Festival conversation also reinforces traditional gender roles. A female tourist to the Alan Minge Victorian home reported that it was clear the home's owner was a man because "that mirror in the bathroom had obviously not been cleaned recently—probably not for a couple of weeks!" Much discussion also revolved around male responses to the high tea. Men reportedly looked "dazed and bewildered" by the variety of food and drink choices. In one conversation, women reported that some men "looked stunned" by the variety and diversity of food offered during the tea and that these men simply ignored foods they didn't recognize. A female committee member labeled this a "typical male response."

Festival organizers recognize this gender disparity and have moved to attract more men to the event. They added the saloon and the street shootouts. The railroad display also tended to be a male attraction. As a committee member pointed out, "I think [the railroad] added a lot for the men because you could see them all talking, ya' know, visiting about it, ya' know, looking at it, examining it. So that was a good drawing card for gentlemen, I think."[39]

Conclusions

Community festivals like Victorian Days function as civic communion. These festivals are transitory yet intense moments in the community when the town performs civic history, values, and hierarchy. Festival performances are sociocultural texts celebrating important community symbols. By examining the performance of community festivals, scholars may gain insight into a community and view a powerful way in which the community is organized.

It is clear that Victorian Days in Waterville is meant to serve a civic purpose. In a 1999 interview, LueAnn Roepke stated that "the festival was created to give back to the community." In fact, over the life of the festival, the organizing committee has raised and donated over $50,000 to community projects in Waterville. It has also used this cash as seed money to attract outside grants and bequests from private citizens to maintain and renovate historical Waterville sites. Further, the festival is viewed as a vehicle for unifying the community.

The festival is a moment when the town celebrates important community history, people, and symbols. Through the performance of the festival, Victorian Days reminds citizens and outsiders of Waterville's railroad history, its brief period of economic affluence, and its prairie roots. The festival also positively performs an affluence lifestyle and celebrates the role of women in this rural community.

Despite some dissenting community voices, the majority of Waterville citizens—both organizing committee members and outsiders—view Victorian Days as an event that brings the town together. Sandy Harding provides a most powerful and articulate voice on this issue. In the following narrative, she explains her job—organizing an after-festival party which anyone who helped with Victorian Days can attend—and the overall value of Victorian Days.

> I guess our main job was the after-party. What can I say when you get over a hundred people to show up. I thought it was a big tribute to this community. I said, no matter what we made or how many people bought tickets, I think that Victorian Days does something for the Waterville community that is above and beyond any monetary value that we ever gain from it. You looked around the room (the after-party) and you had people from all walks of life in our community gathered together for one cause, having a good time, and to me, that was worth anything and everything we all did together. It was good. I think the value to our community is just above and beyond any work we do, any money we make. I think it unites the Waterville Community.[40]

Finally, community festivals such as Victorian Days function to create and reinforce a public community identity. Victorian Days serves to promote Waterville as a rural community on the prairie, founded in the history of railroads and cattle, but also a community of style, grace, and charm. Both community insiders and outsiders indicate that Waterville is recognized through Victorian Days. LueAnn Roepke, for example, argues that Victorian Days "gives us name recognition for a small town."[41] Sandy Harding echoes this sentiment but also avers that Victorian Days "sets us up to be an example and leader to all surrounding towns and counties. . . . When you say Waterville, people sit up and take notice. We are a model to a lot of communities."

Through Victorian Days, Waterville citizens briefly, but intensely, come together in an attempt to retain and remind citizens of vestiges of the town's affluent prairie past. Through the performance of this community festival, the community reminds citizens and visitors of important civic histories, hierarchies, values, and cultural symbols. Through the organization and production of Victorian Days, Waterville projects a public image to both its citizens and neighboring people and communities.

NOTES

1. Frank E. Manning, "Cosmos and Chaos: Celebrating the Modern World," in *The Celebration of Society: Perspectives on Contemporary Performance,* Frank E. Manning, ed. (Bowling Green, OH: Bowling Green State University Popular Press, 1983), 6.

2. Carole Farber, "High, Healthy, and Happy: Ontario Mythology on Parade," in Manning, *Celebration of Society,* 33.

3. Robert H. Lavenda et al., "Festivals and the Creation of Public Culture: Whose Voice(s)?" in *Museums and Communities: The Politics of Public Culture,* Ivan Karp, Christine Mullen Kreamer, and Steven D. Lavine, eds. (Washington, DC: Smithsonian Institution Press, 1992), 77.

4. Michael T. Marsden, "Summer and Winter Festivals in Thompson, Manitoba," in *The Cultures of Celebration,* Ray B. Browne and Michael T. Marsden, eds. (Bowling Green, OH: Bowling Green State University Popular Press, 1994), 157.

5. Raymond J. Schneider, "Tampa: Tale of Two Cities," *Text and Performance Quarterly* 14 (October 1994): 334.

6. Michael T. Marsden and Ray B. Browne, introduction to *Cultures of Celebration,* 6.

7. Roger D. Abrahams, "The Language of Festivals: Celebrating the Economy," in *Celebration: Studies in Festival and Ritual,* Victor Turner, ed. (Washington, DC: Smithsonian Institution Press, 1992), 163.

8. Alessandro Falassi, "Festival: Definition and Morphology," in *Time Out of Time: Essays on the Festival,* Alessandro Falassi, ed. (Albuquerque: University of New Mexico Press, 1987), 4.

9. Lavenda, "Festivals and the Creation of Public Culture," 77.

10. Falassi, "Festival," 4.

11. Lavenda, "Festivals and the Creation of Public Culture," 80.

12. Ibid.

13. Manning, "Cosmos and Chaos," 4.

14. Robert Lavenda et al., "Festivals and the Organization of Meaning: An Introduction to Community Festivals in Minnesota," in *The Masks of Play,* Brian Sutton-Smith and Diana Kelly-Byrne, eds. (New York: Leisure Press, 1984), 49.

15. Ibid., 34.

16. Ivan Karp, "Festivals," in *Exhibiting Cultures: The Poetics and Politics of Museum Display,* Ivan Karp and Steven D. Lavine, eds. (Washington, DC: Smithsonian Institution Press, 1990), 282.

17. Farber, "High, Healthy, and Happy," 36.

18. *Victorian Days,* supplement to the *Waterville Telegraph,* April 28, 2001.

19. Don Fitzgerald, *Pleasant Valley: Waterville, Revisited* (Waterville, KS: Yellowjacket, 1987), 12.

20. "Waterville Celebrates Its Heritage," *Victorian Days,* 1.

21. Ibid.

22. Fitzgerald, *Pleasant Valley,* 48

23. Interview with LueAnn Roepke, April 24, 1999, and April 17, 2001.

24. Falassi, "Festival," 3.

25. "Waterville Man Uncovers 'Buried Treasure' in Home," *Waterville Telegraph,* February 20, 1999, 1.

26. Falassi, "Festival," 4–5.

27. Ibid., 4.

28. Ibid., 5.

29. *Victorian Days.*

30. In 1999, school children recited and performed poems by Emily Dickinson. In 2001, the children performed the poems of Robert Louis Stevenson.

31. "Depot Highlights Heritage," *Victorian Days,* 6. For a discussion of the importance of railroads in creating commerce and building towns, see John F. Stover, *American Railroads* (Chicago: University of Chicago Press, 1961).

32. The significant influence of religion in the Waterville festival contrasts dramatically with the Tulip Festival in Wamego. In Wamego, organizational meetings are held in the City Hall. Organizers report that religious services were once part of the festival but were discontinued due to a lack of interest.

33. During Victorian Days, the local librarian was encouraging festival-goers to visit the Waterville Methodist Church and view the Biblical murals: "Go into the church basement, stand on the stage, and look around at those murals. You'll feel something when you're in that basement."

34. "Bicycling Was a Victorian Craze," *Victorian Days,* 8.

35. Victorian Days Committee Meeting, May 7, 2001, Waterville, KS.

36. Victorian Days Committee Meeting, April 9, 2001.

37. Interview with Terry Roepke, April 21, 2001.

38. Ibid.

39. Ann Walters, Victorian Days Committee Meeting, May 7, 2001.

40. Victorian Days Committee Meeting, May 7, 2001.

41. Interview with LueAnn Roepke, April 17, 2001.

Part IV

Nation Building

Chapter 9

Can You Celebrate Dissent?
Holidays and Social Protest

Francesca Polletta

Consider three episodes of protest. At a Mardi Gras festival in France in the early nineteenth century, the revelry includes celebrants dressing up as and mimicking the town's mayor and his deputies. At one point, protesters break into the town's granary and begin to distribute grain to the cheering crowd. After the festival, half-hearted efforts are made to identify the ringleaders, but no one is ever prosecuted.[1] Flash forward over a century to East Berlin in the fall of 1989 and to a parade organized by the ruling communist party to celebrate forty years of victorious socialism, complete with a hundred thousand marching party members. Unexpectedly, however, people begin to drift away from the march to join what seems to be a spontaneous dissident march. Over the next few weeks, the thousands become hundreds of thousands as protest marches are launched around the country, culminating with the destruction of the Berlin wall.[2] Now, forward to New York in the fall of 2002. The annual Victoria's Secret lingerie show is expected to draw eleven million television viewers, and tickets for the live show are being scalped for $500 apiece. Animal-rights activists have managed to infiltrate the audience, however, and as supermodel Gisele Bundchen comes down the runway, they leap in front of her to unfurl a banner reading, "Gisele: Fur Scum." The protesters are hustled out and arrested, but the episode is replayed on the evening news and it dominates the fashion press for weeks.[3]

What should we make of these episodes? All three involved public rituals that became the occasion for protest. But clearly they were different kinds of occasions and different kinds of protest. Scholars have tended to treat episodes such as the first one in the literature on carnival. Rebellion that takes place on such occasions has been seen as a challenge to existing structures of power and status, but a challenge without much political punch—in the end, reaffirming the relations of power that it so gaily inverts. Protest in East Germany has always been seen, by contrast, as thoroughly political and instrumental. As a result, analysts have paid little attention to the symbolic spectacles of power and discontent that preceded the full-blown protests and may have played a critical role in spurring them. Finally, it is difficult to see the third episode, the lingerie show, as a public ritual at all.

Yet all three episodes have important things to say about the relations between public rituals—holidays, commemorations, and festivals—and protest. If we recognize that ordinary people have pressed their collective claims against the powerful in diverse ways, the first episode reminds us of the centrality of public rituals and festivals in nineteenth-century Europeans' repertoires of contention. It was not uncommon then for people to protest by usurping public officials' functions on festival days, for example, forcibly distributing the grain that officials were accused of hoarding. To have protested in the ways that we take for granted today—marching to the seat of official governmental power, for example—would have made no sense in a nineteenth-century political context in which power was localized. Challengers' scope of action has always been powerfully shaped by the political contexts within which they have operated, that is, by the institutionalized relationships that exist between authorities, citizens, and challengers. (This applies to both activists' use of holidays as well as their use of other forms of claimsmaking.)

For authorities, public celebrations have often served as means of legitimating the current regime, with participants and viewers performing their assigned roles as appreciative publics. But there is always the risk that the gathered crowds will constitute themselves as a different kind of public and, in so doing, puncture the regime's legitimating myths. To understand why the 1989 German march went so terribly wrong, and with such revolutionary effect, requires that we explore the ways in which Leninist regimes have sought legitimacy through public performances of public acclamation. Finally, one cannot talk about the contemporary American political scene without recognizing the extraordinary role of the media in shaping both mainstream politics and challenges to it. This helps to explain why staging protests at media events like Victoria's Secret fashion shows make good strategic sense. It also reminds us that struggles between challengers and authorities often have the effect of remaking the rituals as well as the movements. If protest becomes a yearly feature of the Victoria's Secret show, that event may move closer to a place among our American pantheon of collective rituals.

So what is the relation between commemoration and dissent? With a few exceptions, sociologists have devoted little systematic attention to the topic.[4] In this essay, I draw on case studies of movements across geographic regions and historical eras in order to flesh out several hunches. Like those historians who have traced the careers of particular holidays, I argue that holidays' meanings and uses are malleable. Still, holidays have spurred protest in patterned ways. I draw on the concept of a repertoire of contention to provide analytic purchase on those patterns. I also show that the process of influence works in two ways: Interactions between challengers and power holders have remade modes of public commemoration as well as protest repertoires. Continuing with holidays as the outcome of protest, I argue, as many activists have, that gaining official recognition for holidays has ambiguous results. Holidays that began by honoring collective action and protest have ended up promoting individual effort and service. Rather than treating that dynamic as inevitable, however, I suggest that it may be the result of competitive relations among those promoting the holiday, people who are ostensibly on the same side. Finally, I agree with public holidays' champions that movement groups' penchant for turning holidays into arenas of contention may undermine holidays' capacity to unite rather than divide. In addition to noting several reasons why that contention may actually be good for democracy, I also argue that movements' own holidays and rituals may provide valuable lessons for how to create public holidays that valorize unity *and* difference. The essay is organized along the lines of these propositions, moving from holidays as spurs to and resources for protest to holidays as outcomes of protest and finally to movement holidays and rituals as the source of democratic innovation.

Order and Dissent

Social historians and folklorists have long recognized the transgressive elements of traditional festivities such as carnivals, charivaris, religious observances, and other collective celebrations. The question is just *how* transgressive they are. Occurring in a time and space separated from the quotidian and parodying the usual hierarchies of power and status, such festivities create *liminal* moments in which structure is suspended.[5] But do those moments create the temporary experience of *communitas* that then allows the structure to reemerge, strengthened?[6] Do they serve as a safety valve for discontent or a spur to its expression?

Critics have rightly pointed to a degree of struggle and contention in ritual that is missing from analyses that rely on a safety-valve metaphor.[7] But neither side has specified just how organized or just how political a challenge must be to constitute a real threat to the status quo. When Terry Eagleton argues that "carnival, after all, is a *licensed* affair in every sense, a permissible rupture of hegemony, a contained popular blow-off as disturbing and relatively ineffectual as a revolutionary work of art," he never says what an "effectual" rupture of hegemony would look like.[8]

Sociological theories of social movements may help us here by reminding us that collective action of any sort is rarely completely expressive.[9] The question is how groups of people have used public festivities and rituals to formulate and press their collective grievances. We can call this activity "politics," whatever form it takes. According to Charles Tilly, in the eighteenth century, authorized holidays like carnival and saints' days were a familiar setting for political protest.[10] This was not the political protest we are used to today, with collective action targeted at state authorities, unfolding through demonstrations at official seats of power, and organized by formal associations representing sectional interests. In the eighteenth and early nineteenth centuries, before power was centralized by national states, contention was necessarily local, often drew in the whole community, and targeted the residences of perceived wrongdoers. Just as important, eighteenth-century repertoires mingled celebration and politics. Authorized festivals and ceremonies provided occasions for people not only to mock authorities but sometimes to appropriate their functions—distributing the grain that was controlled by royal deputies, for example, in a manner perceived to be more just.

It is in the changing uses of folkloric customs often treated by scholars as simply "quaint," Tilly goes on, that we can also see the mutation of an eighteenth-century repertoire. Take the charivari, a ceremony in which young people gathered outside the home of someone accused of a moral offense, singing and banging pots and pans until the offender paid a negotiated penalty. The offender might be a widower who remarried too early or newlyweds who failed to host the celebration expected of them. The charivari had long been used for purposes of moral control within the community, but in the early nineteenth century it was adapted to new purposes. In Perpignan, the regional prosecutor reported in 1830 that a "charivari had been organized to punish" a deputy named M. Lazerme, who had recently voted with the king and had thereby antagonized "many young people of an extreme persuasion," the prosecutor explained.[11] The young people organized a charivari, but one that departed from formula. Those who participated "shout[ed] wildly: A BAS LAZERME, VIVE LA CHARTE, VIVE LA LIBERTE" ["Down with Lazerme, Long Live the Charter, Long Live Liberty"]. When two of the ringleaders were arrested, posters appeared on town walls that read, "MORT AU TIRAN ... PAIX AU PEUPLE ... LIBERTE ET EGALITE ... AU NOM DU PEUPLE FRANCAIS" ["Death to the Tyrant ... Peace to the People ... Liberty and Equality ... In the Name of the French People"].[12] A form of moral control within the local community was now being used to challenge national political actors in the name of a national people.

By the late 1850s, the political charivari was falling into disuse as new forms of protest took shape. Food riots and skirmishes over taxation yielded to strikes and "demonstrations," in which people massed at formal seats of power with banners and signs indicating their identity and interests. The electoral rally replaced the feast-day processional; the formal meeting, the charivari. Ordinary people's targets and forms of protest reflected a new ecology of power, Tilly argues, one that centers on national electoral politics and one that has endured until our own time. To be sure, it has not endured intact, and in a moment I will argue that features of today's political environment have made for important changes in how challengers have used protest generally and holidays in particular to advance their claims. For now, I want to underscore two points in Tilly's account. One is that public festivities' and rituals' place in challengers' arsenal of protest changed as the locations of political power did. The other is that demonstrations emerged within the shell of the carnivalesque. Challengers put familiar public rituals to new political uses.

In his account of local contention across the channel in England during roughly the same period, Marc Steinberg explores the latter process.[13] On Easter Monday in early-nineteenth-century Ashton, the town's working-class residents paraded, then burned and ripped to pieces an effigy of a fifteenth-century manorial lord. Undamming a reservoir that had been specially constructed for the occasion, and fortified by copious amounts of liquor, celebrants dragged hay and rags through the muddy stream and soaked bourgeois passers-by. Games and street brawls completed the festivities, which brought commerce virtually to a halt. "Riding the Black Lad," as it was called, evinced the inversionary features of the carnival, with public order ceding to gleeful chaos and social superiors brought down to the muddy earth. But celebrants were also resisting an emerging capitalist control of public space, Steinberg argues. By the 1820s, legislators and police forces in Ashton and elsewhere cooperated with mill owners to make town streets and squares into efficient channels for the movement of vast amounts of materials and disciplined labor. New laws permitted the prosecution of individuals for obstructing any passageway, loitering, or conducting parades. Riding the Black Lad threw a wrench in the works of this new ecology of commodity exchange.

When Ashton's cotton spinners struck for higher piece rates in 1830, they drew on the forms familiar to celebrants of the Black Lad, pelting mill owners with sticks and mud and streaming out of mills to join colorful processions. Led by a musical band, wearing tricolor cockades, chanting in unison, and stopping periodically to harangue mill owners, some twenty thousand marched through Ashton in the first of several marches. "With a combination of carnival cheer and military rigor, the spinners marched through the main streets of the region's mill town proclaiming that the manufacturers were imperious tyrants in workers' territory."[14] In this repertoire-in-transition, then, the defiant appropriation of capitalist space remained central.

The disorder in Ashton was eventually put down and a permanent military presence established; a strategy of occupying capitalist space became impossible in Ashton. But workers' adoption of the firm-by-firm strike, the next innovation in their contentious repertoire, may have forgone that possibility more generally, Steinberg speculates. In any case, the carnivalesque had begun its retreat from organized contention.[15] It was never completely eliminated, but it was increasingly marginal in the lives of communities and to conceptions of the political.[16]

Reconstituting the Public

If charivaris and the Black Lad were recognized occasions for pressing collective grievances, then viewing holidays' disruptive power simply in terms of saturnalian excess posed against the forces of order misses the point. Flash forward a century, then, to a kind of commemoration that would seem to permit little in the way of even "permissible rupture," as Eagleton put it.

Images of public commemorations in state socialist societies are familiar, with long lines of tanks and troops marching in lockstep and a sea of citizens holding up colored placards in a synchronized display of patriotic slogans. It is difficult to see in such carefully coordinated spectacles much in the way of festivity, let alone the potential for disorder. And yet, in 1989, official commemorations played a role in popular uprisings in Czechoslovakia, East Germany, and China. The timing of these protests has long puzzled scholars. As Steven Pfaff and Guobin Yang point out, surveillance and repression made the cost of participating in oppositional action steep, and in 1989, they showed no obvious signs of lessening.[17] Unlike democratic regimes, moreover, where resources of labor, money, publicity, and political influence are diffuse and therefore mobilizable by challengers, in authoritarian regimes, such resources are largely controlled by the state. Dissidents' scope of action in East Germany, Czechoslovakia, and China was limited to small circles of low-key dissent.

Yet one feature of the political setting opened up a surprising opportunity. Leninist regimes depended on large-scale, highly scripted political spectacles to demonstrate the party's power and the public support it enjoyed, Pfaff and Yang argue. For citizens, participating in such events did not require that one actually believe in the regime or its policies. By behaving "as if" one believed, however, the power of the regime was reconfirmed—both symbolically and, thereby, in fact. Lisa Wedeen describes the "politics of pretense" created by such spectacles (in authoritarian regimes generally, she says, rather than only Leninist ones), spectacles "in which all participate but few believe."[18] Still, say Pfaff and Yang, misperception may have been important—but misperception on the part of authorities. By mistaking public compliance for acclamation, they overestimated the support they enjoyed.

This kind of miscalculation seems to have been made by officials in China, Czechoslovakia, and East Germany. In Berlin, a carefully orchestrated commemoration of forty years of victorious socialism complete with a hundred thousand marching party members was derailed when Mikhail Gorbachev's speech calling for greater democratization met with spontaneous applause from spectators. Encouraged, activists launched a simultaneous protest march which gradually drew participants away from the official march and led eventually to clashes with the police. Similar reversals occurred at official commemorative events around the country and in the weeks following the October commemorative debacle. Demonstrations grew from a few thousand to hundreds of thousands, paving the way for the fall of the Berlin wall. In Czechoslovakia, dissidents turned state-sponsored commemorations into protest rallies: Five thousand demonstrators hijacked an official commemoration of the Universal Declaration of Human Rights and staged a protest event; dissident groups orchestrated a rally at the official May Day celebrations; and fifty thousand marched in the streets in opposition to the regime after an official commemoration of a World War II antifascist martyr. In China, unlike East Germany and Czechoslovakia, the challengers were crushed, but not before mobilizing an extraordinary pro-democracy movement. Again, official ceremonies provided unanticipated opportunities for mobilization. Students demanding a dialogue with officials massed in Tiananmen Square after the official funeral ceremony for government reformer Hu Yaobang. When officials refused to meet with the three student representatives who were kneeling in the traditional style of courtiers petitioning the emperor, the symbolism proved galvanizing and launched a mass mobilizing effort by students. Political anniversaries that followed this one were also turned into protest events.

Public commemorations did not on their own cause widespread mobilization, Pfaff and Yang caution, but they did provide dissidents with vital symbolic resources. Not only did such commemorations put large numbers of people in close proximity and away from the routines of daily life; they also offered up the regime's myths for public scrutiny, focused participants' grievances by drawing attention to the gap between ritual and reality, and in several cases, provoked sharp repression. All this made it possible for dissidents to mobilize widespread but previously unarticulated discontent.

Steinberg's celebrants of the Black Lad and Pfaff and Yang's participants in communist martyrs' days are miles and years and repertoires apart. Yet at least one similarity bears mention: In both cases, authorities' power depended on ordinary people visibly constituting themselves as a certain kind of public. Manufacturers in England needed public thoroughfares and spaces to serve as efficient channels for capitalist production and exchange, and they needed a public that constituted itself in an orderly way as a workforce and a market. Similarly, state socialist regimes needed a public that would perform as an appreciative audience for the party's self-described victories. In each case, holidays gave people the opportunity to refuse that role, to constitute themselves unmistakably as a different kind of public. This suggests that we look for other places or moments where power has depended on creating a certain kind of public.

Commemorative events—whether staged by officials or challengers—in such settings have a unique disruptive power. A march on the National Mall in Washington, for example, has the potency of its connection to a long tradition of protest, but it does not have real disruptive potential. Consider, by contrast, a small group of pacifists in New York who sat on a park bench outside City Hall in June 1955, defying an annual air-raid drill by refusing to go inside and beginning what would become an annual ritual.[19] Experts agreed that a nuclear attack would destroy any shelter, yet the public's adherence to the practice effectively constituted the government as protectors and the public as protected. Pacifists' annual ritual of ignoring the air-raid siren refused that construction and enacted a different kind of public. The ritual drew more supporters each year until the city was forced to abandon the ordinance as unenforceable. The protest also generated intense publicity for pacifists and attracted scores to their cause.[20] Activists often try to occupy important public spaces to draw attention to their cause. This line of thinking suggests activists may be especially effective at times and places where those in power depend on visible manifestations of orderly and appreciative publics.

So far, I have described three ways in which holidays have spurred protest. For working people in early-nineteenth-century Britain and France, authorized festivities and the rituals that accompanied them were recognized as legitimate occasions for pursuing collective grievances against power holders, whether local or, increasingly, national. For people in authoritarian regimes, official commemorations enacted the power of the state at the same time as they put its myths on display, making it possible for small groups of dissidents to mobilize discontent. In both settings, as well as in the United States in the grip of the Cold War, protesters drew power from their refusal to constitute themselves visibly as appropriate publics, whether party supporters, disciplined workers, or protected citizens.

Yet another way in which official holidays may inspire antistate action, especially in authoritarian regimes, is by counterpoising a religious discourse to a political one. In many secular authoritarian regimes, religious ceremonies and holidays have been tolerated by the state. Activists have used such occasions to promote a religious vocabulary of motive for participation. So, Ramadan and other religious holidays have served as an important mobilizing tool for Islamists, in part because of the belief that Muslims receive greater reward from God for good deeds during such

holidays.[21] Activists have also drawn from religious rituals normative standards for criticizing the current regime and have been able to legitimately
defend against state interference during the period of the ceremony. For
example, prior to the Iranian revolution, the conditions for protest seemed
as inauspicious as those I have described in China, East Germany, and
Czechoslovakia. But in late 1977, under pressure from dissidents, moderate
to conservative clerics in Tehran began to sponsor public "mourning ceremonies" as a way for people to voice opposition to the regime. Such ceremonies were traditionally held forty days after a death, and the ceremonies
held in 1977–78 helped radical clerics to connect with students, moderate
political leaders, and citizens involved in local mosque activities. These
networks formed the basis for the revolution. The funeral observances also
became occasions for increasingly violent clashes with security forces, and
the resulting deaths led to a new cycle of public funeral observances and
wider mobilization.[22] Holidays' mobilizing power, then, may lie in part in
the fact that they reflect a moral discourse that is alternative to the state
but is legitimated by it.

Finally, holidays may inspire collective action not against the state per
se but against the ethnic groups that are seen as favored by the state. In his
study of ethnonationalist conflicts in postcolonial and newly independent
states, Stanley Tambiah argues that democracy has been not a remedy for
ethnic strife but a condition for it.[23] Ethnic groups have taken advantage
of democratic elections and representation to fight for material resources,
political offices, and linguistic dominance. Violent attacks on ethnic antagonists have been part of that project. By destroying the homes and property of the opponents, one "levels" them, both literally and politically. Ethnonationalist rioting has been purposive, but also performative, Tambiah
maintains, with the syntax of violence drawn from a shared culture in
which ethnic rituals and religious observances have been key attributes.
Processions, festivals, and commemorations have always been occasions
for enacting the form and content of ethnic and religious identities. But
since competing groups' celebrations have often occurred at roughly the
same time or have required celebrants to traverse the territory of other
groups, they have been occasions for symbolic competition—and often
physical conflict. Allen Feldman similarly describes Protestant and
Catholic parades in Northern Ireland: "Marching along the boundaries
transforms the adjacent community into an involuntary audience and an
object of defilement through the aggressive display of political symbols

and music."[24] Unsurprisingly, the involuntary audience has often risen, sometimes violently, to the intended challenge.

Although we can identify common features of public commemorations and festivals that might make them occasions for unruly collective action—large numbers of people are taken out of the routines of daily life and gathered together, symbolism is at a high pitch, and interactions are often lubricated with liquor—the fact is that most such occasions pass off without a hitch or with only minor skirmishes rather than regime-threatening protest. To understand when and why the latter sometimes occurs requires that we acknowledge the ecologies of power and claimsmaking within which repertoires of contention evolve. In early-nineteenth-century France and Britain, public festivities were just beginning to lose their central role in contention as power shifted from local authorities to national ones. In twentieth-century Leninist regimes, public commemorative activities were firmly controlled by authorities, but their importance as rituals of public acclamation made them vulnerable to dissidents' cooptation. And in postcolonial democratic regimes, holidays, like elections, have provided the occasion for violent efforts to "level" ethnic competitors.

Rituals Remade

In Czechoslovakia, East Germany, and Iran, protest nurtured in commemorative rituals brought about the regime's collapse. In China, it led to the execution of dozens of protesters, the imprisonment of hundreds more, and a ban on protest activity. A year after the pro-democracy movement, the festival of Quingming was celebrated in Tiananmen Square with schoolchildren bused in for the occasion, residents barred from the square, and protest of any kind prohibited. China's public commemorative rituals were thus altered as a result of the pro-democracy movement. This should not be surprising. As challengers innovate, authorities do too. The result is change not only in how collective claims are made and responded to, but also in the public rituals on which they draw.

We can see this process in the American history of parading. Parades, as they evolved in American cities in the early 1800s, seemed to be a stunning enactment of American pluralism.[25] Citizens from the city's diverse corporate groups were organized into marching platoons and applauded by throngs of fellow citizens as they made their festive way along the city's major thoroughfares. Early in the century, occupational groups predominated in urban parades; later, civic and ethnic groups did. As Mary Ryan shows, pluralism came in part at the expense of protest, since the parade both appropriated and preempted a common protest form. Dissatisfied tradesmen had commonly used the processional—or "turning out"—as a way to assert their grievances and demonstrate their strength. City-sponsored parades effectively incorporated both the form and the groups. With officials and leading businessmen at the head of the parade and occupational groups rank-ordered behind them, urban parades turned workers into players in an idealized social order. Parading was a form of social control.

Perhaps inevitably, however, the players sought to use the parade to advance their positions in the real social order. By the 1850s, Irish immigrants were determinedly marching in public parades as well as in their own unauthorized ones. Scuffles broke out for a time between Irish contingents and native-born ones, before the Irish won out. But they won at a cost, if not to them, then to the idealized social order the parades were supposed to enact. By 1858, the *New York Herald* observed that parading had become an Irish affair. The native-born middle class stopped participating in parades, preferring to celebrate holidays in private or with their own kind. As an idealized image of the urban social order, the parade was also thus a terrain for real battles over groups' place in that order. But the contenders were mismatched; the powerful could withdraw altogether. Ryan's main point is to contrast the early-nineteenth-century parade, open to most of a city's corporate groups, to one that had emerged by the latter part of the century. Narrower in its social composition, but with a few women or girls costumed to represent "the Goddess of Liberty" or "the Ship of State," the parade had become democratically representative in a symbolic sense rather than a descriptive one. But Ryan's account also shows powerful groups variously using means of formal exclusion (of blacks and women), incorporation (of native-born workers), informal violence (against Irish workers), and withdrawal to enforce the idealized social order of the parade. And it shows relatively powerless groups seeking a place in the parade and the political status that place implied. Such interactions, and successive ones, made American parades what they are today.

American Protest Today

National political representatives in nineteenth-century France or even 1950s America encountered their publics infrequently. Today, political officials' positions, opinions, personal lives, and political fumbles are the subject of constant scrutiny. And officials spend an enormous amount of time canvassing, interpreting, and striving to shape public opinion. What does this mean for people pressing political claims outside the normal channels of political influence? Certainly, it opens up opportunities for challengers as well as constituents. By influencing public opinion, movement groups can exert powerful pressures on political decision-makers. Since the attention of the public is limited, however, activists must struggle to generate public attention and support for their cause. They must do so against politicians' better-resourced efforts to "spin" political issues to their own advantage. "The mass media forum is *the* major site of political contest," Myra Marx Ferree and her collaborators write, "because all of the players in the policy process *assume* its pervasive influence."[26] Two other features of the contemporary American political landscape are important in shaping activists' relations to public holidays and rituals. Both within the state and outside it, power is diffused across numerous offices, agencies, and levels of governance. This means that activists have numerous points of leverage in trying to change policies or institutionalized practices. Challengers to the policy of the Catholic Church, for example, may work through lawsuits or petitions and through appeals to local or national bodies or to the Vatican. In part as a result of the prominence of the media and the diffusion of authority within and across institutions, movement groups operate in a much more competitive environment, striving to be heard above the clamor of allied movement groups, opponents, media commentators, and elected officials.

What consequences have these developments had for movement groups' relation to public commemoration? In their study of media coverage of protest events, Pamela Oliver and Gregory Maney found that events that were tied to holidays received more coverage than those that were not.[27] By staging demonstrations, meetings, and direct actions on holidays or on the anniversary of notable political events, challengers legitimate their own cause by linking it to hallowed values—of democracy, freedom, or patriotism.[28] Activists want to send the message that they, and not those in power or their opponents, are staying true to the values enshrined by the holiday. That, in turn, can provide a valuable news peg. So, for example, a *Washington Post* story on anti–Iraq War protests began, "Antiwar activists marked International Human Rights Day yesterday in Washington with several demonstrations."[29] The actions' commemorative quality gave them an air of seriousness as well as continuity with a noble tradition of human rights—a tradition, they declared, that the United States was violating.

Movement groups also pose their values against those enshrined in public rituals in a more parodic and colorful way. Indeed, the media's preference for strong graphics and striking footage has probably contributed to a revival of the carnivalesque in protest generally. Take, for example, the "Billionaires for Bush" who paraded at the presidential inauguration or the environmentalists who celebrated the Fourth of July by symbolically ousting the owners of an electrical energy plant, singing their version of "Yankee Doodle": "Power profits going up, profits are so thrilling; when you use the power up, we really make a killing." Activists see public holidays and rituals as enshrining social values, but the point they make is that such events often implicitly enshrine values that are less than noble.[30] When "Billionaires for Bush" parade at the presidential inauguration, they point out that electoral politics in our society is infused by values not only of democracy but of commerce. When campus activists celebrate "Vagina Day" rather than Valentine's Day, they draw attention to the sexual exploitation that has gone unchallenged under the guise of "romance."[31]

Activists are speaking to more than the media on such occasions. They also want to build solidarity among their members, support among bystanders, and even irritation among opponents. But media coverage assists in those tasks as well. Activists' strategic orientation to the media helps to explain another striking feature of public rituals today. The line distinguishing civic holidays like the Fourth of July and Presidents Day from televised entertainment and sports events like the Miss America Pageant, the Super Bowl, and the Academy Awards is not so clear. We see animal-rights protesters at Victoria's Secret lingerie shows, feminists picketing the Masters golf tournament, and antiwar activists at the Academy Awards. Ironically, the protests that come to be associated with such events may help to lodge them in the pantheon of American collective rituals. So, for example, many people watch the Academy Awards in anticipation of another Vanessa Redgrave or, now, a Michael Moore. Thus, protest may contribute to making spectacles into public rituals.

Challengers in democratic regimes, like authoritarian ones, also create their own commemorative occasions. Of course, much of protest *is* collective ritual: marches, demonstrations, sit-ins, teach-ins, die-ins, lie-ins, kiss-ins are all periodic, coordinated group actions that enact the group's relations to its members and to the larger polity. But activists also commemorate past protest events and heroes to assert their continuity with a tradition of struggle. This campaign becomes just one episode in a narrative of overcoming, and activists become heirs to a victorious or martyred generation of activists.[32] Activists also commemorate the anniversaries of injustices against the movement or its constituency: The militia movement publicly marks Ruby Ridge and Waco, and pro-life activists, like pro-choice ones, commemorate the anniversary of the Supreme Court's *Roe v. Wade* decision. Such observances spur the indignation that recommits activists to the cause and bring new people into the fold. But they are also an opportunity to speak to an even larger audience via the media coverage they elicit.[33]

Two of the standard features of news reporting are an emphasis on getting both sides of the story (in the interest of objectivity) and an emphasis on portraying conflict (in the interest of telling a sellable story).[34] This encourages the familiar media images of groups shouting at each other across police barricades. The media's emphasis on florid conflicts may also help to explain the proliferation of battles over whether and how to celebrate particular holidays. Columbus Day, Thanksgiving, Christmas, St. Patrick's Day, Gay Pride Day—these and other holidays have been the target of lawsuits, demonstrations, and sometimes violent altercations.[35] We can read these conflicts as part of the continuing struggle to define who counts as an American—and who counts as an Irish-American, in the case of gay and lesbian protests against St. Patrick's Day parade organizers. As ethnic or ethnicity-modeled conflicts, they are not so different from those that unfold over St. Patrick's Day and Orange Day parades in North Ireland or Buddhist processions in Sri Lanka. But we should also see in these controversies efforts on the part of activists to get public attention for their agenda that they would not get otherwise. American Indian Movement (AIM) activists in Denver were pleased with the arrest of their media spokesperson, who poured blood over a statue of Columbus during that city's Columbus Day parade. "We had the action, we had the arrest, we had a little trial, we had the media statements, we had no outrageous demands, and they were forced to hear us," said one.[36] Without being especially manipulative, activists know that the arrest of an articulate spokesperson is a way to get issues into the public arena.

Does it work? Does the media coverage, the often incendiary rhetoric on both sides, the arrests, and sometimes violent stand-offs translate, in the end, into gains for the movement? Activists themselves are ambivalent. Gay activist Brendan Fay broke with the Irish Lesbian and Gay Organization in New York City several years ago because he felt it was wasting its time and energy fighting to be in Manhattan's St. Patrick's Day parade. Since then, he told a reporter, he has come to recognize the power of parades as a "significant cultural expression." Indeed, he organized a gay and lesbian contingent at 2003's St. Patrick's Day parade in Queens, which does allow gay and lesbian marchers under their own banner.[37] But Fay did not say whether he believed that the battles over the Manhattan march were worth it. Nor can sociologists of social movements answer the question; we do not yet have systematic comparative data on the longer-term impacts of battles over cultural performances.

In his study of Columbus Day protests by Native American activists in the early 1990s, Timothy Kubal identifies a wide range of impacts.[38] The protests stimulated art exhibits, documentaries, media stories, and new student organizations. The National Council of Churches passed a resolution condemning the colonization of Native Americans, and Catholic leaders publicly questioned Columbus's fitness as a national hero. While school textbooks published in the 1990s continued to handle the settlers' treatment of Native Americans circumspectly, students' essays emphasized the exploitation and brutality to which Native Americans were subjected. South Dakota and Alabama renamed Columbus Day "Native American Day," and in 1994, Bill Clinton's Columbus Day proclamation acknowledged explicitly the experience of colonized Native Americans.

By no means were all groups supportive of the protesters and their claims. Native American senator Ben Nighthorse Campbell criticized the protests, the National Endowment for the Humanities cut off funding for a documentary that associated Columbus with the "genocide" of native peoples, and numerous journalists, academics, and politicians attacked the movement's use of the Holocaust analogy.[39] Still, the protests clearly seem to have led people in diverse institutional spheres to confront Native Americans' counterhistory, recognize their institution's responsibility for correcting that history, and in many instances, begin to transform the institution's cultural practices.

These kinds of cultural changes were not merely symbolic, for at least two reasons. One is that, where authority is diffuse, changes within institutions of art, religion, the media, education, and so on may have more impact on people's lives than changes in law or governmental policy.[40] The other is that, even if we limit our focus to changes in governmental policy, public debates that unfold in settings other than explicitly political ones may be important in shaping public opinion. As Benjamin Page and Robert Shapiro have demonstrated, public opinion is shaped less by movement organizations or interest groups speaking in their own name than it is by those groups' impact on media commentators, policy experts, and institutional elites.[41] Sensitive to favorable public-opinion ratings, policymakers are likely to be responsive to cultural groundswells in nonpolitical institutions.

Domesticating Dissent?

What happens when activists get not only a place in the parade but their own parade? In the last several decades, activists have been part of coalitions that gained recognition for Martin Luther King Jr. Day, Cesar Chavez Day, Earth Day, and World AIDS Day. Parents across the country take their children to the office on Take Our Daughters to Work Day. In some states, as I noted, Columbus Day has been joined or replaced by Native American Day.

Many activists have mixed feelings about movement holidays. On one hand, widely observed movement holidays raise public consciousness about a group's cause and involve people in activities that promote the values of the movement. In 1970, for example, the first Earth Day was celebrated as a "nationwide teach-in on the environment."[42] Twenty years later, 200 million people in 140 countries participated in conservation activities on Earth Day. Movement holidays are also an opportunity to gain national attention for pending policies on an issue that movement groups favor or dislike. Official recognition of a holiday often comes with government funding for educational programs as well as with public declarations of support for the cause by for-profit organizations. However, activists also worry about the commercialization of holidays. Earth Day, say critics, is an opportunity to market "green" products to customers.[43] Martin Luther King Jr. Day is one more in the sequence of department store sales days.[44] Kwanzaa, which was created as an explicitly political and antimaterialist black alternative to Christmas, is now associated with family values and gift giving.[45]

Activists have another worry about movement-inspired holidays, that is, that a day intended to encourage activism as the way to make substantive change may become part of a triumphalist narrative in which only government tinkering and individual volunteer efforts are necessary. "King was no idle dreamer," says Dr. King's associate Jesse Jackson, complaining about the portrayal of the man now enshrined in the holiday. "He was a practical man of action, a leader who understood that change required challenging the structure of entrenched arrangements."[46] An environmentalist makes a similar point: "I worry that folks will emerge from Earth Day perceiving that if you inflate tires and use cloth grocery bags you will save the Earth. That's what corporations/polluters want—to keep folks out of public policy debates."[47] In fact, corporations were major sponsors of the 1990 Earth Day, thus buying environmental credibility at a time when they were seen by activists as the chief threat to environmental sustainability.

What concerns critics is the political domestication of movement holidays. They worry that the holiday will become increasingly about service rather than protest, that its critical, oppositional edge will be dulled. Rather than treat that process as inevitable, however, my own research and that of others point to the contingent dynamics through which it occurs. Consider the career of Martin Luther King Jr. Day.[48] The holiday was established in 1983, with funding for the federal King Holiday Commission to come from private sources. However, difficulties in raising adequate sums led to congressional appropriations and, in 1994, Harris Wofford and Carol Moseley-Braun in the Senate and Ralph Regula and John Lewis in the House proposed legislation to reauthorize the appropriation. In hearings and Senate debate on the issue, Wofford gave numerous versions of the following rationale:

> Nothing would have ticked Martin off more than people supposedly honoring him by sitting on their duffs watching the tube or sleeping late. The King holiday should be a day on not a day off. A day of action, not apathy . . . Fixing parks, tutoring children, rebuilding schools, feeding the hungry, immunizing children, housing the homeless.[49]

What King "would have liked" was "action"—meaning "service." Senator Moseley-Braun noted that "the day could be used to donate blood or volunteer at a hospital, to clean up a park or plant flowers in an inner-city neighborhood, to volunteer for the Boy Scouts or Girl Scouts or the Special Olympics, to tutor children or to work with those who have AIDS." Wofford and Moseley-Braun's brief for the legislation was echoed in re- marks by other bill supporters. In some of these statements, King's com- mitment to nonviolence was restyled as a commitment to ending youth violence. Indeed, when Coretta Scott King, who had tirelessly lobbied Congress for the holiday, and the commission appeared before a congres- sional hearing on the bill, she was quizzed on strategies to end teenage crime.[50]

Surely Wofford and his colleagues believed that emphasizing King's commitment to service would secure them the congressional support they wanted, which it did. What is interesting, however, is that African American legislators who commemorated King in their speeches on the House and Senate floor, which they did fairly frequently before and after this, also described King's legacy as one of individual volunteer efforts rather than organized collective action. Why? One reason may lie in black elected officials' competitive relations with the civil rights move- ment establishment. Black legislators are in a tricky position: They must convince their constituents not only that they are the best politicians for the job, but also that the job is better done through legislative politics than protest. The civil rights past has been a critical terrain for this com- petition.[51]

In my analysis of House and Senate speeches between 1993 and 1997, I found that African-American legislators frequently represented their own positions as the fruits of King's movement, saying, for example, "My own story is a testament to King's dream," "I along with many of my colleagues am here today as a direct result of the struggles of the sixties," and so on.[52] Speakers were clear that their careers were made possible by an earlier generation of movement activists. But they also styled themselves as legiti- mate heirs to that earlier activism. Their own careers became the next stage in a saga of African American struggle. For example, Jesse Jackson Jr. stated the following:

> I was born, as a matter of African American history, on March 11, 1965. On
> March 7, 1965, in our history, it is known as bloody Sunday. It is the Sunday
> that the gentleman from Georgia [John Lewis], Martin Luther King, and
> Jesse Jackson and many others in our history walked across the Edmund
> Pettus Bridge for the right to vote. Because of the struggle that they engaged
> in in 1965, I now stand here as the 91st African American to ever have the
> privilege of serving in the U.S. Congress.[53]

Representatives did not claim exclusive guardianship of the movement's legacy. They shared it, they said, with people who are working in "the tradition of Reverend King," who are "shining examples of his legacy," and who are the "unsung heroes" of the movement. These were rarely activists, however. Rather, they were teachers, ministers, a founder of a homeless shelter, a leader of a boys' club, a president of a city growth association, a director of a family care center, a local high school coach, and so on. King's legacy, as congressional speakers told the story, was electoral representation and service, *not* insurgency.

This is just one example of the competitive political dynamics that led, in this case, to the representation of King's legacy—and his holiday—as about service rather than activism. Have such dynamics operated with the same effects elsewhere? If cultural stewardship of an insurgent past is frequently a terrain for fighting out continuing leadership claims between protest and electoral elites, we might examine whether other groups that have ostensibly made the shift from protest to politics—Green Party members in European parliaments, African National Congress members in South Africa, and Irish elected officials associated with Sinn Fein come to mind—have similarly sought to reorient commemorative rituals so as to valorize electoral activity and/or service rather than protest. It should be noted, finally, that domesticated holidays can be repoliticized. In 2002, Martin Luther King Jr. Day was used as an occasion for protests against the war in Iraq. The King recalled that day was the more radical, anti–Vietnam War King—not the "I have a dream" King. In a similar dynamic, in Naples, Italy, a festival honoring the city's monuments that was originally sponsored by a local civic association was taken over by the city's tourist office when its capacity to generate tourist revenues became clear. Funding for the *Maggio dei Monumenti* (May of Monuments), as it was called, increased as a result, but residents were disturbed by the festival's increasingly commercial tone. In 2000, leftist groups launched a counterfestival called the "*Contro*maggio dei Monumenti."[54] Competition, in other words, can lead to politicizing holidays as well as depoliticizing them.

Commemoration, Contention, and Democracy

I have discussed movements and holidays mainly from the perspective of those wanting to bring about radical change. What about the perspective of those who are interested not in movement groups' success but in that of

American democracy? Should we worry about turning holidays into arenas of contention? I argued above that conflicts over holidays' celebration have sometimes generated valuable reappraisals of American history. In this last section, I want to take a different tack: I argue that we can derive lessons on how to create a more democratic polity from movements' own experiments with holidays and collective rituals.

Why should what movements do have any relevance to what government or civil society does? Because movements offer an alternative to both tradition and utopia as the source of social values. As John R. Gillis and others have pointed out, many of our most traditional holidays are of recent vintage.[55] The historical record shows that, again and again, authorities or activists have created new holidays such as the Fourth of July, May Day, and Kwanzaa. But in most cases, those promoting the holiday have striven to assert its deep roots in traditional values and practices. For example, Kwanzaa's founder, black nationalist Maulana Karenga, claimed to have modeled the holiday on traditional African harvest rituals, despite the fact that he had invented the holiday's name, date, and practices.[56] So, traditions can be invented. But some groups do not have the luxury of such invention. Gays and lesbians, for example, cannot claim any tradition of homosexual marriage; the ritual cannot avoid asserting its newness. Similarly, it is difficult to find holidays valorizing real equality across difference. Even the nineteenth-century American parade, in some ways a high point in enacting American pluralism, excluded African Americans and, usually, women; the positions of occupational groups that were permitted to march were ordered by their status.[57]

Of course, there is an alternative to tradition as warrant for a collective ritual: utopia. The justification for the ritual is not, "this is how things have always been done," but rather, "this is how they should be done." Revolutionaries have often sought to create new holidays as a way to enact values of the future rather than the past. And yet, such efforts, from French revolutionaries' new calendar to Soviets' alternative to Christmas, have rarely been successful. Without roots in the lived practice of communities, they risk seeming like one more obligation imposed on citizens by the state.

There is still another alternative to tradition as the source of collective ritual, however. It lies in the prefigurative practices of social movements. Many movements are utopian, of course, in the sense that they want to bring about changes in values as well as formal policies. But they also often operate on the belief that they should enact in the here and now the values that they want to bring about on a larger scale.[58] Since movement groups also want to get things done, however, they are forced to wrestle with the challenges of living radical values. They must find ways to balance their commitment to individual freedom with the unity necessary for concerted action, create a community that does not foreclose organizational growth, and enact equality in a way that does not insist on members' sameness. Movement groups' use of collective rituals to do those things may offer insights into how to develop the kinds of public rituals that can strengthen unity while celebrating difference.

For example, the "affinity group" has become a key feature of contemporary progressive activism, serving not only as a support group for participants in direct action but as a basic unit in radically democratic decision-making.[59] Affinity groups can be formed around any shared commitment—veganism, for example, or Marxist-Leninism or lesbianism. Traditional political creeds are only one among many bases for solidarity, activists recognize. Such groups provide the support for people with minority interests or views to stand up to the larger group, making a false consensus less likely. But activists are also encouraged to "go outside their comfort zone" in choosing affinity groups, joining people with different backgrounds. Affinity groups' internal bonds and their relations to other affinity groups are affirmed in rituals at the beginnings and ends of meetings, in group parties and gatherings, and in their choice of group names and symbols. Affinity groups point to the variety of ways in which collective identity can be constructed. Imagine a public parade in which citizens were encouraged to march in any formation that was meaningful to them, in which they could march in several formations, and in which they could create hybrid formations (groups wearing different colors might, in a synchronized way, mingle as they marched, then separate, then mingle). One can imagine parades and public celebrations organized to enact the many ways in which unity and difference can coexist.

Affinity groups also point to democracy's dependence on novel relationships. In my study of groups that styled themselves as radical democracies, I found that activists often drew informal norms for deliberating from familiar nonpolitical relationships like religious fellowship, tutelage, and especially, friendship.[60] Those relationships supplied the mutual trust, respect, and care that made it fairly easy to make decisions by consensus—and to avoid the endless meetings and subtle coercion that have been seen as inevitable in radical democracies. The problem was that familiar relationships also came with norms that undercut a democratic project. For example, friendship's natural exclusivity made it difficult to bring new people into a group, and its natural informality made people resistant to implementing rules that would have gained newcomers a place in the organization. Participatory democracy has worked better where activists have made a point of forging new relationships that combine the respect, care, and trust characteristic of familiar nonpolitical relationships with the inclusivity, openness to dissent, and openness to some degree of formality that are *not* often characteristic of those relationships.

How have activists done that? Through holidays and rituals. The insight is Durkheimian with a twist. Holidays and rituals strengthen group solidarity by taking people out of the routine of daily life and reenacting their essential "groupness." But holidays and rituals may be used to strengthen new forms of group solidarity as well as older ones. They can be crafted to foster norms both of solidarity and of openness to disagreement, trust *and* accountability, all of which are necessary to successful participatory democracies, outside movements as well as inside them.

NOTES

Thanks to Amitai Etzioni for suggesting the topic, to Edwin Amenta, Charles Tilly, and the participants in the "Ways We Celebrate" conference for valuable comments, to the many members of the Amsoc listserv for their leads to movement case studies and intriguing hypotheses, and to Lesley Wood for vital research assistance.

1. Charles Tilly, "Charivaris, Repertoires, and Urban Politics," in *French Cities in the Nineteenth Century,* John Merriman, ed. (New York: Holmes and Meier, 1981): 73–91.

2. Steven Pfaff and Guobin Yang, "Double-Edged Rituals and the Symbolic Resources of Collective Action: Political Commemorations and the Mobilization of Protest in 1989," *Theory and Society* 30, no. 4 (2001): 539–589.

3. Michael Specter, "The Extremist," *New York Times,* April 14, 2003, 52.

4. For exceptions, see Pfaff and Yang, "Double-Edged Rituals"; and Charles Tilly, *The Contentious French* (Cambridge, MA: Harvard University Press, 1986).

5. See, among others, Victor Turner, *The Ritual Process: Structure and Anti-Structure* (Ithaca, NY: Cornell University Press, 1969); David Kertzer, *Ritual, Politics, and Power* (New Haven, CT: Yale University Press, 1988).

6. Turner, *Ritual Process*; Emmanuel Le Roy Ladurie, *Carnival in Romans* (New York: George Braziller, 1979).

7. See Nicholas Dirks, "Ritual and Resistance: Subversion as a Social Fact," in *Culture/Power/History: A Reader in Contemporary Social Theory,* Nicholas Dirks,

Geoffrey Eley, and Sherry Ortner, eds. (Princeton, NJ: Princeton University Press, 1994): 483–503; and Peter Stallybrass and Allon White, *Politics and Poetics of Transgression* (Ithaca, NY: Cornell University Press, 1986)

8. Terry Eagleton, *Walter Benjamin: Towards a Revolutionary Criticism* (London: Verso Press, 1981), 148; quoted in Dirks, "Ritual and Resistance," 486.

9. Of course, even the most instrumentalist and explicitly political mobilizations have expressive elements. Indeed, the self-consciously hard-nosed instrumentalist style that some groups adopt can be seen as just that, a style, whose ability to advance a concrete objective is less important than its ability to symbolize effectiveness, seriousness, or perhaps, masculinity. For more, see Francesca Polletta, "Culture in Contention," in *Authority in Contention,* Dan Myers and Dan Cress, eds. (Elsevier Press, forthcoming). This view is not inconsistent with one of people using holidays to advance their claims.

10. Tilly, "Charivaris, Repertoires, and Urban Politics"; Tilly, *Contentious French.*

11. Tilly, "Charivaris, Repertoires, and Urban Politics," 79.

12. Ibid., 80.

13. Marc Steinberg, "The Riding of the Black Lad and Other Working-Class Ritualistic Actions: Toward a Spatialized and Gendered Analysis of Nineteenth-Century Repertoires," in *Challenging Authority: The Historical Study of Contentious Politics,* Michael P. Hanagan, Leslie Page Moch, and Wayne te Brake, eds. (Minneapolis: University of Minnesota Press, 1998), 17–35.

14. Ibid., 9.

15. Stallybrass and White, *Politics and Poetics of Transgression,* 179.

16. Among those who lost out in the process were women; see Steinberg, "Riding of the Black Lad." Women had been prominent in the Black Lad as well as in carnival forms generally. Strikers, with their display of firearms, their violence to property, and the military style of their marches, transformed protest into a masculinized zone in which women had little place. They would regain a place in nineteenth-century contention only symbolically, as incarnations of civic order and virtue. See also Mary Ryan, "The American Parade: Representations of the Nineteenth-Century Order," in *The New Cultural History,* Lynn Hunt, ed. (Berkeley: University of California Press, 1989): 131–153; and Susan G. Davis, *Parades and Power: Street Theatre in Nineteenth-Century Philadelphia* (Philadelphia: Temple University Press, 1986).

17. Pfaff and Young, "Double-Edged Rituals."

18. Lisa Wedeen, *Ambiguities of Domination: Politics, Rhetoric, and Symbols in Contemporary Syria* (Chicago: University of Chicago Press, 1999), 19.

19. James Tracy, *Direct Action: Radical Pacifism from the Union Eight to the Chicago Seven* (Chicago: University of Chicago Press, 1996).

20. Ibid.

21. Quintan Wiktorowicz, personal communication, March 9, 2003.

22. Karen Rasler, "Concessions, Repression, and Political Protest in the Iranian Revolution," *American Sociological Review* 61 (1996): 132–152.

23. Stanley J. Tambiah, *Leveling Crowds: Ethnonationalist Conflicts and Collective Violence in South Asia* (Berkeley: University of California Press, 1996).

24. Allen Feldman, *Formations of Violence: The Narrative of the Body and Political Terror in Ireland* (Chicago: University of Chicago Press, 1991), 29; quoted in Tambiah, *Leveling Crowds,* 240.

25. See Ryan, "American Parade."

26. Myra Marx Ferree, William Anthony Gamson, Jurgen Gerhards, and Dieter Rucht, *Shaping Abortion Discourse: Democracy and the Public Sphere in Germany and the United States* (New York: Cambridge University Press, 2002), 10.

27. Pamela E. Oliver and Gregory M. Maney, "Political Processes and Local Newspaper Coverage of Protest Events: From Selection Bias to Triadic Interactions," *American Journal of Sociology* 106, no. 2 (2000), 484–485.

28. This is not a new tactic. In the 1790s, abolition societies in several states began to hold their annual meeting on Independence Day in order to take advantage of that holiday's association with the Declaration of Independence and, especially, with the value of equality it enshrined. See Matthew Dennis, *Red, White, and Blue Letter Days: An American Calendar* (Ithaca, NY: Cornell University Press, 2002), 22–23.

29. Manny Fernandez, "Demonstrators Raise Voice against War; Protests in D.C., Nationally Observe Human Rights Day," *Washington Post,* December 11, 2002, B1.

30. See Amitai Etzioni, "Toward a Theory of Public Ritual," *Sociological Theory* 18, no. 1 (2000): 44–59.

31. Jennifer L. Pozner and Jim Naureckas, "The Media Crowns George II," *Ms.,* April/May 2001, 30; Duke Helfand, "Patriotism, Protest on the 4th; Holiday: Parades and Free Speech Mark Celebrations around Southland," *Los Angeles Times,* July 5, 2001, B1; John Leo, "V-Day without Hearts: Giving New Meaning to an Annual Ritual of Romance," *U.S. News and World Report,* February 21, 2000, 16.

32. Michael Walzer, *Exodus and Revolution* (New York: Basic Books, 1985).

33. Jo Mannies, "Both Sides in Abortion Struggle Gear Up for the Anniversary of Its Legalization," *St. Louis Post-Dispatch,* January 19, 2000, A1; "Government—and Militias—Tread Softly on Bombing Anniversary," *St. Louis Post Dispatch,* April 19, 1997, 14.

34. Todd Gitlin, *The Whole World Is Watching: Mass Media in the Making and Understanding of the New Left* (Berkeley: University of California Press, 1980).

35. On Thanksgiving protests by Native American activists, see Robert Knox, "An Equal Share of History: Plymouth County Indians Seek Museum of Their Own," *Boston Globe,* January 17, 2002, 3.

36. Timothy Kubal and Rhys Williams, "Columbus the Cruel Colonizer:

Symbolic Production, Reception, and the Puzzle of Cultural Change," unpublished paper, 2002, 11.

37. Lynda Richardson, "Marching Out of Step, by Some Irish and Gay Norms," *New York Times*, March 7, 2003, B2.

38. Kubal and Williams, "Columbus the Cruel Colonizer."

39. Ibid.

40. See Mary Fainsod Katzenstein, *Faithful and Fearless: Moving Feminist Protest inside the Church and Military* (Princeton, NJ: Princeton University Press, 1998); Polletta, "Culture in Contention."

41. Benjamin I. Page and Robert Y. Shapiro, *The Rational Public: Fifty Years of Trends in Americans' Policy Preferences* (Chicago: University of Chicago Press, 1992).

42. Amy Fried, "U.S. Environmental Interest Groups and the Promotion of Environmental Values: The Resounding Success and Failure of Earth Day," *Environmental Politics* 7, no. 4 (1998): 5.

43. Ibid.

44. Dennis, *Red, White, and Blue Letter Days*.

45. Elizabeth Pleck, "Kwanzaa: The Making of a Black Nationalist Tradition, 1966–1990," *Journal of American Ethnic History* 20, no. 4 (2001): 3–30.

46. Jesse L. Jackson Sr., "Expanding the Marketplace: Inclusion, the Key to Economic Growth," speech delivered in New York City, January 15, 1998, in author's possession.

47. Quoted in Fried, "U.S. Environmental Interest Groups," 13.

48. See Francesca Polletta, "Legacies and Liabilities of an Insurgent Past: Remembering Martin Luther King, Jr., on the House and Senate Floor," *Social Science History* 22 (1998): 479–512.

49. Harris Wofford, *Congressional Record*, Senate, April 3, 1993, THOMAS database.

50. Carol Moseley-Braun quoted in the *Congressional Record*, Senate, May 23, 1994, THOMAS database; "King Holiday and Service Act of 1993. Hearing before the Committee on the Judiciary, U.S. Senate, April 13, 1994" (Washington, DC: GPO, 1995).

51. See Adolph Reed, *The Jesse Jackson Phenomenon* (New Haven, CT: Yale University Press, 1986).

52. Carol Moseley-Braun quoted in the *Congressional Record*, Senate, April 3, 1993; Bennie Thompson in the *Congressional Record*, House, June 21, 1994; Jesse Jackson Jr. in the *Congressional Record*, House, February 11, 1997; all in the THOMAS database.

53. Jesse Jackson Jr. in the *Congressional Record*, House, February 11, 1997; in the THOMAS database.

54. Eleanora Passotti, "From Clients to Citizens: Public Opinion Mobilization in Naples," PhD diss., Columbia University, 2003, 273–274.

55. John R. Gillis, "Memory and Identity: The History of a Relationship," in *Commemorations: The Politics of National Identity,* John R. Gillis, ed. (New Brunswick, NJ: Rutgers University Press, 1994).

56. Pleck, "Kwanzaa."

57. Ryan, "American Parade."

58. See Wini Breines, *Community and Organization in the New Left, 1962–1968: The Great Refusal* (New Brunswick, NJ: Rutgers University Press, 1989); Barbara Epstein, *Political Protest and Cultural Revolution: Nonviolent Direct Action in the 1970s and 1980s* (Berkeley: University of California Press, 1991).

59. Francesca Polletta, *Freedom Is an Endless Meeting: Democracy in American Social Movements* (Chicago: University of Chicago Press, 2002).

60. Ibid.

Chapter 10

The Invention of
Martin Luther King Jr.'s Birthday

Matthew Dennis

Until quite recently, African Americans—unlike Irish, Italian, or Norwegian Americans, who trumped Columbus as "discoverer" of America with their own Leif Erikson—had no broadly recognized patron saint of their own (Abraham Lincoln was the Great Emancipator, but he was not black) and no publicly sanctioned holiday.[1] Blacks—like other Americans—had advanced their claims on the Fourth of July and celebrated other particularly African American holidays, such as Juneteenth and Emancipation Day, but they lacked a Columbus or St. Patrick's Day, occasions when they could perform their "doubleness"—as both African Americans *and* as Americans—publicly, without contradiction, and when others marched in *their* parades. Yet, within two decades of Martin Luther King Jr.'s assassination, King's birthday achieved the status of a national public holiday. Indeed, it became a St. Monday, a moveable feast culminating a three-day weekend observed in the middle of each January.

Does such status confer on the day the legitimacy, the moral authority, and the popular appeal of such events as Presidents' Day, Memorial Day, or Labor Day? Keepers of King's memory fear such "success." Indeed, one might ask, does such federal holiday status, even as it institutionalizes the day, actually diminish it, orchestrating leisure and historical amnesia rather than memory, civic education, reverence, and social action? To adopt Amitai Etzioni's proposed terminology, King's birthday seems designed to function as a "recommitment" rather than as a "tension management" holiday (see introduction). But does such a typology work, or more specifically, work in the ways proposed?

A key to the power of special occasions like Columbus Day or Labor Day is their dual function and legitimacy—as particular fetes for particular groups (defined ethnically, politically, or socially) and as general American festivals, appropriate for and commanding attention and respect among a majority of citizens. A monument to African American achievement and to the modern civil rights movement generally—one that celebrated a great *American* hero—merged, then, in the creation of an annual national holiday honoring Martin Luther King Jr. on his natal day, beginning in 1986. But what is the meaning—and what will be the ultimate fate—of that new red letter day? While all traditions must originate in particular times and places, however obscure, as E. J. Hobsbawm has argued, traditions derive their legitimacy and sanctity in part from their apparent timelessness.[2] Yet Martin Luther King Jr.'s birthday, an invented tradition erected conspicuously so recently, in the penultimate decade of the twentieth century, lacks that patina of antiquity. The holiday's youth and historical transparency, in addition to its focus on the most troubling dilemma in U.S. history—the conflict between American ideals of equality and the endurance of discrimination and inequality, based particularly on race—thus make it a telling case study in our efforts to understand the creation of the American public calendar, the public negotiation of identity and historical memory in the United States, and the historical challenges of pluralism in America, especially with respect to the strains between the particularism of diverse Americans and the claims of a more universal American nationalism.

Inventing Martin Luther King Jr. Day

Within four days of Martin Luther King Jr.'s assassination on April 4, 1968, outside the Lorraine Motel in Memphis, Tennessee, U.S. Representative John Conyers Jr. introduced legislation seeking to make King's birthday a federal holiday. The bill failed initially to garner the necessary support, but within fifteen years both houses of Congress endorsed the proposal, and a skeptical President Ronald Reagan signed it into law on November 3, 1983. Just over two years later, on the third Monday in January—January 20, 1986—the United States celebrated the birthday of Martin Luther King Jr. for the first time as a national holiday. If promoters of the observance felt frustration over delays in achieving their objective, historians can only be struck by the velocity of this development.[3] But, then, King's public career—lasting a mere thirteen years—was itself a whirlwind, as was its impact on American life. At the time of his death, King—only thirty-nine years old—was world famous, the recipient of the 1964 Nobel Prize for Peace. Yet he was nonetheless at the ebb of his popularity, as he moved from the "glory years" of the civil rights struggle in the South in the early 1960s to tackle the even more obstinate problems of racial and economic inequality in the North as well as the South, and to become an outspoken critic of the United States' involvement in Vietnam. In 1967, King failed to make a Gallup Poll list of the ten most popular Americans. Yet, by 1986, as reflected in a *New York Times* editorial on January 15, King was conventionally placed in an American holy trinity with America's two loftiest heroes: "If George Washington symbolizes the creation of the Union and Abraham Lincoln its preservation, Martin Luther King symbolizes the continuing effort to confer its benefits on every citizen."[4]

Like King's life, his public holiday emerged amid controversy and continues to evolve in surprising and unpredictable ways. Conyers's bill encountered opposition, from Representative Larry P. McDonald of Georgia, for example, who declared that King was "not the caliber of person suitable to be made into a national hero." The arguments of McDonald and other detractors aside, the Georgia congressman assumed too much in his suggestion that a national hero can be "made" by any legislative or executive action. In fact, heroes and holidays are not simply erected by government or business but are produced in untidy cooperation with a mass public, which influences officials and then revises their acts through the improvisations of life. The meaning of Martin Luther King Jr. Day, in other words, is not merely what its inventors prescribe, but what the American public has made and will make of it.

America's immediate reaction to King's assassination was despair, fear, anger, and violence. Riots erupted in over a hundred cities across the country, with forty-six deaths reported; within a week, twenty-seven thousand people nationwide, mostly African Americans, had been arrested.[5]

Eventually, Martin Luther King in death — as a symbol and inspiration—became part of a desired solution to this unrest, a means of restoring peace through justice and reform. Some hoped the designation of a day to honor his memory, to remember his public life, and to promote his message of nonviolent social change would advance this goal by claiming a place in the calendar when Americans might suspend normal activities, reflect, and focus attention on America's continuing struggle to achieve equality. If no other living African American leader could "keep hope alive, could galvanize the struggle, could inspire dreams," then perhaps a deceased King still could.[6]

January 15 memorial events emerged spontaneously and without official sanction, even as elected officials in Washington, D.C. and states throughout the country pushed for government recognition of King's birthday. According to Cornelius Williams, student-body president and leader of a boycott at Federal City College in the District of Columbia soon after King's death, "We have declared classes suspended today in honor of a great man. We have not waited for someone else to declare this a national holiday. We must establish our own heroes and holidays of our own."[7]

African Americans mobilized to do just that. In 1971, the Southern Christian Leadership Conference (SCLC)—the group that Martin Luther King had helped to found in 1957—delivered a petition to Congress containing three million signatures calling for a King holiday. Though unsuccessful, efforts continued. While localized January 15 events continued to take place, ebbing and flowing according to the energies of Americans dispersed in various communities nationwide, several states sanctified the day, beginning with Illinois in 1973. In 1982, the Martin Luther King Jr. Center for Nonviolent Social Change gathered over six million signatures on a petition again calling for the creation of a federal holiday on Martin Luther King's birthday, and soon thereafter the House of Representatives complied, voting overwhelmingly in favor of the legislation. A year later, in October, the Senate followed suit, and President Reagan signed the bill on November 3, 1983.[8]

With some notable exceptions (which I haven't space to discuss), those states which had yet to create a day honoring King quickly followed the federal government's lead. By 1990, only Arizona, Montana, and New Hampshire had yet to mandate the holiday in some form; by 1995, in only its ninth year as an official national event, the holiday was observed at least in some fashion on the third Monday in January by all fifty states and four territories. Yet the rapid success of the new American holiday was neither easy nor complete. Reluctant states offered various explanations for their reticence in creating a day recognizing Martin Luther King specifically. Their expressed reservations fell into two rough categories: those concerning the holiday's economic impact and those assessing the relative worthiness of "King the hero" (both could work together). While it simmered as subtext, the issue of race virtually never surfaced in the statements provided by King-holiday antagonists as they justified their opposition.

Proponents, on the other hand, frequently interpreted such opposition as racially motivated. The economic objection usually accepted, for the sake of argument, King's worthiness but countered that the economic impact of another paid holiday, for whatever noble purpose, was simply too costly to absorb. The objection to King as a worthy hero, in its most benign form, credited King for his contributions to the struggle for civil rights but suggested that he failed to merit his own official day relative to scores of other deserving champions not similarly honored. In more caustic critiques, King's contributions were obliterated by his alleged shortcomings—particularly the charges of plagiarism and philandering—rendering him an inappropriate idol.

In some states—Kentucky and North Dakota, for example—King's birthday was recognized, but not as a paid holiday. New Hampshire created a state "Civil Rights Day" for the third Monday in January, self-consciously avoiding recognition of Martin Luther King Jr. Utah similarly refused to recognize King by name, celebrating instead "Human Rights Day" beginning in 1986, until Utah governor Mike Leavitt signed a bill in 2000 renaming the January holiday. By the century's end, South Carolina became the only state without an official celebration of Martin Luther King Jr.'s birthday. The state permitted its employees the option of taking off either the day of the federal holiday or one of three Confederate holidays spread throughout the year. On January 17, 2000, South Carolina state offices remained open, and later that year legislation designed to explicitly create a Martin Luther King Jr. Day in South Carolina was amended in the House of Representatives to remove King's name and instead designate the occasion "Civil Rights Day."[9]

Widespread celebration of Martin Luther King Jr. Day by federal, state, and local governments today does not necessarily ensure either the permanence or importance of the holiday in American social and political life. Private employers—particularly those whose employees are not members of labor unions—have been much slower in recognizing the occasion. In 1994, only 22 percent of businesses surveyed by the Bureau of National Affairs gave employees a paid holiday on King's birthday; a 1990 survey of Fortune 500 companies found that only 18 percent offered their employees the day off. On the other hand, observance of King's birthday may be increasing, in the private as well as the public sector. The Martin Luther King Jr. Federal Holiday Commission, established by Congress in 1984 to promote the commemoration, found that participation increased from 23 percent in 1991 to 31 percent in 1993, for example. Although such figures lag well behind those for Christmas, New Year's, Thanksgiving, Independence Day, Memorial Day, and Labor Day—which are paid holidays for nearly all (some 99 percent of American businesses)—they compare favorably with Presidents' Day (45 percent in 1985) and Veterans' Day (20 percent). Nonetheless, the holiday remains a work in progress, and only time will tell if and how Martin Luther King Jr. Day will become woven into the fabric of American life in the twenty-first century.[10]

The Meaning of St. Martin's Day

Disagreement over the holiday's rightful name, its proper means of celebration, or even the legitimacy of its claim to a place in the United States' public calendar all reflect an ambiguity or indeterminacy in the commemoration's meaning, as various Americans contest or collaborate in the invention of Martin Luther King Jr. Day. Is the holiday a forum for the expression of black pride and an occasion to recognize specifically the historical contributions of African Americans to the nation? Or is it, on the other hand, a day for all Americans to embrace King as their hero, celebrate his accomplishments simply as an American, and follow his prescriptions for the nation? Is Martin Luther King Jr. Day a time for education, inspiration, and reflection? Should King be remembered for his dreams? Or is the holiday a call to action, a time for deeds—political activism or community service—over words? Is King primarily a symbol of racial integration, nonviolent social change, the fight for economic equality, or the resistance to the economic and human costs of militarism? Is King an emblem of moderation and reform, or of radicalism and revolution? Is he a convenient or unsettling hero? Does Martin Luther King Jr. Day or April 4—the day of his assassination—commemorate more than a mere political figure or mortal champion? Is it as much a holy day as it is a holiday, dedicated to "St. Martin"? Or should Americans see the occasion as an opportunity to embrace a fully human hero, a great man despite—or even because of—his flaws? Or, finally, is King's birthday an opportunity to dispute his worthiness, challenge his status as hero, or revise the historical meaning of his life and the struggle for equality and justice, which he helped to lead?

The short historical record dictates that we answer yes to all these questions. Though tethered to a particular historical figure whose real life history constrains the range of potential meanings that might be assigned to his work and legacy, Martin Luther King Jr. Day, like all American holidays, is nonetheless a protean public festival, particularly because the holiday is young and the issues it raises are old and ongoing—racism, inequality, poverty, and violence. King's birthday, as a complex public event celebrated variably across the country, expresses contradictory messages; while some of these contradictions may be resolved over time, others no doubt will linger, both because people often do not think and act with perfect consistency and because Americans continue to disagree politically and express those differences in the arena provided by the public calendar, on Martin Luther King Jr. Day or on other holidays.

King's birthday is thus an official commemoration in which African Americans celebrate themselves, build solidarity, and steel themselves for continuing battles against discrimination. In this sense, it builds on earlier commemorative occasions adopted by blacks—such as Emancipation Day—and parallels some of the goals of another recently invented African American fete—Kwanzaa. Kwanzaa's African American, nationalist objective is congruent with one of the King holiday's purposes—to cultivate black pride and solidarity—but its particular ethnic or racial constituency makes its task easier. Unlike Martin Luther King Jr.'s birthday, Kwanzaa neither seeks nor requires official endorsement; it need not be all things to all people. Indeed, it continues to exist in part because the King holiday cannot be an exclusively African American fete. As the Kwanzaa Information Center observed in 2001—fifteen years after Martin Luther King Jr.'s birthday had become a federal holiday—"African-Americans did not observe a holiday that was specific to our needs. A review of the major holidays celebrated in the United States would reveal that not one related specifically to the growth and development of African-Americans."[11]

Martin Luther King Jr.'s birthday *is* an African American festival, one that does express something vital about "the growth and development" of black people in the United States, but it is also an ecumenical, multicultural holiday, one that uses the exemplary public life of King to teach larger truths about America to all Americans. Are these two purposes of the festival at odds with each other? No, according to Alan Minton, chief of staff of the King Federal Holiday Commission, which has worked "to make sure it's an American holiday, not just an African-American holiday."[12]

In a sense, Martin Luther King Jr. Day embodies the dilemma and possibility outlined brilliantly by W. E. B. Du Bois in *The Souls of Black Folk*, which spoke of the "double-consciousness" of African Americans: "One ever feels his two-ness,—an American, a Negro; two souls, two thoughts, two unreconciled strivings; two warring ideals in one dark body, whose dogged strength alone keeps it from being torn asunder." Writing in the gendered language of his day, Du Bois argued that black Americans have struggled to merge these selves in a way that preserves them both: "He would not Africanize America," nor would he "bleach his Negro soul in a flood of white Americanism. . . . He simply wishes to make it possible for a man to be both a Negro and an American, without being cursed and spit upon by his fellows, without having the doors of Opportunity closed roughly in his face." The apparent paradox of Martin Luther King Jr. Day—as both a black holiday and an American holiday—may be resolved through Du Bois's concept of "two-ness": the fete might be both things simultaneously and without contradiction by expressing African American experience as American experience, with African American moral leadership—exemplified by Martin Luther King Jr.—redeeming the entire American nation.[13]

Is it surprising that participants at Martin Luther King Jr. Day programs are often disproportionately black, given the significance of King as the sole African American hero celebrated prominently and officially by the United States? In their 1998 study of the popular uses of history in American life, historians Roy Rosenzweig and David Thelen found that African Americans generally possessed greater historical consciousness than white Americans. The former more frequently identified with historical figures—particularly with Martin Luther King Jr.—and had a stronger sense of a public, American past than did white Americans. Surely some white Americans eschew King festivities due to their bigotry, but most who fail to attend express political apathy, not antipathy. Such disinterest keeps white Americans away from similar public functions—Columbus Day parades, Labor Day marches, or Fourth of July speeches (though not fireworks)—as they choose self-indulgent leisure over historical and political engagement.[14]

If the establishment of King as an American hero and the designation of the third Monday in January as a red letter day was a cause for celebration among African Americans, it also produced some consternation within the black community. Some feared that remembering King might allow the public to forget other black heroes. Others became suspicious of the very acceptance of King that a federal holiday signified. For some in African American circles, mainstream endorsement almost by definition undermined King's status as a champion of black resistance. Were white

motives pure? Was King—or rather, the particular King sanctified in public—too convenient a hero?[15]

Yet if some African Americans remained skeptical, blacks generally expressed annoyance toward those who publicly challenged King's status,
not merely as a black hero but as an American hero. And if King's individual star threatened to eclipse other, less-famous black champions, the
metamorphosis of Martin Luther King Jr.'s birthday into a more generic
Civil Rights Day or a broader and more diffuse celebration of civil rights
figures of various races outraged African Americans afraid that their sacred day might be diluted. In Arizona in 1994, just two years after Martin
Luther King Jr. Day had been created by state referendum, the festival's
popular, multicultural approach troubled some black Arizonans, who pre-
ferred not to share the spotlight. One community activist called Phoenix's
efforts to honor the late Cesar Chavez, founder of the United Farm Workers' Union, along with King, "stupid," arguing that it "shows no respect to
the black community." Such sentiments clumsily expressed the challenge
that Martin Luther King Jr. Day faces as a festival establishing itself both as
an African American and an American holiday. The event continues, paradoxically, to cleave the country, in both senses of the word—to divide as
well as to bind Americans.[16]

Martin Luther King Jr. Day embodies a certain doubleness in other
ways. Is it a time for words or actions, a political occasion for liberals or
conservatives? President Ronald Reagan, who initially opposed the holiday
and most of King's agenda (including the Civil Rights Act of 1964), emphasized the inspirational side of King's legacy and linked himself to the
civil rights leader in remarks to the Council for a Black Economic Agenda
in 1986: "Dr. King believed in the great promise of America and an America in which all of us can progress as fast and as far as our ability, our vision and our heart will take us. . . . That is the very promise that I came to
Washington to restore."[17] Not surprisingly, Reagan's words provoked skep-
ticism among black leaders, such as M. Carl Holman, president of the National Urban Coalition, who said, "Frankly, it's easier for a lot of people to
honor Martin when he's safely dead and deal with him as though he were
just a visionary, and not a practical and very pragmatic protester against
the status quo."[18]

The Reagan administration also invoked King's message of nonviolence, not as a recommended strategy for civil disobedience during social
protest (which it did not seek to encourage), but rather to preach against
youth violence, particularly within urban black communities. Ironically—

and disturbingly to King's living compatriots—conservatives even cited King's inspirational "I Have a Dream" oration, delivered at the Lincoln Memorial in 1963, to challenge affirmative action. William Bradford Reynolds, Assistant Attorney General for Civil Rights in the Justice Department during the Reagan administration, criticized affirmative action policies as violations of King's hope for a color-blind society. Selective citation of King's words, of course, obscure other King statements regarding affirmative action, for example his insistence in *Why We Can't Wait* that it "is impossible to create a formula for the future which does not take into account that our society has been doing something special *against* the Negro for hundreds of years." But such manipulation of heroes' words and memories is the stuff of politics and will no doubt continue, particularly as King becomes more firmly established in the American pantheon of heroes. In apparent affirmation of the adage "what's good for the goose is good for the gander," the black conservative and businessman Ward Connerly, who as a University of California regent led the successful effort to dismantle affirmative action in California, officially opened his National Campaign Against Affirmative Action on Martin Luther King Jr. Day in 1997.[19]

"National Nothing Day"?

If Martin Luther King Jr. and his holiday can be employed to make political hay and to promote community, toleration, nonviolence, and equality, it can also function—sometimes to the distress of King Day supporters—as an occasion to promote consumption and indulge leisure. The Reverend Elliott Cuff of Mount Ararat Missionary Baptist Church in Ocean Hill–Brownsville, New York, speculating about the long-term prospects of the holiday, worried, "King's birthday, as we move into the next millennium, will probably go the way of the rest of the holidays, a day to rest and shop. That's unfortunate. I think it is vitally important because these are marks in the sand for what made America what it is today."[20] Ironically, it is often controversy and political contention on public holidays—even challenges to their validity as days of official commemoration—that give these occasions vitality. As they become less contentious, less "political," holidays may become more entrenched and universal, but also blander and less meaningful—more often moments of forgetting. Though it is impossible for historians to predict the future (the past is hard enough), it may be that some of the aspects of the recent observances of Martin Luther King Jr. Day that promoters find most troubling in fact signal the successful arrival of the holiday as an American tradition.

In 1989, on the eve of King's birthday, residents of Memphis were shocked by the local distribution of a whimsical promotional calendar by McDonald's restaurants. Through an embarrassing oversight, an advertising agency employee labeled the entry for January 16 (the Monday officially designated to honor King that year) "National Nothing Day." McDonald's quickly recalled the offensive calendars, but the African American community expressed outrage, calling the gaff an "inexcusable thing." "It's an insult and an effort to degrade what is important to us," a Memphis NAACP official charged. McDonald's spokespersons, on the other hand, maintained that it was simply "a terrible, terrible oversight, . . . an innocent mistake." "National Nothing Day" was intended, according to the advertising agency, to mock all other holidays, to call attention to the clutter of the calendar, inundated with numerous silly occasions, like National Pickle Day. Three years later, a joke book-of-days published in 1992 and prominently featured by the national bookstore chain Walden Books more consciously ridiculed King on his birthday, offering the mildly offensive riddle, "What do you call a civil rights leader from another planet? Martian Luther King." The McDonald's Martin Luther King Jr. Day debacle in Memphis certainly reflected the youth of the holiday and its ongoing fight for full recognition. But, ironically, it may also presage the future fate of the day—as just another space on the calendar, ignored by most Americans or trivialized with tasteless humor—even as it achieves official status in the United States.[21]

For the first time in honor of King, Wall Street closed down on January 20, 1998. Although stores continue to stay open on the holiday, they more often call attention to the special nature of the day, if less to salute King than to sell him. Increasingly, Martin Luther King figures in sales promotions in mid-January, and shoppers take advantage of three-day weekends. A newspaper in Eugene, Oregon, carried an advertisement in a January 17, 2000, edition, for example, which featured a large picture of King and the words "Help us celebrate Martin Luther King, Jr. Day!" over a three-dollar-off coupon for any purchase over ten dollars. In more sophisticated fashion, a computer company—Apple—has featured King (as well as Einstein and Gandhi) in its advertisements, under the banner "Think Different," exploiting King's image as an innovator without much concern that King's career predated the "information revolution" or that he might have been more critical than supportive of the corporate giant. A young man working in New York on King's birthday in 1998 reflected on the shoppers around him: "They think it's a day for recreation, part of a three-day weekend. . . . It surprises me. After everybody fought for it, there's a day of observance and nobody observes it."[22]

In fact, Americans do observe it widely, both with reverence and nonchalance, as a serious political occasion and, unself-consciously, as just another celebration of American capitalism, which has been successful enough to underwrite days of rest and commercial consumption for some—though clearly not all—its citizens. It is a further irony, perhaps, that if commercialization threatens to trivialize the King holiday, the power of commerce—or, rather, the threat to commerce through economic boycotts—proved crucial in its establishment.

The ambiguous Martin Luther King Jr. Day—as a federal holiday—is a sign of the times. As historians such as Michael Kammen and John Bodnar have argued, until late in the nineteenth century, government in the United States had proved hesitant to sanctify its heroes, only reluctantly authorizing funds for statues and monuments or creating public holidays. But since then, the state, as it has grown in power, has acted more frequently to endorse and underwrite the construction of public memory through memorials and red letter days, culminating perhaps during the presidency of Franklin Delano Roosevelt, who sought to unify and regulate the national calendar in unprecedented fashion, declaring which days should be sacred, which should be available for shopping, and which should "live in infamy." Bodnar draws a distinction between "official" and "vernacular" culture—the former represents elite leadership (professional and educational, not simply governmental) and its commitment to clear, ideal, nationalistic statements in commemoration, while the latter "represents an array of specialized interests that are grounded in parts of the whole." Vernacular culture is diverse, changing, and divisive. In Bodnar's subtle analysis, the two cultures work together in complicated ways to fashion public memory.[23]

Yet the King holiday seems not to fit his formulation easily. Certainly Martin Luther King Jr. Day is both official *and* vernacular. It is official because it has been sanctioned by federal, state, and local governments, and vernacular because it emerged in the popular recognition of a martyr and hero—one who had often been at odds with official culture—and is celebrated regularly in private or nongovernmental exercises. In Arizona's 1992 referendum, the official and the vernacular merged as ordinary Arizonans approved the holiday overwhelmingly, yet throughout the United States official endorsement did not necessarily translate into a paid holiday for many citizens because employers proved reluctant to cooperate. Nonetheless, even in such situations, some find ways to craft vernacular celebrations, while others manage to avoid official and vernacular fetes alike. Ironically, endorsement of Martin Luther King Jr. Day by the state—which made the vernacular official—carried liabilities or signaled the limitations of newly won African American status and power. On the one hand, some black critics feared cooptation, as they were unable to imagine that the King so harassed and abused by officials could be embraced by them without fundamental alteration of his memory. On the other hand, some may have wondered how meaningful federal endorsement was in the 1980s, at a moment in American history when Americans were particularly wary of the national state and when leaders in the executive branch sought to dissolve agencies and promote a devolution of authority. And while the law decreed equality, and the executive branch seemed to support it, inequality and discrimination persisted. Perhaps it was less an irony than it had originally appeared, then, that Ronald Reagan—who as a presidential candidate promised to "get government off people's backs" and who cultivated unprecedented suspicion of Washington—had signed the new holiday into law.

If today St. Martin's Day has become another St. Monday for some, the history of King's life and his official stature in America's pantheon of heroes remains a resource for those who promote his legacy or who seek his posthumous support in shaping responses to present or future dilemmas, particularly those that concern the enduring problems of discrimination, inequality, limited opportunity, and poverty in the United States. Martin Luther King Jr. Day, its stakes clearer and higher than older national holidays, is a work in progress, still being shaped, still being contested, and still in the process of becoming "traditional."

NOTES

1. This chapter is adapted from Matthew Dennis, *Red, White, and Blue Letter Days: An American Calendar* (Ithaca, NY: Cornell University Press, 2002), and used by permission of the publisher.

2. See Eric Hobsbawm and Terrence Ranger, eds., *The Invention of Tradition* (Cambridge: Cambridge University Press, 1983), esp. introduction, 1–14.

3. Michael Eric Dyson, *I May Not Get There with You: The True Martin Luther King, Jr.* (New York: Free Press, 2000)—the best treatment of King's reputation and representation in American life—briefly traces the events leading to the creation of King's birthday as a national holiday, see esp. 286–90; Andrew Young quoted in "Looking Back at a Man Ahead of His Time: A Conversation: Andrew Young on Rev. Martin Luther King, Jr.," *New York Times*, January 12, 1986.

4. Dyson, *I May Not Get There with You*, 303; "How to Honor Dr. King—and When," *New York Times*, January 15, 1986, A22.

5. Harvard Sitkoff, *The Struggle for Black Equality, 1954–1992*, rev. ed. (New York: Hill and Wang, 1993), 185–89, 208–9.

6. Ibid., 209.

7. William H. Wiggins, *O Freedom! African-American Emancipation Celebrations* (Knoxville: University of Tennessee Press, 1987), 137; *New York Times*, January 16, 1969, A30; *Washington Post*, January 16, 1969, A2. On the origins of the holiday, see U.S. Congress, House, Subcommittee on Census and Population of the Committee on Post Office and Civil Service, Designate the Birthday of Martin Luther King, Jr., as a Legal Public Holiday, 94th Cong. 1st sess., H.R. 1810 (Washington, DC, 1975); U.S. Congress, House, Subcommittee on Census and Statistics of the Committee on Post Office and Civil Service, Martin Luther King, Jr., Holiday Bill, 98th Cong. 1st sess., H.R. 800 (Washington, DC, 1983); and see esp. Wiggins, *O Freedom!* 134–51.

8. Dyson, *I May Not Get There with You*, 287–88.

9. Richard M. Merelman, *Representing Black Culture: Racial Conflict and Cultural Politics in the United States* (New York: Routledge, 1995), 79–80; Peter Applebome, "King Holiday Seeks Wider Acceptance in U.S.," *New York Times*, January 16, 1994, A1, A10; Nicholas O. Alozie, "Political Tolerance Hypotheses and White Opposition to a Martin Luther King Holiday in Arizona," *Social Science Journal* 32, no. 1 (January 1995): 1–16; "New Hampshire Denies King Holiday Again," *Jet*, April 7, 1997, 16; "Utah Designates Dr. King's Birthday a Holiday; Last State to Adopt the Day," *Jet*, April 24, 2000, 4; David Firestone, "46,000 March on South Carolina Capitol to Bring Down Confederate Flag," *New York Times*, January, 18, 2000, A12; Associated Press, "S.C. Strips King's Name from Holiday," *University of Oregon Daily Emerald* (Eugene), March 2, 2000, 1.

10. Applebome, "King Holiday Seeks Wider Acceptance"; Janice Castro, "Thanks for the Memories: Walt Disney Studios, Universal Studios, and Twentieth-Century Fox Film Corp. Do Not Honor Martin Luther King Day," *Time*, January 25, 1993, 15.

11. Melanet's Kwanzaa Information Center, at www.melanet.com/kwanzaa, accessed March 18, 2001; Leigh Eric Schmidt, *Consumer Rites: The Buying and Selling of American Holidays* (Princeton, NJ: Princeton University Press, 1995), 300–301.

12. Clarence G. Williams, ed., *Reflections of the Dream* (Cambridge, MA: MIT Press, 1996), 26–27; Neville, "Honoring a Legacy for Us All," *Register-Guard*

(Eugene, OR), January 15, 1996, 6A; Applebome, "King Holiday Seeks Wider Acceptance," A1.

13. W. E. B. Du Bois, *The Souls of Black Folk* (1903), in *Writings*, Nathan Huggins, ed. (New York: Library of America, 1986), 364–65, 371, 545; Williams, *Reflections of the Dream*, 39.

14. Roy Rosenzweig and David Thelen, *The Presence of the Past: Popular Uses of History in American Life* (New York: Columbia University Press, 1998), 151–62, esp. 153–54.

15. Susan F. Rasky, "Black History Struggles to Keep Up with the Demand," *New York Times*, January 12, 1986, E28; Dyson, *I May Not Get There with You*, 104, 284–85.

16. Applebome, "King Holiday Seeks Wider Acceptance," A10.

17. Williams, *Reflections of the Dream*, 56, 60; William E. Schmidt, "Top U.S. Educator Calls Dr. King a Fine Teacher," *New York Times*, January 15, 1986, A8; Bernard Weinraub, "Reagan Opens Observances Leading to Dr. King's Birthday," *New York Times*, January 14, 1986, A16.

18. Weinraub, "Reagan Opens Observances," A16; see also "Required Reading: On Dr. King's Birthday," an excerpt from a speech by Jesse L. Jackson, January 12, 1986, *New York Times*, January 15, 1986, B10.

19. Dyson, *I May Not Get There with You*, 22–25 (Reynolds quoted on 22); Edward W. Lempinen, "Connerly Widens Anti–Affirmative Action Campaign; He Announces New Effort on King Birthday," *San Francisco Chronicle*, January 16, 1997, A17. The most offensive appropriation of King's famous "I Have a Dream" speech may be that of John Callahan, the syndicated cartoonist of *Callahan*, who in April 1995—during the anniversary month of King's assassination—drew a comic that showed a frowning woman standing in the doorway of her son's bedroom, while her son stood over his bed, with a puddle in the middle. At the top, a caption read, "Martin Luther King, age 13," while near the boy it read, "I had a dream." See Ann Oldenburg, "A Cartoonist on the Offensive," *USA Today*, November 14, 1995, 8D. Callahan has also published the cartoon in his *Freaks of Nature* (New York: Quill, 1995).

20. Randal C. Archibold, "Celebrating a Milestone for Freedom," *New York Times*, January 1, 2000, A27.

21. Isabel Wilkerson, "Memphis Blacks Charge Calendar Slurs Dr. King," *New York Times*, late city final ed., January 15, 1989, sec. 1, part 1, 16; Alex Chadwick, "Waldenbooks Fires Three over Nasty Calendar," *Weekend Edition*, National Public Radio, September 5, 1992.

22. Barry Bearak, "On Day to Honor Dr. King, Some Pause as Others Shop," *New York Times*, January 20, 1998, A1, A12; advertisement for Value Village, in *Register-Guard* (Eugene, OR), January 12, 2000, 3A (this ad generated at least one objecting letter, urging readers not to commercialize King: "How demeaning and degrading to honor his contribution and achievements by shopping," wrote Mary-

beth M. Nessler, letter to the editor, *Register-Guard* [Eugene, OR], January 19, 2000, 10A); a criticism by the Turning Point Project of the print and television advertising campaign using King appeared in the *New York Times,* July 10, 2000, A13. See also Dyson, *I May Not Get There with You,* 6.

23. Michael Kammen, *Mystic Chords of Memory: The Transformation of Tradition in American Culture* (New York: Knopf, 1991); John Bodnar, *Remaking America: Public Memory, Commemoration, and Patriotism in the Twentieth Century* (Princeton, NJ: Princeton University Press, 1992), 13–14.

Chapter 11

Proclaiming Thanksgiving throughout the Land

From Local to National Holiday

Diana Muir

At the close of the eighteenth century, Thanksgiving was a holiday exclusive to New England. It was celebrated with great enthusiasm, but only in the New England states and in adjacent parts of Long Island and upstate New York that, having been settled by New Englanders, were culturally part of the region. It was also celebrated in Connecticut's Western Reserve, which we now know as northeastern Ohio. People elsewhere did not celebrate Thanksgiving, although they might have heard of it in much the same way that Americans today know of Mardi Gras as a holiday that is celebrated in New Orleans.

The Thanksgiving holiday was created within a generation of the settlement of New England. The impulse to create a new holiday is understandable in the context of Puritan doctrine that regarded Christmas, Easter, and Saints' Days as grave Papist errors and banned their celebration. The Sabbath was central to New England Puritans, but their only holidays were special days of fasting and prayer called when a disaster such as a drought or invasion threatened, as well as special days of prayer and thanksgiving called when a disaster had been averted. A day of prayer and thanksgiving could be proclaimed by a single town that had experienced a great blessing, or it could be called by the colony as a whole. In such an event, a proclamation of Thanksgiving was issued by the governor and a copy sent to each church, where it was read from the pulpit. The proclamation enumerated the particular blessing for which a day of prayerful thanks was being held and specified the date.

It was the innovation of the people of Connecticut to decide in the 1640s that the annual miracle of the harvest was sufficient blessing to warrant an annual proclamation of Thanksgiving. Massachusetts theologians were appalled. To set an annual day of Thanksgiving, predictable in advance, was to take for granted that the "Lord in his mercy" would grant the sunshine and rain required to produce a harvest. It would tend to make people overconfident of God's blessings and insufficiently conscious of their constant dependence upon his mercy. This was good Puritan doctrine, but it failed to take into account the universal human craving for holidays. Despite the objections of the colony's leading theologians, by the end of the seventeenth century, Thanksgiving was as firmly established in Massachusetts as it was in Connecticut.

New England's unique culture—featuring free schools for every child, a religious tradition in which ordinary folk wrestled with complex theological questions, and two centuries of self-government—produced in the early nineteenth century a generation of young people uniquely qualified to fill the demand for educated professionals in the growing urban centers of the republic.

Even as tens of thousands of New Englanders cleared farmland on the western frontier, thousands of their cousins became clerks in the banking houses of New York, shopkeepers in Louisiana, schoolteachers in Virginia, editors in Pennsylvania, lawyers in Ohio, physicians in Missouri, and clergymen in Illinois. In every state of the Union, and overwhelmingly so in the new states of the West, New England disproportionately furnished the professional men and women. Congressman John C. Calhoun, South Carolina's great statesman and a Yale man, reflected this dominance when he remarked that he "had seen the time when the natives of Connecticut, together with the graduates of Yale College, in Congress, constituted within five votes of a majority of that body."

Transplanted Yankees Sow the Seeds of Thanksgiving

In the 1830s and 1840s, this cadre of Yankee editors, teachers, ministers, and citizens began a campaign to make Thanksgiving a national holiday. There was no central leadership, no coordinated strategy, not even an awareness by each individual that others, elsewhere, were working toward the same end. There was only a simple desire of New Englanders living in other states to celebrate this holiday beloved of childhood in their new homes. When virtually the entire population of a territory was made up of New Englanders, as was the case in Michigan and Iowa, this was a relatively simple proposition. Increasingly, however, New Englanders were in a position to persuade governors of such states as Missouri, Maryland, and Mississippi of the desirability of proclaiming Thanksgiving Day.

By the early 1840s, Thanksgiving had spread far beyond the borders of New England. Connecticut, Massachusetts, New Hampshire, Rhode Island, Vermont, and Maine still celebrated the holiday born two centuries earlier along the banks of the Connecticut River, but governors of New York, Michigan, Illinois, Iowa, Wisconsin, and Indiana also proclaimed an annual thanksgiving day, and in 1843 Pennsylvania and Missouri joined the growing list. Governor David Rittenhouse Porter proclaimed Thursday, December 21, 1843, Thanksgiving Day for Pennsylvania and, in contrast to the efforts of earlier governors to establish the holiday, his initiative took root.

Reverend Samuel Lowrie of Pittsburgh recalled as an elderly gentleman how he had spent that first Thanksgiving Day as a seven-year-old boy:

> The part assigned to me was to baste the turkey, which was to be roasting in a reflector oven before the open grate fireplace, while the church service was going on, so as to be ready to be offered to the company promptly when they came from church. . . . The canned oysters that came from Baltimore were properly cooked and served. . . . There were, of course, pumpkin pie and apple butter and, also, sweet cider from Grandfather Thompson's cider mill and press.

The following year there was no Thanksgiving in Pennsylvania, but Thanksgiving Day was proclaimed by Governor Francis Shunk for November 27, 1845, and has been observed every year since.

Folks in Pittsburgh learned how to celebrate Thanksgiving the same way their governors learned how to write Thanksgiving proclamations. Though the Pennsylvanians had never written one before, Yankees showed them how. Pennsylvania governors issued proclamations in the style of governors of Connecticut and Massachusetts, and people celebrated by following the lead of their New England–born preachers, editors, teachers, writers, and neighbors.

Louisiana observed Thanksgiving for the first time on Thursday, January 15, 1846. An exultant New England–born resident of Water Proof, Tensas Parish, Louisiana, wrote to relatives in Indiana:

> You little thought when telling us of the good Thanksgiving dinner you expected to eat at Mrs. Douglass' that we too were going to enjoy the privilege of showing our thankfulness for mercies past by partaking of a sumptuous repast. But it is even so, thanks to His excellency Governor Mouton! He has seen the evil of his ways, and has at length repented and announced that this year and ever after the people of Louisiana must celebrate a day of Thanksgiving. The day set apart is the fifteenth of January 1846. We are going to try to have a real Yankee dinner, pumpkin pies and everything to match.

The promise of Thanksgiving Day "this year and ever after" proved true; Louisiana celebrated Thanksgiving on a Thursday in November or December from November 26, 1846, onward. Thanksgiving Day, December 9, 1847, was especially joyful, coming just six days after General Zachary Taylor led a triumphal parade of soldiers fresh from victory in the Mexican War through the streets of New Orleans.

Governor Thomas Reynolds proclaimed the first Thanksgiving Day in Missouri for December 3, 1843, specifying as did many governors that he addressed his constituents "without any distinction of sect, denomination or creed." William J. Hammond, a newspaperman working for the *Missouri Republican,* described the day in a letter to his mother:

> It was the first Thanksgiving Day ever observed in this State, and you may suppose the most was made of it. . . . There was all sorts of frolicking. . . .
>
> In the morning the . . . Churches were thrown open for religious exercises, and all were crowded to overflowing. The afternoon . . . was observed by the gathering together of all the members of families . . . as I had no fireside to go to . . . nor no relation to talk with . . . the afternoon was spent by me walking around like a lost sheep waiting to be gathered into the fold. But the afternoon would not last always, and night came, and with it brought my time for fun. There were Methodist Sewing Societies, Presbyterian Tea Parties, and Balls in abundance and it was some time before I could make up my mind which to attend. I finally concluded to stick to first principles and go to a Methodist Sewing Society.

The one which I attended was held at Mrs. McKee's. . . . At an early hour quite a company was assembled. . . . All passed very pleasantly till about 8 o'clock, when Miss Mary took a particular spite against the Piano, and commenced hammering it, with vocal accompaniments, which frightened me considerably and I sloped. The evening not being far advanced, I . . . [gave] the Presbyterians a pop by going to their Tea Party; they had a splendid supper, good speeches were made by several gentlemen, and I regretted that I did not go there first as I never spent my time more agreeably.

Missouri's first Thanksgiving was a success, but Thanksgiving did not become an official annual holiday in Missouri until 1855. Between 1843 and 1855, some governors proclaimed the holiday, while others neglected to do so. An editorial from the December 7, 1849, Liberty, Missouri, *Weekly Tribune* scolded, "We observe that many of the States have long since appointed certain days for thanksgiving, and yet the Governor of Missouri is mum on the subject." Governor Austin King was negligent only in 1849; the following year he proclaimed Thursday, December 12, as Thanksgiving Day.

Such erratic proclamations were common. Thanksgiving Day might come in September, October, November, December, or even January, and in many states it was some years proclaimed, some years neglected, according to the whim of the governor. This irregularity of dates had a single, distinct advantage: it was often possible to partake of a turkey dinner with cousins in New York on Thanksgiving Day and still be able to ladle cranberry sauce onto sliced turkey with cousins in Vermont on Thanksgiving Day a week later. But the practical minded, Mrs. Sarah Josepha Hale chief among them, found this variety untidy and confusing.

Mrs. Hale's Campaign

Sarah Josepha Hale was a remarkable woman. Born near Newport, New Hampshire, in 1788 to a Revolutionary War veteran and his wife, Sarah Hale was left a poor widow with five children to support in an era when no profession open to women enabled them to earn an adequate living. Mrs. Hale determined to support her family with her pen and wrote *Northwood; or Life North and South,* a novel that set out to demonstrate the superiority of democratic, virtuous, rural New England by contrasting it with decadent, slaveholding southern society. One entire chapter was devoted to a description of Thanksgiving Day in the hero's New Hampshire farm family and to the author's opinion that Thanksgiving Day "should be the same as the Fourth of July, a national holiday." To Mrs. Hale, more than to any other individual, goes the credit for making it so.

The success of *Northwood* led to a job as editor of the *Ladies' Magazine* in Boston, one of the earliest women's magazines and the first to be edited by a woman. In 1837, the *Ladies' Magazine* merged with the *Lady's Book* of Philadelphia, and Mrs. Hale became editor of the new *Lady's Book and Magazine*, published by L. A. Godey. In 1841, she moved her home and editorial offices to Philadelphia.

Godey's Lady's Book was, for the next two decades, the most widely distributed periodical of any kind in the United States. It was read in New York townhouses, on southern plantations, and in cabins on the western frontier. Not precisely comparable to any single periodical today, the *Lady's Book* under Mrs. Hale's direction exercised an influence of the magnitude of *Seventeen, Redbook, Good Housekeeping,* and *Better Homes and Gardens* combined. When *Godey's* printed a new bonnet style, milliners from coast to coast fashioned copies for their customers. *Godey's* published plans for "model cottages," and carpenters from Baltimore to Portland built houses "like the picture in the *Lady's Book.*" Hers was a powerful position, and Mrs. Hale chose to use it to make Thanksgiving a national holiday.

Sarah Hale began her campaign in 1846 to make the last Thursday in November the national Thanksgiving Day. Whether she was inspired by the recent gubernatorial decision to make Thanksgiving a holiday in Pennsylvania or whether she in some way influenced the governor to proclaim the holiday is impossible to say. Old issues of the *Lady's Book* do show that Hale waged an unremitting campaign for a nationwide Thanksgiving holiday beginning that year.

Each year, Mrs. Hale wrote a rhapsodic editorial on the desirability of a national Thanksgiving Day. November issues of the *Lady's Book* featured Thanksgiving poetry and stories of families reunited on Thanksgiving Day. Household advice columns carried directions on how to stuff a turkey and bake a mince pie. Mrs. Hale intended to tell her readers about Thanksgiving and teach them to celebrate it until the holiday became as familiar a household custom in Mississippi and Nebraska as it was in New Hampshire.

Thanksgiving Takes Root

In addition to her editorials, Mrs. Hale wrote letters. Each summer the governor of every state and territory received a letter from her urging them to proclaim the last Thursday in November as Thanksgiving Day. Her requests, and the similar efforts of others, fell on fertile soil. America, always a God-fearing nation, was experiencing a groundswell of religious fervor in the 1840s and 1850s. Protestant churches, leading institutions in the culture of the time, favored officially proclaimed days of thanksgiving.

The Presbyterian Church played an especially important role in introducing Thanksgiving to new states. Presbyterian state synods commonly proclaimed days of thanksgiving for Presbyterians in states where the governors did not, and sometimes they formally petitioned the governor to proclaim Thanksgiving Day. Presbyterian synods began to issue Thanksgiving proclamations after the Revolution, but Presbyterian enthusiasm for Thanksgiving was augmented by the odd circumstance that when New England Congregationalists moved west, they usually became Presbyterians.

The old New England doctrine of congregational autonomy proved unequal to the task of establishing churches throughout the rapidly expanding frontier. Presbyterianism was doctrinally compatible with Congregationalism and had the advantage of a strong, centralized hierarchy. Presbyterian churches with New England–bred congregations led the way in establishing Thanksgiving Day in new states, but churches of other denominations also endorsed the holiday. Ministers, as a rule, were in favor of anything that brought people into church.

Thanksgiving had the additional advantage of being introduced to people who, while not accustomed to celebrating it, were at least familiar with it as a New England custom, much as Americans today recognize Mardi Gras as a customary holiday in New Orleans. Young Rutherford B. Hayes, sent East to a Connecticut prep school in 1838, wrote home to his family in Ohio:

> Thanksgiving was the 30th of November. I suppose you have heard of the richness of the dinner in this Yankee Country on that day; but it beat everything all hallow I ever saw. Our dessert alone, I should think, would cost fifty dollars . . . we had things [I] never dreamed of there being such. . . . There are divers things in this blue country I like better than Ohio; for example, Thanksgiving dinner.

The holiday that appealed to the future president appealed to other Americans as well, and a steadily increasing number of governors issued Thanksgiving proclamations for their states.

Jonn Munn, a Connecticut Yankee by birth, ran a store and a bank in Canton, Mississippi, when the first Thanksgiving Day ever observed in that state was proclaimed for November 25, 1847. He recorded the event in his journal:

> An unusual scene has been witnessed in our village and state this day. By appointment of Governor Brown it was selected as a day of "Thanksgiving"—and for the first time in this state has such a date been set apart for such purpose. This good old New England custom was a long time confined to those states—in time it was adopted by the Western and middle states and for the last few years had gradually come to be observed in many of the Southern states, and on this day and this year about two thirds of the states unite in rendering thanks for the mercies and benefits received during the year now drawing to a close. There is something grateful and pleasant to the feelings of any man of right thought and mind in contemplating such a scene, but how much more so to one who was born on the soil of New England as he sees state after state adopting so advisable a custom. Far away from that birthplace, the observance of the day here brings a flood of early recollections. . . .
>
> In our village the day has been observed in a manner that would have given ample satisfaction to the most rigid observer of such days in the times of its earliest appointment. All business was suspended and quiet prevailed in our streets. There was a general attendance at church to listen to the Rev. Mr. Halsy of Jackson, and seldom have I listened to a more interesting and appropriate sermon. It was well adapted for a people who were assembled for the first time for such a purpose, and those listening attentively could not but have been instructed in the objects of those who first established the custom and the reasons that demand its observance.

New Englanders were not shy about instructing their fellow Americans in the reasons that demanded the observance of Thanksgiving. They were, in fact, accustomed to arrogating to themselves the prerogative of instructing their fellow citizens on whatever topic they chose. Boston was the cultural center of early-nineteenth-century America. Virtually every reform movement of the era was born either in New England proper or in the New England–settled areas of upper New York State. Abolition, women's suffrage, the movement for free public schools, the campaign to establish public insane asylums, and America's first health food crusade were among the movements led by Yankees. A people who felt free to tell their reluctant fellow citizens to educate their children, free their slaves, and give women the vote were unfettered in their eagerness to suggest that other regions join their home states in celebrating Thanksgiving Day.

Governor Thomas Drew proclaimed the first Thanksgiving Day in Arkansas for December 9, 1847. Newspapers throughout the state reprinted the governor's proclamation. The *Arkansas Gazette* also printed a poem written for the occasion in its December 2 issue:

> Th' appointment's gone forth from the Halls of the State,
> Inviting all ranks to the Church to repair,
> And the bountiful goodness of GOD celebrate,
> In the rapture of praise and the fervor of prayer. . . .

Thanksgiving Day was officially proclaimed in California even before that state was admitted to the Union, and it was observed by individual Californians well before it was officially proclaimed. A New England forty-niner noted in his journal that "we celebrated Thanksgiving Day (or what we supposed to be so) . . . by an extra dinner." In the burgeoning cities of the territory, the first official Thanksgiving Day, November 29, 1849, was celebrated with somewhat greater formality.

Since California was not admitted to the Union until 1850, that first Thanksgiving proclamation was issued over the signature of Military Governor General Riley, at the urging of his New York–born adjutant. Although the proclamation was issued in both Spanish and English, Spanish inhabitants seem to have ignored the holiday, probably wondering what all the fuss was about. The day was observed by eastern immigrants with services in the handful of churches that then existed. Reverend Albert Williams and the congregation of the First Presbyterian Church of San Francisco, not yet having constructed a church building, held their worship service in a tent. In Monterey, Reverend Samuel H. Willey commented on the day in his journal:

> A clear, bright, beautiful day. But only a beginning to Thanksgiving Day keeping in Monterey, where so small a proportion of the inhabitants care for any Protestant observance. There are fewer Americans in this town than were expected to be here when the rains came. But who ever saw

Americans leave places where they can make money. . . . A few attend worship and seem to remember their education and principles even in California.

Undaunted by the meagerness of the turnout, Reverend Willey held services and preached a Thanksgiving sermon that expressed gratitude for the abundant resources and bright future of the territory, but nevertheless expressed a wistful longing for old New England.

Though very few can procure the luxuries and delicacies or even the substantial comforts of life to compare with the loaded tables in New England homes, the very absence of these things will make the sacred memories of the day more vivid in their minds.

The mention of Thanksgiving calls up each one's home, with its antique structure, the venerable halls, rooms, windows all as we left them years ago. The same elms spread out their branches to shade them. The little brook comes leaping down over the stones merrily as ever. Though thousands of miles away, it seems as if we could hear the measured tick of the old clock in the corner.

Reverend Willey was not alone in his homesick ruminations. Although those eastern families that had set up housekeeping prepared Thanksgiving dinners as traditional as resources allowed and invited their acquaintances among the many single men of the community, Thanksgiving Day was a lonely time for many pioneers. Reverend R. F. Putnam confided to his diary in 1863,

Thanksgiving, which was here as in Massachusetts, on the 26th of November, was a solemn and unsatisfactory day. In the morning we had services at church, but the congregation was very small. After the services we returned to our homes and spent the remainder of the day in quietness. We thought of home and longed to be there.

Our dinner was plain and simple, for we had no heart for a sumptuous repast. We had been invited to dine out, but declined all such invitations, preferring to remain alone and think of the dear ones who gathered around the Thanksgiving table at home.

We felt a sense of relief when the day was over. Holidays in California are to us homesick days of which we have an instinctive dread. Commonly, they are the gloomiest days of the year.

Although Reverend Putnam seems to have been a gloomier character than the average Californian, his holiday depression was at least partially induced by circumstances. The good reverend's Christmas entry for the same year was cheerful enough, noting the attendance of a "large congregation" at morning services, but Thanksgiving was a newly transplanted holiday, with shallow roots in the West and South. Years would pass before Thanksgiving was as joyfully and spontaneously celebrated in other states as it was in New England.

As long as the western states remained a young land of new immigrants, one of the fixed customs of the day was for as many citizens as could manage the trip to return East to spend the holiday with family. Even after the railroads came through, the trip from Washington State or Minnesota back to New York or Connecticut was long and expensive, but almost everyone wanted to go home at least once before the old folks would be there no longer, and every year some westerners made the trip.

Among New Englanders settled in the cities of the mid-Atlantic states, the pilgrimage home to Thanksgiving became an annual ritual. The custom was acknowledged by Horace Greeley, the Vermont-born editor of the New York *Herald Tribune,* who printed this poem addressed "To All New Englanders" in 1846:

> Come home to Thanksgiving! Dear children, come home!
> From the Northland and the South, from West and the East,
> Where'er ye are resting, where'er ye roam,
> Come back to this sacred and annual feast.

From Greeley's perspective, and from that of many Americans, Thanksgiving was a holiday that Yankees went home to New England to enjoy. Franklin Benjamin Hough, a New Yorker who wrote a history called *Proclamations for Thanksgiving* in 1858, estimated that upwards of ten thousand people left New York City each year to return to New England for Thanksgiving. The holiday these pilgrims sought on Vermont farms and in Connecticut villages was the traditional one of family gatherings and church services, turkey dinners, and village socials.

It was the New England model of Thanksgiving Day that Sarah Hale knew, loved, and promoted in her magazine. Each year, along with Thanksgiving poems, recipes, and editorial admonitions directing governors to proclaim the last Thursday in November as Thanksgiving Day, short stories about Thanksgiving appeared. Many a story featured a family gathered on Thanksgiving Day in a spacious old New England home when, miraculously, just as the family prepared to say grace, a son who had gone to sea and was presumed drowned or who had gone west and not been heard from for many years or who had stormed out in anger a decade before would reappear to great rejoicing and thanksgiving.

Alternate plots featured spoiled city youngsters who learned the virtues of charity, humility, and gratitude by visiting country cousins for Thanksgiving or girls who met their true loves while at home on Thanksgiving Day. Sometimes these girls wanted to be in New York at the opera or at a ball, but they were dragged off to the country by old-fashioned parents and, while rusticating, met young men handsomer, wealthier, and more virtuous by far than their city beaus.

Mrs. Hale was joined in her campaign to make Thanksgiving a holiday familiar to the nation by the popular pictorial magazines of the day. These oversized periodicals, featuring pen-and-ink drawings of news events, interesting places, and famous people, found in "An Old-Fashioned Thanksgiving Day" the perfect feature for their November issues. Magazine articles were instrumental in teaching Americans how to celebrate Thanksgiving Day at a time when growing numbers of governors were proclaiming the holiday for their constituents.

Governor John Gaines issued the first Thanksgiving proclamation for Oregon Territory in 1852, stating that he did so "in conformity to a usage in most of the States of the Union," and this was true. By that year, the Northeast and Midwest, along with many parts of the South and several territories, celebrated Thanksgiving as an annual holiday. Oregon did not have another Thanksgiving until it achieved statehood in 1859—and a most begrudgingly proclaimed Thanksgiving it was. The economy was bad, Indians were attacking and burning settlements in the southern part of the state, and the threat of civil war hung over the nation. "For what," complained the *Oregon Statesman*, "should the people of Oregon especially give thanks?"

Seventy-six Oregon City women knew the answer: the time for Thanksgiving had come, and there were always sufficient blessings to encourage a God-fearing people to offer thanks. Accordingly, they petitioned Governor John Whiteaker for a Thanksgiving proclamation. In response, he issued one of the most niggardly proclamations on record: "Be it known that in conformity with the wishes of many citizens of Oregon," not, apparently, including his own, "I appoint and set apart Thursday, the 29th of December, 1859, as a day to be kept for PUBLIC THANKSGIVING, to be observed throughout the state in such manner as the good people thereof may deem appropriate."

Governor Whiteaker did not list any of the many causes for which the people of Oregon might give thanks, nor did he suggest, as other governors usually did, that they should suspend their regular activities and spend the day at prayer and family gatherings. But the people of Oregon knew how to celebrate Thanksgiving. They prayed and feasted and enjoyed the holiday that soon became a regular part of Oregon life.

Nebraskan editors appear to have been cast from a more optimistic mold than the Oregonian variety, for when the state's first Thanksgiving Day was proclaimed, Nebraska's only newspaper, the *Bellevue Palladium*, commented that "although we have, as in all new countries, comparatively little to be thankful for, we have sufficient to inspire our gratitude and blessing." The editor of the *Bellevue Palladium* noted that he was a guest "at an excellent Thanksgiving dinner," but we do not know whether anyone thought to invite the grumpy editor of the *Oregon Statesman* to Thanksgiving dinner.

Acting Governor Thomas Cuming set the first Thanksgiving Day in Nebraska on November 30, 1854, just six months after Nebraska Territory was established by the Kansas-Nebraska Act. The settlers were Yankees moving into the new territory from nearby Iowa and other northern states, and they would keep their old New England holiday in this new free-soil territory. The introduction of Thanksgiving to Kansas would prove more controversial and bloody.

Settlers in territories where Thanksgiving was not yet a holiday grew impatient. "November passed and week by week New Englanders looked for the announcement of their ancient and beloved festival," wrote Mrs. Isaac Atwater, a Minnesota pioneer, "but even the sacred last Thursday went by without it, and dismay and homesickness filled all hearts. Our good governor must have been of Scotch or Dutch pedigree to have overlooked a duty of such importance; but at last a hint was given him, a brief proclamation was forthcoming, and the day duly celebrated."

On that first Thanksgiving Day, December 26, 1850, St. Paul was a frontier village of about 225 buildings, and St. Anthony was the next largest town with but 115 houses; indeed, the entire Minnesota Territory, including both Dakotas as far as the Missouri River, held only six thousand settlers. New and sparsely populated though the territory was, a "magnificent ball" was held in St. Paul in a hall decorated with "paintings, pictures, transparencies and chandeliers in a style of superb elegance," while the three hotels in town "each served elaborate dinners of buffalo, bear, and venison."

Such gaudy celebrations fit poorly with our more stereotypic images of sturdy pioneers leading the way west in buckskin shirts. But typical immigrants to a young western city had not come west to enjoy the simple life—they had come in the hope of getting very rich, very fast. Founders of town sites surveyed land and laid out grid-patterned streets on acres of vacant prairie, hoping that theirs would be a new Chicago, making them overnight millionaires by land speculation alone. Even before their fortunes were made, these would-be millionaires aspired to live in style. Thanksgiving entertainments were arranged to demonstrate that society in the territories lacked none of the refinement of Philadelphia or Boston. An 1854 visitor to tiny Excelsior, Minnesota, recorded his pleasure in the Thanksgiving exercises held by the local lyceum during which ladies and gentlemen offered "addresses appropriate to the occasion" and "music upon the piano," all of which, in the visitor's flattering opinion, compared well with "the most selected gatherings in many portions of the east."

Governors of the young Minnesota Territory proclaimed Thanksgiving every year, a practice regularized by the first legislature after Minnesota became a state in 1858. A statute was enacted providing that "the governor shall by proclamation set apart one day each year as a day of solemn and public thanksgiving to Almighty God, for his blessings to us as a state and a nation."

Edward J. Pond recalled his family's simple celebration of Minnesota's first Thanksgiving in their home at Chief Shakopee's village on the shore of Lake Harriet, where his father was a missionary to the Indians: "I know that we had venison we got from the Indians. We had cranberries too." High-bush cranberries grew wild in Minnesota; picked and boxed, they earned important cash for the early settlers. "We always had pumpkin pies. Then we had bread and butter and that was about all."

The simple fare of the Pond family is probably representative of what Minnesota farm families ate, both on Thanksgiving and on other days. Simple food, hard work, and faith in God marked the lives of these pioneers, circumstances that led Reverend Edward D. Neill, in his well-received sermon on that first Thanksgiving Day in Minnesota Territory to a congregation of thirty-eight worshipers, to compare "the infancy of our favored territory with that of the Puritan colonies."

Settlers throughout the West compared themselves with the Puritan colonizers of New England as self-consciously as New England settlers had once compared themselves with the biblical children of Israel. Perhaps no group of pioneers took these comparisons more to heart than the five thousand Latter-Day Saints whom Brigham Young led over the Rocky Mountains in 1847 to settle the Great Salt Basin of Utah. No crops had ever been raised in this desert with its late-spring and early-autumn frosts; many believed that none could be grown here. That first harvest, then, was like the first harvest of the Pilgrims at Plymouth—it proved that land could be farmed and settlements planted where no Englishmen had lived before. To these pilgrims, driven from home by religious prejudice, it meant new homes and the opportunity to worship in the wilderness according to their own beliefs.

When the harvest was gathered, Utah, or Deseret as the first settlers called it, held a celebration much like the 1621 harvest Thanksgiving at Plymouth.

> On the tenth of August [1848] we held a public feast under a bowery [bower built of poles and branches] in the center of our fort. This was called a harvest feast; we partook of a rich variety of bread, beef, butter, cheese, cakes, pastry, green corn, melons, and almost every variety of vegetables. Large sheaves of wheat, rye, barley, oats, and other productions were hoisted on poles for public exhibition, and there was prayer and thanksgiving, congratulations, songs, speeches, music, dancing, smiling faces and merry hearts. In short, it was a great day with the people of these valleys, and long to be remembered by those who had suffered and waited anxiously for the results of a first effort to redeem the interior deserts of America, and to make her hitherto unknown solitudes "blossom like a rose."

The Mormon pioneers who founded Utah were from many states and from England, but their leader, Brigham Young, was a son of Vermont. Before long, he began to issue Thanksgiving proclamations as other governors did, but in a style unique to the Latter-Day Saints. In one proclamation, issued in 1851, Governor Young gave thanks for the harvest, good health, general prosperity, and peace, but went on to incorporate uniquely Mormon concepts of priesthood and to emphasize such Christian virtues as brotherhood and charity.

Territory of Utah
Proclamation
For a day of Praise and Thanksgiving
It having pleased the Father of all good to make known His mind and will
to the children of men, in these last days; and through the ministrations of
his angels, to restore the Holy Priesthood unto the sons of Adam . . . and
influencing them to flow together from the four quarters of the earth, to a
land of peace and health; . . . reserved of old in the councils of eternity for the
purposes to which it is now appropriated; a land choice above all others; . . .
I, Brigham Young, Governor of the Territory aforesaid, in response to the
time-honored custom of our forefathers at Plymouth Rock . . . DO PRO-
CLAIM . . . A Day of Praise and Thanksgiving . . . in honor of the God of
Abraham . . . And I recommend to all the good citizens of Utah . . . that they
rise early in the morning . . . and wash their bodies with pure water; that all
men attend to their flocks and herds with carefulness; . . . while the women
are preparing the best of food for their households . . . ask the Father to
bless your food; and when you have filled the plates of your household, partake with them, with rejoicing and thanksgiving. . . . I also request of all
good and peaceful citizens, that they refrain from all evil thinking, speaking,
and acting on that day; that no one be offended by his neighbor . . . that all
may cease their quarrels and starve the lawyers . . . I further request, that
when the day has been spent in doing good; in dealing your bread, your
butter, your beef, your pork, your turkeys, your molasses, and the choicest
of all the products of the valleys and mountains . . . to the poor; . . . that you
end the day . . . on the same principle that you commenced it . . . preparing
for celestial glory.

One after another, the western states proclaimed Thanksgiving, welcoming, as the *Iowa City Standard* put it in 1844, "the good old Pilgrim
custom to our midst." The widespread acceptance of the idea that the Pilgrims founded this nation at Plymouth Rock and that Thanksgiving was
worthy of adoption by every state in the Union because it was first observed at Plymouth was a triumph of Yankee persuasiveness. English
colonists with a variety of motivations founded several colonies along the
Atlantic seaboard in the 1600s. Jamestown, of course, was the first to become permanently established. Pennsylvania was the true haven of religious freedom. But it is the footfall at Plymouth Rock that American
schoolchildren are taught to venerate.

The landing of the Pilgrim Fathers did not become the honored myth of our nation's birth because of a realistic understanding of who these people were — after all, they themselves were intolerant religious fanatics—but because of who their descendants became. Virginia grew into a prosperous, hierarchical colony led by aristocratic slave owners. Massachusetts became an almost pure democracy, inhabited by freehold-ing, self-sufficient farmers. Virginia gave the country great statesmen. New England produced teachers, ministers, lawyers, men and women of letters, and merchants. The New England ideals of free education and respect for learning, citizen participation in government, equality of opportunity, and centrality of religious faith became the ideals of a nation. For these rea-sons, Plymouth, and not Jamestown, became our national myth.

When the republic was young, the creation of a national mythology was a deeply felt necessity. George Washington, the father of his country, as-sumed the status nearly of a demigod. His portrait hung in parlors and schoolrooms, adulatory biographies sold tens of thousands of copies, and myths grew up around his every action and utterance. Lafayette, returning in 1824 to visit the nation in whose revolutionary army he had served as a young man, was hailed by worshipful crowds of thousands. The states needed heroes, myths, and legends to make them one nation. To fill this need, New England offered the Pilgrims and the first Thanksgiving. Here was a third holiday for the nation to celebrate together along with Wash-ington's birthday and the Fourth of July. Here was a new constellation of mythic Pilgrim heroes to place in the firmament alongside Washington and Lafayette. Just as Thanksgiving had been created to fill a need for hol-idays in Puritan New England, so it was adopted by western and southern states that needed national myths and nationwide holidays.

NOTES ON SOURCES

This essay first appeared as a chapter in Diana Karter Appelbaum, *Thanksgiving: An American Holiday, an American History* (New York: Facts on File, 1984).

John C. Calhoun is quoted from Horace Bushnell, *Work and Play: Literary Va-rieties* (London: Alexander Strahan, 1864; repr., New York: Charles Scribner's Sons, 1903), 1:220.

Information on Thanksgiving in Pennsylvania was communicated to me by the Pennsylvania Historical and Museum Commission in Harrisburg. Reverend Samuel Lowrie's memoir is in the collection of the Historical Society of Western Pennsylvania in Pittsburgh.

The letter describing the first Thanksgiving in Louisiana is from the Samuel Merrill Collection, of the Indiana Historical Society in Indianapolis. Dated December 23, 1845, it was written by Julia Merrill to Catharine Merrill. There is an article, "The First Thanksgiving in New Orleans," by T. E. Tedd, that appeared in *Inn Dixie* in November 1946, 15–16. Two dates in the article are incorrect. January 15, 1845, should read January 15, 1846, and December 21, 1841, should read December 21, 1848.

Missouri Thanksgiving proclamations are reprinted in *Messages and Proclamations of the Governors of Missouri*. I quote from vol. 1, 520–21. This, along with the Hammond letter, information on dates of early Thanksgivings, and the quote from the *Liberty Weekly Tribune*, were obtained from the State Historical Society of Missouri in Columbia.

Dates of early Thanksgiving days in Maryland were obtained from the Hall of Records, Department of General Services, in Annapolis.

Richard Collins, *History of Kentucky*, vol. 1, first published in Covington, Kentucky, 1874, discusses Thanksgiving on pp. 49 and 52 (Frankfurt: Kentucky Historical Society, 1966).

Early Thanksgivings in Florida are mentioned in Sidney Walter Martin, *Florida during Territorial Days* (Athens: University of Georgia Press, 1944), 104; and Bertram Groene, *Ante-Bellum Tallahassee* (Tallahassee: Florida Heritage Foundation, 1971), 149.

The best source on the activities of Sarah Josepha Hale is her monthly column, "The Editor's Table," in *Godey's Lady's Book*. See also Ruth Albright Finley, *The Lady of Godey* (Philadelphia: Lippincott, 1938).

The passage on Mississippi is quoted from the journal of John Munn, vol. 17, 148–50, manuscript collection of the Chicago Historical Society.

Arkansas information was drawn from Diane Sherwood, "When Arkansas Had Its First Thanksgiving Day—1847," *Arkansas Historical Quarterly* 4 (autumn 1945): 250–56.

California material is drawn from several sources: "Life in Early California in 1849—Journal of I. Kent," *California Historical Society Quarterly* 20 (1941): 40; and Jay Ellison, "The Struggle For Civil Government in California," *California Historical Society Quarterly* 10 (1931), which contains a copy of Governor Riley's proclamation. The R. F. Putnam diary, which mentions Thanksgiving on p. 236, is manuscript no. 1734 in the collection of the California Historical Society in San Francisco. In the library of the same society is an article by W. W. Ferrier on Thanksgiving Day from a November 1924 edition of the *Berkeley Daily Gazette.*

Gubernatorial proclamations for Oregon were obtained from the collection of the Oregon Historical Society in Portland. Further information is found in Charles Oluf Olsen, "Thanks to the Gracious Author of All Our Mercies," *Portland Sunday Journal*, sec. 5, *Pacific Parade Magazine*, November 18, 1945, 1–2; and Dorris

Holmes Bailey, "Thanksgiving in Pioneer Days," *Portland Sunday Journal, Northwest Living Magazine,* November 1, 1954, 17.

Information on Nebraska comes from the Western Heritage Society in Omaha.

Information on Minnesota Thanksgivings is quoted from Glenn Hanson, ed., *The Frontier Holiday* (St. Paul: North Central, 1948), and from an address by Solon J. Buck, "The Minnesota Historical Society and Some Early Thanksgiving History," delivered on November 29, 1928, in the collection of the Archives and Manuscripts Division, Minnesota Historical Society, Ms. #FF602 B92. Further information was gleaned from Ruth Thompson, "First Thanksgiving Day in Minnesota Territory," *Minneapolis Tribune,* November 22, 1948, and from a newspaper clipping, "Mary Knopik Uncovers an Early Thanksgiving Here," dated November 23, 1977, in the collection of the Hennepin County Historical Society, Minneapolis.

Governor Young's 1852 proclamation for Utah was reproduced in the *Deseret News* of November 25, 1939, on p. 1 of the Church section. A very useful article is by E. Cecil McGavin of the Church Historian's Office, "The First Thanksgiving in Utah," *Improvement Era* 49 (November 1946): 696–97.

Chapter 12

"Our Hearts Burn with Ardent Love for Two Countries"

Ethnicity and Assimilation

Ellen M. Litwicki

In 1876 Chicagoans marked the centennial of American independence with two massive displays of patriotism.[1] In the first, military and fraternal societies, led by the Second Regiment of the newly organized Illinois National Guard, paraded through downtown streets lined with cheering spectators waving American flags. Afterward, the regiment sponsored holiday exercises, which featured a ritual reading of the Declaration of Independence, oratory, patriotic recitations and music, and military drills. Across town on the Fourth, a second, three-day centennial celebration culminated in another procession and rhetorical exercises, followed by a balloon ascension, a "grand illumination of the grove," dancing, and a fireworks display.[2]

Although Chicago's celebrations looked very much like other centennial commemorations across the country, they differed in one remarkable way.[3] Their sponsors and participants came from the city's immigrant neighborhoods. The Second Regiment had been created from Irish-American militia companies, and the organizations invited to join its procession included the Ancient Order of Hibernians (AOH) and Irish Catholic total abstinence societies, as well as the Polish Guards and the Kosciuszko Corps. The three-day centennial extravaganza was the product of the *Turngemeinde*, a federation of German-American gymnastic associations, which preached physical fitness as a means of instilling patriotism and preparing its members to defend liberty.[4]

In addition to these celebrations, the city's predominantly German-American socialist unions, militia companies, and Turners had organized a third, more subversive, commemoration on the eve of the centennial. Although this celebration, like the others, featured speechmaking, dancing, games, and fireworks, the highlight was the adoption of an alternative declaration of independence offered by the Workingmen's Party of Illinois. This document urged workers to organize politically to challenge the current government, which repudiated American ideals by favoring the rights of capital over those of the people.[5]

In marked contrast to their ethnic fellow citizens, native-born, nonethnic Chicagoans declined to celebrate publicly the centennial, which should have had much more meaning to them. Many deserted the city for lake excursions and picnics, while others took in baseball games or horse races. The *Chicago Tribune* complained caustically that

> the Chicagoan celebrated the Fourth in his own inimitable style. He didn't celebrate as a component part of Chicago or as an American citizen. . . . he did not march in procession. . . . He would be blessed first before he would stand in a crowd, and listen to the reading of the Declaration of Independence. . . . All that kind of business he left to our German and Irish fellow-citizens.[6]

The lack of a central centennial celebration by native-born Chicagoans is not in itself surprising; nineteenth-century Chicagoans were notoriously apathetic when it came to community holiday celebrations and had marked the Fourth of July and other occasions with unified celebrations only on rare occasions.[7] That the city's two largest immigrant populations did sponsor lavish celebrations is more noteworthy. The centennial celebrations were no aberration. An examination of Chicago's foreign- and English-language newspapers reveals that between 1876 and 1918, immigrants and their children regularly observed a variety of U.S. holidays, including the Fourth of July, Memorial Day, Washington's Birthday, and Flag Day. Neither every ethnic group nor every individual celebrated all of these, but a sufficient number did to make these occasions worthy of study.

Curiously, given the recent spate of studies of ethnic commemorative activities, ethnic celebrations of American holidays have been largely overlooked by scholars. The most extensive work on this topic has been done by Roy Rosenzweig, who included an analysis of Irish, Swedish, and

French-Canadian Fourth of July celebrations in his larger study of working-class leisure in turn-of-the-century Worcester. His main concern, however, was ethnic and class styles of leisure and the extent to which ethnic-centered recreation inhibited the formation of a broader working-class identity.[8]

The fact that so many immigrants and their children celebrated American holidays has broader implications for the study of ethnicity and assimilation. A burgeoning scholarly literature has reconceptualized ethnicity, and other forms of collective identity, as socially constructed rather than primordial and has interpreted public commemorations as significant sites of this process of invention. If, as these historians contend, on ethnic holidays immigrants and their children invented ethnicity, then we might expect that on American holidays they constructed American identities.[9] Indeed, one reason for scholarly neglect of these celebrations may be this perceived assimilative function. If one assumes the traditional view of assimilation as a linear process, the celebration of American holidays looks like a step toward Americanization and away from ethnic identity. Elliott Barkan, for instance, posits American holidays as a part of the American "core culture" to which immigrants assimilate.[10]

A closer examination of these celebrations, however, quickly shatters the classic image of immigrants shedding their cultures and marching lockstep into Americanization. For one thing, individual ethnic groups or organizations rarely joined general celebrations, preferring to mark such occasions by themselves, apart from both native-born Chicagoans and other ethnic groups (notwithstanding the Irish invitation to the Polish militias in 1876). Just as important, these celebrations featured prominent displays of ethnicity and avowals of ethnic loyalty. At 1913 Memorial Day exercises at the Bohemian National Cemetery, for example, a Czech orator praised the cause for which the dead had fought but reminded his audience that "we who are assembled here are not Americans, only. Our hearts burn with ardent love for two countries." Similarly, the Highland Association of Illinois declared on Memorial Day 1890 that its members "desired to show their equal love for Scotland and America."[11]

To make sense of these celebrations requires a more complex reading of the relationship between ethnicity and assimilation. After a period in the 1960s and 1970s of rejecting assimilation and seeing ethnic persistence everywhere, scholars have recently begun to reexamine the concepts of assimilation and Americanization.[12] Some have been concerned with developing better models to describe the assimilation process. Barkan, for instance, has proposed a sophisticated six-stage model of assimilation that, despite its complexity, still depicts assimilation as an essentially linear process.[13] Other scholars have turned to assimilation to illuminate issues of ethnicity and class, positing a more complex ongoing dialectic of accommodation and resistance, embrace and subversion of "American" culture, along with efforts by immigrants themselves to define Americanism to fit their own needs.[14]

The celebrations of Chicago's ethnic groups support Werner Sollors's contention that "the opposition between 'pluralism' and 'assimilation' [is] a false one."[15] On these occasions, ethnicity and assimilation not only coexisted, they were interdependent and even mutually reinforcing. They constituted the intertwined products of the traditions and history of immigrants' homelands and their responses and adaptation to life in the United States. Ethnic celebrations of American holidays stood at the intersection of ethnic and American cultures and thus can illuminate the dialectical relationship between ethnicity and assimilation.

On these occasions, immigrants and their children constructed both ethnicity and Americanism. Their ethnicity informed the way that they defined their Americanism, in ideological terms that allowed for cultural pluralism and dual loyalties. Some even contended that continuing loyalty to one's homeland was a prerequisite to successful Americanization. Oscar Haugen, for example, told Norwegian Chicagoans at a 1915 commemoration that "the man who remembers the home of his forefathers makes a better citizen in his adopted country because of his loyalty and his love for the land of his ancestors."[16] At the same time, ethnic Chicagoans' understanding of American culture and values penetrated their construction of ethnicity, leading them to focus on homeland heroes and values in a distinctly American mold.

It is not surprising, then, that American holiday exercises included affirmations of ethnicity or that ethnic Chicagoans celebrated these holidays separately. At general celebrations, ethnicity would be subsumed to American identity, while at separate celebrations immigrants could interweave their story with America's, demanding incorporation into American culture on their own, pluralistic, terms. They celebrated separately precisely because American holidays were not simply about becoming Americans but about becoming ethnic Americans.

This ethnic Americanism was primarily, although not exclusively, the project of the ethnic middle class—the publishers and journalists, merchants and businessmen, clerics and attorneys, along with leaders of ethnic associations such as the Turners and the Polish National Alliance—who were the most visible sponsors, organizers, promoters, and participants in these holiday celebrations.[17] There has been some tendency among scholars of immigration to see ethnicity as a characteristic of working-class more than middle-class immigrants, who allegedly shed ethnicity as they move up the class ladder. Although Olivier Zunz has argued that the formation of the ethnic middle class may be the key to immigrant assimilation, it was that very cohort that was also most active in promoting and constructing ethnic identities.[18] That the middle class could simultaneously promote ethnicity and assimilation becomes less paradoxical if one stops treating these as binary oppositions. The combination of ethnicity and assimilation served as a strategy to build the ethnic community as a cultural, economic, and political power base for the ethnic middle class and to legitimize its leadership of this community.

That the stakes were high is evident in the conflicts over these issues within the ethnic middle class. Bourgeois factions within each ethnic group competed to win the hearts and minds of the majority working class to their vision of ethnic Americanism and, thus, to their leadership. Holidays, both ethnic and American, provided apt occasions to do so. The rituals, symbols, and oratory of holiday celebrations served as means of promulgating and affirming ethnicity and Americanism as if they were primordial truths. The middle-class organizers and promoters of these commemorations sought to unify under ethnic Americanism those with whom they shared a common homeland or descent, but often their celebrations revealed as much about what divided their ethnic groups as what united them. The role of religion and the political economy provided particularly heated debates, sometimes spilling into holiday celebrations. In addition, low attendance plagued many ethnic celebrations, both of ethnic and American holidays, suggesting that the majority of ethnic Chicagoans may have been indifferent to the middle-class goal of ethnic unity.

Turn-of-the-century Chicago provides a fertile field for the exploration of the relationship between ethnicity and assimilation on American holidays. Chicago was one of the nation's fastest-growing cities, skyrocketing from a population of 109,000 in 1860 to almost two million in 1900, with the majority of that growth coming from immigrants and their children. In 1870 approximately half the population was foreign born. Although the percentage of foreign-born Chicagoans subsequently declined, the percentage of Chicagoans of foreign stock (the first and second generation) rose. In 1890 this group constituted 78 percent of Chicago's population. The surge of immigrants after 1890 kept that percentage high, even as the second generation had children. As late as 1920, immigrants and their children still constituted close to three-quarters of the city's population.[19]

Not only did the city have a large and diverse immigrant population, it also offers scholars an excellent resource for studying them in the Chicago Public Library's massive *Chicago Foreign-Language Press Survey*, completed in 1942. This survey compiled topically organized articles translated from the hundreds of foreign-language newspapers that circulated in Chicago from the 1870s through the late 1930s, making accessible a rich lode of firsthand information on the city's ethnic groups.

Little research has been done on the role of the foreign-language press in America, despite the fact that it is one of the best primary sources available for the study of immigrants and ethnic Americans. Robert Park's 1922 comprehensive study *The Immigrant Press and Its Control* has yet to be updated or superseded, although there has been some recent work on individual ethno-linguistic groups.[20] Park found that although the main function of the foreign-language press was "to preserve the foreign languages . . . and to maintain contact and understanding between the home countries and their scattered members," it nevertheless promoted assimilation as well. The ethnic press, Park concluded, produced a reader who "is not American, at least according to the standards of an earlier period, but that is not foreign either, according to existing European standards."[21] Recent studies focusing on the newspapers of specific ethnic groups have generally confirmed this argument that, as one scholar has put it, the ethnic press served as both "a carrier of ethnicity" and "a means of assimilation." The press, while providing coverage of homeland events, focused primarily on the activities of immigrants and their descendants in America. Even the earliest Polish-American journalists, according to one historian, recognized that "their journalistic enterprise was connected with their adjustment to the New World."[22]

The foreign-language press, like its English-language counterpart, was primarily a bourgeois institution that articulated a middle-class viewpoint, with only a few exceptions, primarily socialist and union papers.[23] Chicago's foreign-language papers provided extensive coverage of ethnic celebrations, including those of American holidays, and used their editorial pages to exhort immigrants and their children to participate in them. Through their coverage of these events, publishers, editors, and reporters, overtly and covertly, promoted both ethnicity and assimilation.

The two American holidays celebrated most regularly by ethnic Chicagoans between the centennial and the First World War were Memorial Day and the Fourth of July. Not coincidentally, both of these occasions were tailor-made for the commingling of ethnicity and Americanism. Irish, German, Czech, and Norwegian immigrants, many of them refugees of the revolutions of 1848 in their homelands, had fought for the Union cause in the Civil War, and the veterans and their families annually commemorated this contribution to their adopted land. The observance of Memorial Day provided what one Czech paper called a "practical answer" to the "maligning" of immigrants in the American press by proving that they "do not come to this land merely to enjoy its freedom,—but that whenever the occasion requires it, they are willing to defend this freedom with their lives."[24]

The Fourth of July, for its part, held particular resonance for immigrants whose homelands had gone through similar struggles for nationhood, such as Germans and Norwegians, or whose homelands were seeking independence, such as Irish, Poles, Serbs, and Czechs. Serbs, for example, celebrated the Fourth in 1892 at the Graeco-Slavonian church with the "liturgy of Servian [*sic*] freedom." In his sermon, the priest "spoke enthusiastically of the freedom of this country and the benefits it confers upon those of his own and other races who were the victims of oppression." After comparing the American Revolution to the five-hundred-year fight of Slavs for freedom from Austrian and Turkish tyranny, he concluded with the hope "that a united Slavic nation would yet be like the United States, free and independent and happy."[25]

Ethnic celebrations of American holidays adhered to the basic structure of civic commemoration that had characterized American national holidays since the Revolution. Militias, war veterans, bands of music, labor unions at times, and a plethora of voluntary associations paraded, bearing flags, banners, and other visual symbols of nationality. Orators outlined the significance of the day, constructing the historical memory that provided the glue of collective identity. Participants joined in singing national anthems. On stages decorated in the national colors, leading men read hallowed national documents, and young men and women, even children, recited patriotic verse and performed patriotic music. Nor did the ethnic commemorations lack the more popular entertainments, which serve to remind us that most participants were enjoying a rare day off work. Revelers ate, drank, and made merry; they danced and played games; they gasped at fireworks displays.

Two examples will illustrate. In 1900 some nine thousand Irish Americans, comprising members of the Clan na Gael Guards, an Irish republican organization, and their families, converged on Oswald's Grove for the Clan's annual Fourth of July picnic. The festivities included orations on the Irish American and on the Irish republican cause, exhibition drills by the boys' cadet corps, plenty of food and alcohol, games and races, and dancing. Six years later, Free-Thinking Czechs gathered for their annual Memorial Day services at the Bohemian National Cemetery. Czech veterans and members of voluntary societies met at the Liberal (Free Thought) School, from which they paraded to the cemetery, halting at the monument to Czechs who had fought in the Civil War. There they heard addresses in both English and Czech on the Civil War and on the role of Czechs in America. Milwaukee attorney J. J. Vlach, the Czech orator, reminded the veterans and other participants of their homeland's troubles and struggles for freedom. Between orations and the decoration of the soldiers' graves, the students of the Liberal School presented Czech and American songs and recitations.[26]

As these examples suggest, what made ethnic versions of American holidays distinctive from other American holiday celebrations was their incorporation (and invention) of ethnicity. The holiday programs conceived by the ethnic middle class featured speakers, recitations, and songs in the national language of the homeland. Orators addressed their audiences in German, Czech, Polish, or Norwegian, as well as in English. On the Fourth of July in 1895, the Sons and Daughters of the Heather Hills presented a program of Gaelic and English songs, while on Flag Day in 1905, Chicago Poles heard a program of twenty Polish and American songs. Czech Memorial Day services featured Bohemian folk songs and the music of Dvořák. Ethnic national anthems, especially those created for nations that did not currently exist, took special pride of place, along with the U.S. anthem, on holiday stages. Czech Chicagoans, for instance, sang "Kde Domov Muj" ("Where My Homeland Is"), and Polish Chicagoans concluded their holiday exercises with "Boze Cos Polski" ("God Save Poland").[27]

Participants in these celebrations also imbibed ethnicity through performances by nationalist gymnasts and folk dancers. Gymnastic exercises and drills by uniformed Turners (called Sokols by Czechs and Falcons by Poles) were a standard feature at German, Norwegian, Danish, Polish, and Czech celebrations in Chicago.[28] The incorporation of folk culture into holiday celebrations provided particularly colorful and compelling reminders of ethnicity. Scottish programs included Highland dancing and games and bagpipe music, while the Clan na Gael's Fourth of July picnics spotlighted Irish songs, dance, and athletics. Fraternal and military organizations wore historical or folk costumes. The Kosciuszko Corps, for example, sported the uniforms of their name-sake's troops, while members of the Polish National Alliance wore the uniform of the Uhlans, the Polish cavalry, topped off by four-cornered caps of blue velvet.[29]

These interjections of ethnicity into the celebration of American holidays might be explained in assimilationist terms. Addresses in the audience's native language, for example, were surely necessary for practical reasons, to reach recent immigrants who did not speak English. Songs of the homeland, folk dances and costumes, and even Turners might be read as the type of apolitical, celebratory cultural nationalism (or ethnicity) acceptable in the pluralistic American culture to which immigrants and their children were assimilating.

But these phenomena had nationalist implications as well, complicating the picture of assimilation. Immigrants from the bourgeois and artisanal classes often had come to the United States as ardent nationalists. Indeed, nationalism, Eric Hobsbawm has suggested, was an eminently middle-class ideology and strategy for cultural and political power, and ethnicity was its kissing cousin. The majority of peasants and laborers, in contrast, may have identified themselves with a place or region but had little sense of national identity. Ethnicization was thus partially a process of nationalization. Matthew Frye Jacobson provides a useful distinction between ethnic consciousness, which he defines as primarily cultural and nonpolitical, and nationalism, which he sees as requiring some level of political commitment to homeland causes. He argues that ethnicization among immigrants often served as a vital step toward the development of political nationalism.[30]

Hobsbawm and Benedict Anderson have both pointed out the importance of the development of "national" languages for the rise of national consciousness. A national language provided a standardized language of communication to unite speakers of regional dialects, who could begin to conceive of themselves as part of a greater, national unit. Immigrants from different villages and regions came to the United States and, in part through this shared national language, which they read in their ethnic newspapers and heard at public celebrations, began to conceive of themselves not as Bavarians but as Germans, not as Sicilians but as Italians.

Hearing and singing anthems and other songs in the national language served a similar nationalizing function.[31]

The Turner movement and folk culture also had nationalistic aims. The Falcons, for instance, had been founded by members of the Polish National Alliance. The key characteristic of the gymnastic organizations was the belief that physical fitness built patriotism. The purpose of Turners' performances on American holidays was to provide an object lesson and stimulus to patriotism, to both the homeland and the adopted land. Folk culture served efforts to create ethnic sentiment, in the service of nationalism, by celebrating the alleged common "folk" history of the nation. As John Bodnar has shown, this folk culture was the product of both a genuine folk revival among European peasants and middle-class nationalists' "discovery" of peasant culture and appropriation of its costumes, music, and dances to create and mobilize nationalism.[32] Thus, the inclusion of folk performances and dress in American holiday programs suggests the organizers' desire to disseminate political nationalism, as well as to construct a pluralistic American identity. On a practical level, folk songs, dances, and costumes surely helped the organizers reach the many immigrants to whom these things represented not abstract notions of the nation but a lived and vividly recalled culture.

Other aspects of the celebrations demonstrate even more clearly the commingling of the ethnic and assimilative goals of the ethnic middle class. In 1905 the Kosciuszko Monument Committee, without a trace of irony, urged Chicago's Poles "to institute and observe an annual Kosciuszko holiday" on the American Flag Day, in order to demonstrate that "we remember about all our Fatherland's warriors, that we remember the Fatherland itself and we never want to forget about it." In that and subsequent years, Polish Americans did gather at the Kosciuszko monument in Humboldt Park to honor not only their heroic forefather but also the flag of their adopted country, because, the editor of *Dziennik Zwiazkowy* explained, "under it we find security and freedom.[33]

Ethnic Chicagoans frequently celebrated milestones in their homeland's histories on American holidays. The Society of Danish Veterans held an annual Fourth of July picnic to commemorate not just American independence but also the battle of July 4, 1849, when the Danes drove the Prussians out of Denmark. Likewise, an orator at the Bohemian National Cemetery urged Czech Chicagoans in 1905 to commemorate on Memorial Day the heroes of the battle of Lipan as well as their Civil War martyrs.[34]

Holiday journalism and oratory often contained healthy doses of ethnic history as well. Speakers and ethnic journalists proudly detailed their forebears' contributions to American independence. On Washington's Birthday, for example, *Dziennik Chicagoski* reminded Polish Chicagoans that they should "take pride in the knowledge that by the side of Washington, at critical times, stood the Poles Tadeusz Kosciuszko and Casimir Pulaski who fought staunchly for freedom." Similarly, an orator at a German-English school's exercises for the Washington inaugural centennial listed "Muhlenberg, Steuben and Kalb as evidence of the support which Germans lent to the establishment of the government in this country."[35] On Memorial Day, ethnic Chicagoans honored their countrymen who had fought to preserve the Union in the Civil War. Irish, Czech, and German Chicagoans erected monuments to their soldier dead in their cemeteries. In 1887, for example, German-American veterans and Catholic civic societies gathered at St. Boniface Cemetery to unveil a monument "honoring the heroes who have died for our great and free country."[36]

American holidays also proved opportune times to celebrate homeland freedom fighters and compare them favorably with American heroes. Polish Chicagoans, for example, adopted the new holiday for Abraham Lincoln in the 1890s but celebrated it jointly with Kosciuszko's birthday on February 14, thereby equating America's savior and the hero who had fought so valiantly to save Poland from partition. Ethnic Chicagoans imbued their national heroes with those characteristics celebrated in their American counterparts. A speaker at an Italian commemoration of Washington's Birthday, in comparing Italian nation builder Giuseppe Garibaldi to Washington, explained that "both were soldiers, each was a leader of men, . . . and each was a statesman and a patriot, loving and holding his country above all else."[37]

The most obvious intrusion of political nationalism into American holidays was the promotion of ethnic causes, both in the United States and in the homeland. This was particularly prevalent among those immigrants whose homelands were engaged in struggles for independence. Agitation for the Irish republican cause was part and parcel of the Clan na Gael Guards' annual celebration of American independence, for instance. In 1885 the speaker of the day was the former secretary of the Irish Land League, which advocated reform of Ireland's odious tenant laws, and in 1900 it was Richard O'Sullivan Burke, who had orchestrated an 1867 rescue of Fenian prisoners and spent years in English prisons for his deed.[38]

In addition to agitation, ethnic nationalists used American holiday celebrations for the practical purpose of soliciting funds for ethnic causes,
both in the United States and in their homelands. The Clan na Gael
sought to raise two thousand dollars for the Irish republican cause at its
Fourth of July picnic in 1890. Six years later, when fund-raising efforts for
a Kosciuszko monument stalled, the leaders of the drive announced that
the Fourth of July, "being an American national holiday, has been happily
chosen as the date for the great summer festival for the benefit of the
Tadeusz Kosciuszko monument." They hoped that the picnic would attract
the entire Polish population and bring in enough money that construction
could begin. Even if they chose not to attend the celebration, Chicago's
Poles were urged by *Dziennik Chicagoski* to "fulfill their patriotic duty by
contributing something for the monument."[39]

Czech solicitations on Memorial Day 1915 give some idea of the range
of causes supported by ethnic Chicagoans. Women at St. Adalbert's cemetery that day requested donations for three separate causes: the Bohemian
Charitable Association, a philanthropic organization for Czech Americans;
a monument to Saint Vaclav (Wenceslaus), a tribute to their Catholic
faith; and Polish war relief, support for the war raging in Europe, through
which Czechs, no less than Poles, sought independence for their homeland. At the Bohemian National Cemetery, meanwhile, Free Thinkers sold
picture postcards of the crematorium to benefit Free Thought schools in
Chicago, which were educating the second and third generations of Free-
Thinking Czech Chicagoans.[40]

Although ethnicity pervaded ethnic celebrations of American holidays,
this should not fool us into believing that Chicago's immigrants and their
children considered themselves any less American or that the exercises had
no assimilative functions. The Chicago Hebrew Institute, for example,
hosted annual celebrations of American holidays in an "effort to interest
our immigrants in national and civic affairs."[41] But the impossibility of
separating the ethnic and assimilative aspects of the celebrations suggests
the porosity of the alleged line between ethnicity and assimilation. For immigrants, becoming ethnic was part and parcel of becoming American,
and in the ethnic aspects of their celebrations, they carved out a niche for
themselves in their adopted land. The organizers and promoters of American holiday celebrations linked their own national heroes, history, values,
causes, and aspirations with those of their adopted land to show that they
shared American values. In selectively recounting both their homeland's
and their adoptive land's history and heroes, ethnic Chicagoans gave evi-

dence of their fitness for American citizenship. Like native-born Americans, they claimed to possess an innate spirit of liberty. *Skandinaven,* for example, asserted that "democracy and love of liberty ever have characterized the Norwegian people," while a Czech Memorial Day orator waxed rhapsodic on "the sense of justice and the feeling of pity for the weak and enslaved which is inborn in Bohemians."[42] *Dziennik Zwiazkowy* reported that Polish Americans on Flag Day "did homage to our emblem, the symbol of national liberty." Indeed, the paper noted that the holiday in 1908 "became prominently Polish, because of the noticeable absence of Yankees," and chastised native-born Americans for their nonparticipation, remarking that "it was deplorable to observe native born Americans lying on the lawn, unmindful of the near-by celebration."[43]

Like this Polish journalist, ethnic Chicagoans not infrequently implied that they were better Americans than those whose families had been here for generations. They claimed, with some justification, that their status as voluntary migrants to the United States gave them a keener appreciation of American principles and ideals than those who had grown up taking these values for granted. In a Washington's Birthday editorial in 1914, the *Jewish Courier* asserted that "the noblest people from all parts of the world have sympathized with the revolting [*sic*] farmers of the New World" and come to the United States "because they coveted a land where all men would be equal." American holidays, the editor noted caustically, had been taken over by immigrants because of native-born Americans' apathy. Thus, "Washington's Birthday, like every other holiday that reminds us of lofty ideals, is . . . chiefly a holiday for the immigrants, who still believe in those ideals and are ready to fight for them."[44]

As the *Courier* editorial suggests, immigrants and their children made American holidays their own. The version of ethnic Americanism created by the primarily middle-class organizers, however, did not go unchallenged. Indeed, their celebrations revealed the internal divisions that wracked Chicago's ethnic groups, as well as challenges to middle-class notions of ethnicity and Americanism. One flashpoint was the role of religion in defining ethnicity and nationalism. The "religionist" camp, led by the clergy and its lay supporters, contended that nationalism and ethnicity were subordinate to religion and that a nonbeliever could not be a member of the nation. The "nationalist" camp, in contrast, subscribed to the view that religion was not a defining characteristic of the nation.[45] The Irish-American centennial celebration in Chicago provides a case in point. In 1876 advocates of an Irish republic, led by the Clan na Gael Guards, a militia group, had founded an umbrella organization known as the United Irish Societies of Chicago (UISC), for the purpose of unifying Chicago's Irish organizations and promoting the republican cause, in part through the celebration of Irish and American holidays. The leaders of the UISC, in the tradition of the eighteenth-century United Irish movement, insisted on religious neutrality, illustrated vividly in their choice of the birthday of the martyred Protestant United Irishman Robert Emmet as one of the organization's main holidays. Catholic temperance societies and the Ancient Order of Hibernians vehemently disagreed, avowing that Catholicism was a necessary ingredient of Irish identity. The conflict over the role of religion in Irish ethnicity led the Clan and other religiously neutral organizations to decline to participate with the Catholic societies on the Fourth. Thus, the religionist view of Irish ethnicity triumphed in the centennial exercises. This rift continued after 1876, with the Hibernians and Clan na Gael holding separate Fourth of July celebrations well into the twentieth century.[46]

Polish and Czech Chicagoans fought just as ferociously over the role of religion. The Polish Roman Catholic Union (PRCU), led by clergy, competed with the religiously neutral Polish National Alliance (PNA) for the loyalties of Chicago Poles.[47] The conflict peaked in the 1890s, disturbing celebrations of American holidays as well as Polish ones. The PNA, for example, refused to march with societies affiliated with the PRCU in Chicago's 1892 Columbian quadricentenary procession, despite the religionist *Dziennik Chicagoski*'s plea that Poles present a united front, "regardless of their imaginary or real differences, irrespective of whether some are referred to contemptuously as ecclesiastics and others as nationalists."[48] Czechs in Chicago divided more profoundly, as a large percentage were Free Thinkers who believed, as one Memorial Day orator explained, that "no one can be a free citizen politically, if, on the other hand, he is a slave to religion."[49] Free Thinkers and Czech Catholics had separate schools, organizations, and cemeteries, and each group annually sponsored its own Memorial Day exercises at its cemetery.

Although they were not always as visible on American holidays, class divisions also wracked ethnic Chicagoans. Czechs, Germans, Poles, Italians, and Jews also parted on political economy, each group having a strong socialist minority that refused to let the middle class paper over class differences with ethnic or national sentiment. James Barrett has argued that organized labor developed its own version of Americanism, which emphasized civil liberties, access to an "American" standard of living, and cultural pluralism. Chicago's radical socialists were particularly active proponents of this type of ethnic Americanism, with a socialist bent. The alternative declaration of independence proclaimed at the socialist centennial celebration urged immigrant and native-born workers "to alter their former systems of government and production" by joining the Workingmen's Party, so as to secure their "inalienable rights" of "life, liberty, and the full benefit of their labor." The *Chicagoer Arbeiter Zeitung* lambasted the 1889 Washington Inaugural Centennial, which had been organized by leading capitalists expressly as a vehicle for assimilating the immigrant working class to their version of Americanism. It was, the editor proclaimed, "a real miserable affair" that demonstrated how the American Constitution had been destroyed by the "perfidy" of the capitalist class. He condemned German Civil War veterans, whom he termed "mercenaries," for marching in the procession and praised those German groups "smart enough not to participate in the whole humbug."[50]

Socialist immigrants made class solidarity an integral part of ethnic and American identity at celebrations of the Fourth of July, Labor Day, and May Day, which became the socialist Labor Day. Turners, labor unions, fraternal societies, and paramilitary organizations participated in these celebrations, which, unlike other ethnic celebrations, were often multiethnic in character. An 1880 Fourth of July celebration, for instance, featured socialist Turners, a German workers' militia, the *Lehr und Wehr Verein,* Roddy's Hibernian Band, and the Bohemian Sharpshooters, a Czech paramilitary group. In 1891, May Day celebrants could hear speeches in German, Czech, and Polish, in addition to English. Similarly, the 1910 May Day procession included a division of Jewish unions and organizations and a Czech division comprising labor unions, Socialist Party branches, Turners, and socialist educational clubs.[51]

Although they disagreed on the nature of ethnic Americanism, socialists and middle-class ethnic leaders could agree that a program of Americanization was not particularly necessary, because immigrants came to America virtually assimilated in all that counted—their commitment to liberty and their willingness to fight for it. Both groups constructed ethnic American identity in ideological and pluralistic terms that enabled ethnic Chicagoans to maintain dual loyalties as good Americans. This construction grew increasingly problematic, however, beginning in the late nineteenth century. Bouts of nativism and the organization of immigration restrictionists put pressure on ethnic Americans to conform to a narrower vision of Americanism, which had no room for dual loyalties. In 1889, for example, the nativist American League sponsored an "Old-Fashioned" Fourth, at which the main speaker condemned immigrants who waved two flags at their celebrations. "We want no flag," he asserted, "but the one our forefathers loved; we haven't room for any other. The red flag has nearly vanished; the green will follow." The orator singled out the Clan na Gael for particular opprobrium, remarking that "while we are celebrating in a quiet way here the Clan-na-Gaels are making merry at Whisky Point." In addition to drinking, the Irishmen's alleged offenses included their republicanism and their placing Irish patriotism on an equal footing with their loyalty as Americans. The speaker acridly noted that "on the flaming poster of that band of midnight assassins . . . the Stars and Stripes modestly peeps forth from under the green flag."[52]

Most Chicagoans were not so overtly nativist, and ethnic Chicagoans continued to celebrate American holidays in their own inimitable ways. Nevertheless, by the early twentieth century another kind of pressure emerged from the progressive reformers who sought to preserve and celebrate immigrants' cultures while Americanizing them politically and civilly. Progressives, that is, reconstructed pluralism and sought to depoliticize ethnicity, particularly by depriving it of its nationalism and ending the dual loyalties. This aspect of progressive pluralism ethnic Americans resisted, stubbornly insisting on their own conception of pluralism.[53]

Two of the largest multiethnic celebrations of American holidays in Chicago, on the Fourth of July in 1911 and 1918, provide case studies of progressive aims and the ways that ethnic Chicagoans responded to these. The first celebration was the product of the Sane Fourth movement and the Americanization push, while the second grew out of wartime Americanization efforts and ethnic Americans' own efforts to demonstrate their patriotism in their most challenging hour. Although ethnic Chicagoans bowed to the pressures of Americanizing forces by joining in these celebrations, they also used their participation to help shape the vision of Americanism promulgated on these occasions. Most important, they consistently refused to accept an Americanism that required them to disavow their loyalty to their homelands.

In 1911 progressive Chicagoans, organized as the Sane Fourth Association (SFA), sponsored a "Safe and Sane Fourth" intended to provide a "wholesome" alternative to the dangerous holiday mix of guns and fireworks.[54] As on the centennial, immigrants and their children dominated the day, by the design of the SFA and allied ethnic leaders. Despite stifling heat, an estimated two to three hundred thousand Chicagoans watched a grand procession featuring marchers and floats from seventeen ethnic groups, lined up in alphabetical order from Bohemians (Czechs) to Swiss. The parade also included floats depicting scenes from American history and one with a tableau of "Woman's Service to the State" contributed by suffragists, who had been denied permission by the SFA to enter a float with the theme of women's suffrage. Afterward, paraders and spectators dispersed to city parks for patriotic exercises with speakers provided by the SFA and various patriotic organizations. In addition, the city's Playground Association sponsored a Sane Fourth play festival, at which children from various playgrounds and settlement houses performed folk dances and gave exhibitions of "native games."[55]

Commentators hailed the celebration as an overwhelming success. The SFA modestly proclaimed that it offered a "dignified and instructive" alternative to the "savage" celebrations of years past; the *Chicago Tribune* agreed, noting that only one Chicagoan had died and four had been injured in holiday-related accidents. Progressives and the press also commended the Americanizing results of the celebration. The SFA's president proudly asserted that the procession had included "a greater number of nationalities than has ever before co-operated in this country in a patriotic demonstration." Speaking at Douglas Park, John P. McGoorty took as his subject the "lesson taught by the commingling of the various races in celebration of the American Independence Day." The *Tribune* described the parade as the "nations of different races, creeds, and attainments, paying their respect to the country into which they have been welded."[56]

The actual events of the day belied such simple interpretations of the Sane Fourth's assimilative effect, however. Ethnic editors, for instance, demonstrated more concern with their ethnic group's showing in the procession than with the overall patriotic effect. The Czech-language daily boasted that "even though today's English newspapers did not mention it, the spectators recognized the Bohemian float as one of the most beautiful." *Dziennik Zwiazkowy* begged to differ, claiming that the Polish section had made the best showing. The German-language *Abendpost*, for its part, professed amazement at the parade's demonstration of the "cultural accomplishments" of "races whose ability to create something unique has always been doubted," among which it counted the Irish, Croatians, and Lithuanians.[57]

As in 1876, Chicago's immigrants participated in the exercises first and foremost as ethnic Americans, not as melted or welded Americans. They paraded by ethnic group and held separate exercises in the parks. The

Chicago Hebrew Institute sponsored its own play festival, and the Clan na Gael held its thirty-sixth annual Fourth of July picnic. The editor of *Denní Hlasatel* informed readers that the Fourth of July had "triple significance" for Czechs that year: to honor the Declaration of Independence, "to prove to the other nationalities of this country that we lead all others in deeds . . . and general interest in the matter," and to tag for the Bohemian Charitable Association.[58]

Ethnic Chicagoans had various reasons for participating in the SFA's celebration, but providing a living demonstration of the melting pot was not high among them. Many ethnic leaders, like the middle-class reformers of the SFA, supported the movement to make the Fourth safe. As early as 1893, long before the Sane Fourth movement emerged, the German-language *Illinois Staats-Zeitung* had attacked the way that Americans celebrated their national holiday, with "nothing but senseless and dangerous noise and murderous shooting." For a more properly dignified commemorative style, Americans need look no further than Memorial Day, which the paper described rather condescendingly as "evidence of the fact that the American people are capable of ideal and noble sentiments." In 1910 *Skandinaven* suggested that the SFA might build on the good example of Norwegian Americans. "There is a lesson for Americans in the manner in which Norwegians celebrate their great national holiday [Norwegian Independence Day, May 17]," the editor proclaimed. "There is no insane use of fire arms, cannon, toy pistols, and other means of noise and human destruction, that disgrace our own national day. There is no list of dead and injured." Ethnic Chicagoans who supported the movement met with the SFA's trustees to plan the celebration, organized and solicited funds for their group's contribution to the parade and other activities, and promoted the celebration in their communities.[59]

In addition to their belief in the Sane Fourth idea, ethnic leaders were cognizant of the need to impress native-born Americans with their patriotism in this era of Americanization. They saw the celebration as a way to do so. Dr. W. A. Kuflewski of the Polish parade committee implored all Poles to participate and "demonstrate loyalty to this great country." The editor of *Denní Hlasatel* told Chicago Czechs that they must participate in the procession because "it is of importance to us that the public should have a favorable opinion about us in everything, everywhere." At postparade exercises, an orator praised the Czech section of the procession for presenting "a gratifying example of the Czech population's love for this new fatherland." Participation in American holiday exercises also provided immigrants with the opportunity to correct American misconceptions. "American people know very little about us," *Dziennik Zwiazkowy* acknowledged, "and what they know is not very complimentary, for it was imparted to them by our enemies, Germans and Russians." Poles could change this unfavorable opinion, however, by cooperating with the celebration organized by "the hospitable people whose country we have adopted as our own."[60]

Finally, in contrast to the melting-pot pluralism envisioned by the SFA, the ethnic participants in the Sane Fourth parade and exercises defined their Americanism with the same ethnically distinct pluralism as they had in previous celebrations of American holidays. Rather than acting out the melting pot, ethnic floats articulated homeland heroes, history, and desires or demonstrated ethnic contributions to America. Irish Chicagoans presented "St. Patrick at the Court of Tara," Greek Chicagoans the Parthenon, and Croatian Chicagoans demanded a "United Croatia." Italian Chicagoans depicted "The Progress of the World since the Invention of Marconi [the wireless telegraph]," Czech Chicagoans featured the Czech role in America's development, and Polish Chicagoans offered an allegorical grouping of Polonia, the Spirit of the Nation, and America, the latter represented by Washington, Pulaski, and Kosciuszko.[61]

The SFA encouraged ethnic distinctions by allowing only uniformed societies to march in the procession. Czech participants included mounted Sokols and singing societies on foot, German Turners performed on a "moving gymnasium," and female Polish Falcons were "showered with flowers" from the spectators. Croatian marchers wore "peasant dress," while Greeks favored philosophers' robes, the breastplate of Alexander the Great, or modern "native costume." Polish marchers dressed as the peasant scythemen of Tadeusz Kosciuszko's 1794 insurrection or donned the wool uniforms of the old Polish cavalry, despite temperatures that soared to over one hundred degrees and caused twenty-four deaths.[62]

The passion for retaining ethnic distinction within an American framework continued as the marchers headed to postparade exercises and picnics, which divided as usual along ethnic lines. Czech exercises included Sokol drills, folk dances such as the Beseda, and a performance of the ballet from Smetana's *Bartered Bride,* along with a reading of the Declaration of Independence and speeches in Czech advocating "a quiet, dignified celebration" of American independence and outlining the duties Czech Chicagoans owed the republic in which they lived. The Scottish societies' postparade picnic featured Highland dancing, bagpipe music, and

Highland games. The Norwegian Young People's League celebrated with games, races, and dancing but also listened to an orator who lectured them on "obedience to the law as the controlling element in the American-ization of all immigrants." Finally, a pageant presented that evening by the United Irish Societies, before an estimated ten thousand Chicagoans, fea-tured tableaux of American history interspersed with Irish dances.[63]

The Sane Fourth celebration in 1911 thus was the site where progressive and ethnic conceptions of American identity as pluralistic met. Despite the attempts of middle-class native-born reformers to impose their ideal of American pluralism in the procession of ethnic groups and at the park exercises and playground festival, middle-class ethnic leaders stuck stub-bornly by their own ideal of an American identity that was not threatened by fund-raising for Czech charities or calls for an independent Croatia or Poland. Relatively few ethnic Chicagoans marched in the procession, which was itself smallish with approximately five thousand in line. A Pol-ish-language newspaper reported, for example, that eight hundred Polish Chicagoans participated, and *Scandia* noted that the Norwegian turnout was low. Although the heat surely kept some spectators away, a large number of Chicagoans, presumably many of them immigrants and their children, turned out to watch the parade and participate in postparade activities.[64]

Although commentators suggested that the Sane Fourth procession would henceforth "be established as a tradition of the city," the 1911 cele-bration was not repeated. Pleading lack of funds, the SFA in 1912 decided to forgo the parade and instead have smaller, and less expensive, programs featuring stereopticon lectures in the city parks and playgrounds.[65] The celebration of the Fourth moved to the city's neighborhoods and assumed a more didactic form, wherein speakers tapped by the SFA (generally members and trustees) lectured immigrants and their children on patrio-tism. The ethnic elements of the 1911 celebration, added by the ethnic Chicagoans who participated, disappeared. Clearly the progressive reform-ers who funded and promoted the Sane Fourth did not conceive of immi-grants having really made any significant contributions to America. The more limited exercises were one-way distillations of patriotic education, from progressives to ethnic Chicagoans. The programs were wholly "American." Speakers distributed leaflets with the lyrics to the "Star-Span-gled Banner" and "America" and presented patriotic slides on topics such as "Betsey Ross and the Flag," "Washington and the Revolution," "Perry and the War of 1812," and "Lincoln and the Civil War."[66] Ethnic culture, dual loyalties, and ethnic contributions to America were conspicuous by their absence. Ethnic Chicagoans had to return to their own celebrations for these.

Chicago did not see another central celebration of the Fourth until 1918. While in 1911 the main purpose had been the reform of the Fourth, with Americanizing immigrants a secondary goal, in the war year of 1918 the exercises were intended as a demonstration of ethnic Americans' loyalty. Although progressive reformers participated in the planning of the celebration, this time the instigators were ethnic Americans. The leading role of ethnic Americans in the 1918 celebration meant that they shaped it even more than they had the 1911 exercises. Despite the wartime pressures to renounce dual loyalties, ethnic Chicagoans defiantly sought to demonstrate that they could be patriotic Americans while retaining loyalties to their homelands.

The United States' entry into the First World War had occasioned a surge of hyperpatriotism and an accompanying intensification of attacks on immigrants' dual loyalties, which now appeared to many native-born Americans to be unpatriotic at best and treasonous at worst. A Flag Day orator in 1918, speaking before city school children, urged the passage of a law requiring all residents of the United States to learn English. At other exercises the same day, a speaker condemned German Americans for their lack of sufficient loyalty to the flag of their adopted nation.[67] Chicago's immigrants took keen note of the necessity to demonstrate their patriotism. On the eve of U.S. entry into the war in 1917, a Polish editor told Polish Chicagoans that they should celebrate Washington's Birthday "more than ever because by so doing we will demonstrate more emphatically our loyalty toward this land of ours—adopted, it is true, but equally dear to us." In its report on exercises for the same holiday organized by the women's auxiliary of a Czech Sokol, *Denní Hlasatel* noted that "the atmosphere of the brilliant evening was surcharged with American patriotism, so essential for the upkeep of sentiment in these portentous times."[68]

At the same time, the war brought renewed vigor to central and eastern European immigrants' nationalist dreams and thus fueled their continuing dual loyalties. Ethnic Chicagoans during the First World War embodied Matthew Frye Jacobson's suggestion that fluctuations in ethnic identification are connected to homeland politics. At Memorial Day exercises in 1917, orator Jan Straka urged his fellow Czechs to buy Liberty Bonds but reminded them that "we Czechs are, however, also under obligations to our motherland, Bohemia." Similarly, in a Flag Day editorial, a Polish newspaper called on Polish Chicagoans to "honor [the American] flag, for under its leadership and through its intervention, we will regain . . . the freedom and independence of our homeland."[69]

Native-born pressure for "100 percent Americanism" and ethnic conceptions of a pluralist Americanism met in the Fourth of July celebration of 1918. In May, representatives of ethnic organizations affiliated with the Committee on Public Information's (CPI) Americanization efforts had petitioned President Woodrow Wilson, requesting that he proclaim the Fourth a special day for immigrants across the nation "to manifest, by special celebrations, our loyalty to this country and to the cause for which we fight." The petition revealed their conception of Americanism as being more internationalist than that of the "100 percenters." "The higher interests of the races which we left behind have become identical," they asserted, "with the higher interests of the United States. We regard ourselves now not only as members of an American commonwealth, one and indivisible, but of a world commonwealth, equally indivisible." The ethnic leaders asked the president's assistance in publicizing this commemoration of "the anniversary not only of national freedom but of universal freedom."[70] In other words, they redefined the Fourth of July as a universal holiday of freedom. The Czech National Alliance in 1918 proclaimed its agreement with Wilson's war goal of making the world safe for democracy, saying that "sons of the Czech nation died for this principle when they fought under the banner of John [Jan] Hus."[71]

Ethnic leaders in Chicago established a foreign-born citizens' committee to coordinate the various ethnic celebrations in the city. This committee, along with the State Council of Defense and a variety of local civic and labor organizations, sponsored the Fourth of July exercises. In addition, organizers established a committee, with representatives from seventy-five nationalities, to promote the celebration in the immigrant communities.[72] These representatives, along with other ethnic leaders and organizing committees, promoted the celebration heavily. The Greek organizing committee "urgently invited" all Greeks to "publicly express our interest in the celebration of American Independence." The Italian consul urged Italian Chicagoans to take part and demonstrate "the great sentiment of unity which today binds Americans of every race to the starry flag." A Russian Orthodox priest called on his countrymen to "make on this day parades with the flags and different signs." The Czech National Alliance and the National Alliance of Catholics issued a joint appeal to Czechs "to celebrate in an impressive, dignified manner." The Czech organizations asserted that participation was the patriotic duty of all Czechs, proclaiming, "He is not a good citizen—that Czech is an enemy of this country—who will not participate in the manifestation of the Czechoslovak people to the Republic of the United States and its President."[73]

Immigrants understood that this patriotic performance was not optional. Addressing Jewish Chicagoans in the pages of the *Sunday Jewish Courier,* J. Leibner informed them that "in order to know the loyalty of each and every national group, [the government] stipulates that alongside of the American flag, the group must unfurl its own flag, the flag of the native land." Ironically, of course, ethnic Americans were happy and eager to carry the flags that native-born Americans saw as merely a marker to tell the ethnic groups apart but that they knew to be symbols of their loyalty to their beloved homelands. Nevertheless, it was clear to ethnic Chicagoans that native-born Americans would be watching them and checking for signs of disloyalty. Leibner urged Jewish Chicagoans to celebrate, explaining that "the more Jews there are marching, the better it will be for our community, and the more it will indicate Jewish loyalty." He warned them neither to be indifferent nor to take the occasion lightly, "because we don't want the Chicago Jews to go on record as not being in sympathy with America."[74]

German Chicagoans' dual loyalties now proved particularly problematic, and some did take steps to distance themselves from America's enemy, their homeland. On the eve of the holiday, the German Club announced it was changing its name to the American Unity Club. Remarkably, however, another group of German Chicagoans found a way to maintain their ethnic loyalty while demonstrating American patriotism. They asserted that it was not their beloved homeland but only the current German leaders who did not deserve their support. Calling themselves the Friends of German Democracy, they resurrected the flag of the 1848 rebellion to be borne on the Fourth.[75]

The celebration organized by ethnic Chicagoans took a familiar shape. The committees for each ethnic group planned morning processions, to be followed, as in 1911, by separate meetings at city parks. Swedes, Assyrians, and Germans organized meetings at Lincoln Park, Czechs and Slovaks at Douglas Park, "Jugo-Slavs" (Croats, Serbs, and Slovenians) at Dvořák Park, Norwegians at Humboldt Park, Chinese in Chinatown, and African Americans at Institutional Church. Residentially scattered or otherwise divided groups planned more than one celebration. In addition to exercises at Humboldt Park, for example, Poles planned six other meetings. Italians organized six celebrations, Hungarians five, Lithuanians and Jews three apiece.[76]

In an effort to create a unified expression of national loyalty, the program prepared by the National Council of Defense (NCD) prescribed uniform exercises for each meeting. At precisely 3:00, each group was to raise the national flag, sing the "Star-Spangled Banner," and salute the flag. At this point, a speaker was to read President Wilson's holiday address, which had been cabled ahead for "reading and publication in foreign hands." This would be followed by a reading of the governor's message and the Declaration of Independence, a "patriotic address," and a "welcome to new citizens." The program was to conclude with a rendition of "America."[77] The rigid, "pure" Americanism and simultaneity of the prescribed exercises suggest the CPI and NCD's desire to project an image of national unity behind the war effort, while the ethnically based and arranged exercises indicate that the proof of immigrants' loyalty would lie in the intensity and magnitude of their celebrations. There was no room for "slackers" in the ethnic community, from either the draft or the required demonstrations of patriotism.

The overall intent was not so much to display an ethnically homogeneous nation as one in which ethnicity was submerged to national identity. Echoing its 1911 commentary, the *Tribune* called the holiday "a melting pot Fourth." The proof of immigrants' loyalty was to be preserved forever on film, which would show the kaiser that "the Americans of foreign blood are 100 percent Americans." A native-born journalist, after observing the Washington, D.C. meeting of representatives from thirty-three ethnic groups (including a Chicagoan representing Belgians), commented that although the representatives' "complexions [varied] from the pinkish white of the Scandinavian to the brown of the Syrian," they possessed "American ways" and "the imprint of America on their faces."[78]

The celebration was wildly successful in accomplishing the patriotic goals of its organizers. Tens of thousands of immigrants marched in processions, accompanied by some three hundred bands. An estimated half million participated in sixty afternoon meetings, where they pledged their allegiance, took in the president's words, and sang American anthems. Many groups publicly avowed their loyalty, such as the Czechs and Slovaks, who read a manifesto of loyalty sent to President Wilson, and Germans, who passed resolutions declaring their "whole-hearted and individual allegiance to the United States." Russians asserted that they were "neither for the Bolsheviks nor for the czar" but supported "a democratic Russia and the cause of the allies."[79]

An examination of the accounts of the processions and exercises for that wartime Fourth, however, reveals that the melting pot rhetoric, as in 1911, was misleading. Although immigrants and their children demonstrated their loyalty to the United States, they clearly did so as ethnic Americans, as they had done on American holidays for the past forty years. The very ethnic celebrations designed to prove each group's loyalty could not help but reinforce immigrants' continuing ethnic identification as well. Ethnic Chicagoans followed the prescribed program of exercises but added ethnic touches to make the day distinctively their own.

The joint Czech and Slovak celebration illustrated the intertwining of ethnic and American identities and causes. Czech Free Thinkers and Catholics united, along with their new Slovak allies in the struggle for an independent homeland, to stage a massive civic procession led by future mayor Anton Cermak. As in 1911, mounted Sokols led the way, followed by Czech police officers, Czech and Slovak Boy Scouts, veterans of the Spanish-American War, and unions. Czech breweries lent their wagons and horses, and the Czech Artists Club donated its members' talents to creating allegorical floats that united American ideals and Czech and Slovak goals. The first represented the arrival of immigrants in America, the second depicted Columbia as protectress of small nations, and the third showed Slavs paying tribute to Columbia. The women's auxiliary of the newly constituted Czech-Slovak army sold buttons with the slogan "Czech-Slovaks for America" to marchers to raise money for the soldiers' tobacco fund. Children from the Free-Thought schools, clad in Czech dress, marched in the parade, charmingly "chanting death to the kaiser in childish voices and enthusiasm," according to the *Chicago Tribune*. At the afternoon exercises, the children once again were visible, arranged on the grass as a living American flag. In addition to the set program and the manifesto of loyalty, Czechs and Slovaks heard oratory in Czech, Slovak, and English and sang British, American, and Czech anthems.[80]

Other ethnic Chicagoans similarly combined symbols and professions of American and ethnic patriotism. Swedish Chicagoans' parade featured Swedish societies in national costumes and a float depicting John Ericsson, inventor of the Union's ironclad *Monitor*, and Abraham Lincoln "clasping hands in front of the figure of Columbia, holding aloft an American flag." In a poignant touch, Swedish women with relatives and friends serving in the armed forces marched, bearing American flags and wearing hats on which American eagles "perched."[81]

Veterans of the Balkan Wars and riders depicting the heroes of the 1821 war for Greek independence headed the procession of Greek Chicagoans. Other paraders wore Greek military or national dress, and a float featured women depicting ancient Greece and Columbia, symbols of "the ancient and modern democracies." After their exercises at Grant Park, in a rare display of interethnic friendship, Greeks marched over to the French demonstration and played the "Marseillaise." In return, the French band played the Greek national anthem.[82]

As on previous occasions, however, competitive patriotism overshadowed such friendly gestures, as well as the larger goal of patriotic unity, as ethnic leaders focused on the showing of their own particular group. In the planning stages of the holiday, the leading Czech newspaper had urged Czechs "to participate as intensively as possible so that our manifestation will excel all others." A Greek newspaper asserted that, in addition to the war, the main reason for the magnitude of the Greek celebration was "the rivalry among the various nationality groups living in Chicago."[83] Not surprisingly, Greeks announced that they had "received by the unanimous voice of the city's press due credit for excelling all others with their parade." *Denní Hlasatel* begged to differ, chauvinistically declaring that "Czechs and Slovaks, always in the forefront in their demonstration of patriotic ardor, carried off first honors this time." Poles as well proclaimed their own exercises to be the best.[84]

Thus, although Chicago's ethnic groups in 1918 responded enthusiastically to pressures to prove their loyalty, their Fourth of July exercises followed the familiar pattern of intertwining their American and ethnic identities. Even in the face of "100 percent Americanism" they refused to deny the importance of their ethnic heritage to their American identity. Ethnic leaders did bow to the constraints of the war era by working to ensure respectably large turnouts in 1918, in contrast to the smaller crowds that joined the 1911 celebration. Many, perhaps most, of those who participated did so because they supported the American war effort. For the time being, even the internal divisions over religion and class were muted, although they would reappear in the postwar years. Unlike many native-born Americans, immigrants and their children knew that their continuing loyalty to their homelands did not signify any lack of patriotism to their adopted land. In 1918, as for the preceding forty years, ethnic Chicagoans used an American holiday celebration not primarily to satisfy nativist demands for patriotic performance but to construct ethnic American identities that situated them firmly in two cultures, the one they had left and the one they had entered. For Chicago's ethnic population, ethnicity and Americanism remained mutually reinforcing identities. Their inseparability was perhaps captured best by the *Jewish Courier*, which told Chicago's Jewish population in 1918 that the Fourth was "a most welcome opportunity for the Jews to display their patriotism for America," but insisted that "we must celebrate this occasion as Jews."[85]

NOTES

1. This essay previously appeared as Ellen M. Litwicki, "'Our Hearts Burn with Ardent Love for Two Countries': Ethnicity and Assimilation at Chicago Holiday Celebrations," *Journal of American Ethnic History* 19, no. 3 (2000): 3–34.

2. *Chicago Tribune*, July 5, 1876.

3. For a description of centennial celebrations, see Robert Pettus Hay, "Freedom's Jubilee: One Hundred Years of the Fourth of July, 1776–1876" (PhD diss., University of Kentucky, 1967), 274–88; Louise L. Stevenson, *The Victorian Homefront: American Thought and Culture 1860–1880*, Twayne American Thought and Culture Series, ed. Lewis Perry (New York: Twayne, 1991), 182–95.

4. *Chicago Tribune*, July 5, 1876; *Illinois Staats-Zeitung*, July 4, 1876, in the Chicago Public Library Omnibus Project, comp. and trans., *The Chicago Foreign Language Press Survey* (Chicago, 1942), section III.B.3, "Holidays" (hereafter cited as CFLPS). On the Second Regiment, see Alfred T. Andreas, *History of Chicago* (Chicago: A. T. Andreas, 1886; repr. ed., New York: Arno Press, 1975), 3:585, 587–88. On the Turner movement, see Eric L. Pumroy and Katja Rampelmann, "Historical Overview of the Turner Movement in the United States," in *Research Guide to the Turner Movement in the United States*, comp. Pumroy and Rampelmann, Bibliographies and Indexes in American History (Westport, Conn.: Greenwood Press, 1996), xvii–xxiii.

5. *Chicago Tribune*, July 4, 1876; "Declaration of Independence by the Workingmen's Party of Illinois," in *We, the Other People*, ed. Philip Foner (Urbana: University of Illinois Press, 1976), 100–103.

6. *Chicago Tribune*, July 5, 1876.

7. See Ellen M. Litwicki, "Visions of America: Public Holidays and American Cultures, 1776–1900" (PhD diss., University of Virginia, 1992), 99–102, 143–47.

8. Roy Rosenzweig, *Eight Hours for What We Will: Workers and Leisure in an Industrial City, 1870–1920* (Cambridge: Cambridge University Press, 1983), 74–79, 81–85. Another perspective is provided by David A. Gerber, "'The Germans Take Care of Our Celebrations': Middle-Class Americans Appropriate German Ethnic

Culture in Buffalo in the 1850s," in *Hard at Play: Leisure in America, 1840–1940,* ed. Kathryn Grover (Amherst: University of Massachusetts Press, with the Strong Museum, Rochester, New York, 1992), 39–60. Gerber argues, not entirely convincingly, that native-born Americans in Buffalo adopted German forms of leisure and celebration. Also see Litwicki, "Visions of America," 138–56.

9. The best summaries of the concept of ethnicity as invention are Kathleen Neils Conzen, David A. Gerber, Ewa Morawska, George E. Pozzetta, and Rudolph J. Vecoli, "The Invention of Ethnicity: A Perspective from the U.S.A.," *Journal of American Ethnic History* 12 (fall 1992): 4–6; Werner Sollors, "Introduction: The Invention of Ethnicity," in *The Invention of Ethnicity,* ed. Werner Sollors (New York: Oxford University Press, 1989), ix–xvii. Also useful are April R. Schultz, *Ethnicity on Parade: Inventing the Norwegian American through Celebration* (Amherst: University of Massachusetts Press, 1994), 10–20; Werner Sollors, *Beyond Ethnicity: Consent and Descent in American Culture* (New York: Oxford University Press, 1986), particularly 3–39.

Among the most compelling of the recent studies of ethnic commemoration are Schultz, *Ethnicity on Parade*; Kathleen Neils Conzen, "Ethnicity as Festive Culture: Nineteenth-Century German America on Parade," in Sollors, *Invention of Ethnicity,* 44–76; John Bodnar, *Remaking America: Public Memory, Commemoration, and Patriotism in the Twentieth Century* (Princeton: Princeton University Press, 1992), 41–77; Shane White, "'It Was a Proud Day': African Americans, Festivals, and Parades in the North, 1741–1834," *Journal of American History* 81 (June 1994): 31–41; Roland L. Guyotte and Barbara M. Posadas, "Celebrating Rizal Day: The Emergence of a Filipino Tradition in Twentieth-Century Chicago," in *Feasts and Celebrations in North American Ethnic Communities,* ed. Ramón Gutiérrez and Geneviéve Fabre (Albuquerque: University of New Mexico Press, 1995), 71–86; William B. Gravely, "The Dialectic of Double-Consciousness in Black American Freedom Celebrations, 1808–1863," *Journal of Negro History* 67 (winter 1982): 302–17; Robert Anthony Orsi, *The Madonna of 115th Street: Faith and Community in Italian Harlem, 1880–1950* (New Haven: Yale University Press, 1985); Richard Handler, *Nationalism and the Politics of Culture in Quebec* (Madison: University of Wisconsin Press, 1988).

10. Elliott R. Barkan, "Response," *Journal of American Ethnic History* 14 (winter 1995): 99.

11. *Denní Hlasatel,* May 31, 1913, CFLPS; *Chicago Tribune,* May 31, 1890.

12. A number of articles examine the historiography of assimilation, with particular focus on the recent resurgence of interest in the concept. See, for example, Russell A. Kazal, "Revisiting Assimilation: The Rise, Fall, and Reappraisal of a Concept in American Ethnic History," *American Historical Review* 100 (April 1995): 437–71; Gary Gerstle, "Liberty, Coercion, and the Making of Americans," *Journal of American History* 84 (September 1997): 524–58; Olivier Zunz, "American History and the Changing Meaning of Assimilation," *Journal of American Ethnic*

History 4 (spring 1985): 53–72; Philip Gleason, *Speaking of Diversity: Language and Ethnicity in Twentieth-Century America* (Baltimore: Johns Hopkins University Press, 1992), 47–90.

13. Elliott R. Barkan, "Race, Religion, and Nationality in American Society: A Model of Ethnicity—From Contact to Assimilation," *Journal of American Ethnic History* 14 (winter 1995): 51–60. In response to Barkan's model, Herbert J. Gans suggests what he calls a "bumpy-line" theory to replace the straight-line concept of assimilation, in "Comment: Ethnic Invention and Acculturation, a Bumpy-Line Approach," *Journal of American Ethnic History* 12 (fall 1992): 42–52.

14. John Bodnar, for one, has argued that "assimilation is not described best as a process of co-option of ordinary people by social superiors but as a process of simultaneous accommodation and resistance." Bodnar, "Comment," *Journal of American Ethnic History* 4 (spring 1985): 75. A good summary of this view of assimilation is also found in Schultz, *Ethnicity on Parade*, 10–17. Labor historians have also examined the ways in which workers of different ethnic groups forged a unifying working-class Americanism. See, for instance, James R. Barrett, "Americanization from the Bottom Up: Immigration and the Remaking of the Working Class in the United States, 1880–1930," *Journal of American History* 79 (December 1992): 996–1020; Rosenzweig, *Eight Hours for What We Will*.

15. Sollors, "Introduction," xiv.

16. *Skandinaven*, May 20, 1915, CFLPS. Schultz finds similar expressions among Minnesota Norwegians in *Ethnicity on Parade*, 97. Matthew Frye Jacobson discusses the dual development of ethnic and American nationalism among immigrants in *Special Sorrows: The Diasporic Imagination of Irish, Polish, and Jewish Immigrants in the United States* (Cambridge, Mass.: Harvard University Press, 1995). Also see Mona Harrington, "Loyalties: Dual and Divided," in *Harvard Encyclopedia of American Ethnic Groups*, ed. Stephan Thernstrom (Cambridge, Mass.: Harvard University Press, Belknap Press, 1980), 676–86.

17. On the middle-class nature of nationalism for such organizations, see John Bodnar, *The Transplanted: A History of Immigrants to Urban America* (Bloomington: Indiana University Press, 1985), 120–30; Conzen, "Ethnicity as Festive Culture," 49–59. On the middle-class nature of nationalism in general for particular ethnic groups, see Kerby A. Miller, "Class, Culture, and Immigrant Group Identity in the United States: The Case of Irish-American Ethnicity," in *Immigration Reconsidered: History, Society, and Politics*, ed. Virginia Yans-McLaughlin (New York: Oxford University Press, 1990), 96–129; Victor Greene, *For God and Country: The Rise of Polish and Lithuanian Ethnic Consciousness in America 1860–1910* (Madison: State Historical Society of Wisconsin, 1975); Schultz, *Ethnicity on Parade*.

18. Zunz, "American History," 60, 66–67. On working-class encounters with ethnicity and assimilation, see Barrett, "Americanization from the Bottom Up."

19. These figures come from Bruce C. Nelson, *Beyond the Martyrs: A Social History of Chicago's Anarchists, 1870–1900* (New Brunswick, N.J.: Rutgers Univer-

sity Press, 1988), 16, table 1.2; Melvin G. Holli and Peter d'A. Jones, eds., *Ethnic Chicago* (Grand Rapids, Mich.: William B. Eerdmans, 1981; rev. and exp. ed., 1984), 548–50.

20. Robert E. Park, *The Immigrant Press and Its Control* (New York: Harper and Brothers, 1922). On specific ethnic groups and their newspapers, see Sally M. Miller, ed., *The Ethnic Press in the United States: A Historical Analysis and Handbook* (New York: Greenwood Press, 1987).

21. Park, *Immigrant Press*, 55, 87–88. Philip Gleason briefly discusses the ethnic press as an agent of Americanization in *Speaking of Diversity*, 53. Also see Conzen et al., "Invention of Ethnicity," 23–24. Matthew Frye Jacobson, in contrast, emphasizes the ethnic press's role in promoting nationalism, in *Special Sorrows*, 57–64.

22. Andrew T. Kopan, "The Greek Press," in Miller, *Ethnic Press*, 175; A. J. Kuzniewski, "The Polish-American Press," in ibid., 275. Similar points are made by Arthur A. Goren, "The Jewish Press," in ibid., 216; Arlow W. Andersen, "The Norwegian-American Press," in ibid., 262.

23. Miller, introduction to *Ethnic Press*, xv; Andersen, "Norwegian-American Press," 266; James M. Bergquist, "The German-American Press," in Miller, *Ethnic Press*, 135–36.

24. *Svornost*, May 30, 1892, CFLPS.

25. *Chicago Tribune*, July 5, 1892.

26. *Chicago Tribune*, July 5, 1900; *Denní Hlasatel*, May 31, 1906, CFLPS.

27. *Chicago Tribune*, July 4, 1895; *Dziennik Chicagoski*, June 14, 1905, CFLPS; *Denní Hlasatel*, May 31, 1913, May 31, 1914, May 31, 1915, CFLPS.

28. For examples of Turners, Falcons, and Sokols at celebrations, see *Skandinaven*, July 9, 1878, CFLPS; *Abendpost*, July 5, 1911, and April 15, 1890, CFLPS; *Dziennik Zwiazkowy*, July 5, 1911, CFLPS; *Dziennik Chicagoski*, June 6, 1896, CFLPS; *Denní Hlasatel*, July 5, 1911, February 22, 1913, and February 23, 1917, CFLPS; *Chicago Tribune*, July 5, 1890.

29. *Chicago Tribune*, July 5, 1890, July 5, 1895, July 5, 1900, and July 5, 1911; *Dziennik Chicagoski*, October 22, 1892, CFLPS.

30. Eric Hobsbawm, *Nations and Nationalism since 1780: Programme, Myth, Reality* (Cambridge: Cambridge University Press, 1990), 117–22; Jacobson, *Special Sorrows*, 15–20. On ethnicization as a process of nationalization, also see Conzen et al., "Invention of Ethnicity," 22–23.

31. Hobsbawm, *Nations and Nationalism*, 103–8, 110–19; Benedict Anderson, *Imagined Communities: Reflections on the Origins and Spread of Nationalism* (London: Verso, 1983), 41–49. Anderson also discusses the significance of singing national anthems on holidays for the construction of nationalism (132–33).

32. Donald E. Pienkos, *One Hundred Years Young: A History of the Polish Falcons of America, 1887–1987* (Boulder, Colo.: East European Monographs, distributed by Columbia University Press, 1987), 20, 24–47; Jacobson, *Special Sorrows*, 40; Pumroy and Rampelmann, "Historical Overview"; Bodnar, *Transplanted*, 46–48.

33. *Narod Polski,* August 9, 1905, CFLPS; *Dziennik Zwiazkowy,* June 15, 1908, CFLPS. Other Flag Day reports include *Dziennik Chicagoski,* June 14, 1905, CFLPS; *Dziennik Zwiazkowy,* June 4, June 5, and June 15, 1908, CFLPS.

34. *Chicago Tribune,* July 5, 1890, and July 4, 1895; *Denní Hlasatel,* May 31, 1905, CFLPS.

35. *Dziennik Chicagoski,* February 22, 1906, CFLPS; *The Nation's Birthday: Chicago's Centennial Celebration of Washington's Inauguration,* April 30, 1889 (Chicago: Slason Thompson, 1890), 153.

36. *Chicago Tribune,* May 31, 1885; *Illinois Staats-Zeitung,* May 31, 1887, CFLPS; *Svornost,* May 30, 1892, CFLPS.

37. *Chicago Tribune,* February 23, 1900. For accounts of joint Lincoln-Kosciuszko celebrations, see *Dziennik Chicagoski,* February 13, 1896, CFLPS; *Zgoda,* February 18, 1897, CFLPS; *Dziennik Zwiazkowy,* February 10, 1917, and February 14, 1918, CFLPS.

38. *Chicago Tribune,* July 5, 1885, and July 5, 1900. For the history and goals of the Clan na Gael and the Irish National Land League and its American counterpart, see Michael F. Funchion, ed., *Irish American Voluntary Organizations* (Westport, Conn.: Greenwood Press, 1983), s.v. "Clan na Gael" and "Irish National Land League of America."

39. *Chicago Tribune,* July 5, 1890; *Dziennik Chicagoski,* May 9, May 28, and June 6, 1896, CFLPS.

40. *Denní Hlasatel,* May 31 and June 1, 1915, CFLPS.

41. *Chicago Hebrew Institute Observer,* November 1912, CFLPS.

42. *Skandinaven,* April 4, 1910, CFLPS; *Denní Hlasatel,* May 31, 1913, CFLPS.

43. *Dziennik Zwiazkowy,* June 15, 1908, CFLPS.

44. *Sunday Jewish Courier,* February 22, 1914, CFLPS.

45. The descriptive terms are Greene's in *For God and Country,* 10–11.

46. *Chicago Tribune,* July 5, 1876; Funchion, *Irish American Voluntary Organizations,* s.v. "United Irish Societies of Chicago," by John Corrigan; Thomas J. Rowland, "Irish-American Catholics and the Quest for Respectability in the Coming of the Great War, 1900–1917," *Journal of American Ethnic History* 15 (winter 1996): 3–31.

47. The best discussion of the religionist-nationalist debate within American Polonia is Greene's in *For God and Country,* 66–142. Also see John J. Bukowczyk, *And My Children Did Not Know Me: A History of the Polish-Americans* (Bloomington: Indiana University Press, 1987), 45–47. On the ethnic and religious diversity of pre-partition Poland, see Norman Davies, *Heart of Europe: The Past in Poland's Present* (New York: Oxford University Press, 1989), 316–17.

48. *Dziennik Chicagoski,* August 2, August 12, and October 22, 1892, CFLPS.

49. *Denní Hlasatel,* May 31, 1911, CFLPS; Karen Johnson Freeze, "Czechs," in *Harvard Encyclopedia of American Ethnic Groups,* 265–66.

50. "Declaration of Independence by the Workingmen's Party"; *Chicagoer*

Arbeiter Zeitung, May 1, 1889, CFLPS; Barrett, "Americanization from the Bottom Up," 1009–1011.

51. *Chicago Tribune,* July 6, 1880, and May 2, 1891; *Chicago Socialist,* April 27 and April 28, 1910.

52. *Chicago Tribune,* July 5, 1889.

53. On the limits of progressive pluralism, see Rivka Shpak Lissak, *Pluralism and Progressives: Hull House and the New Immigrants, 1890–1919* (Chicago: University of Chicago Press, 1989).

54. For an overview of the Safe and Sane Fourth movement, see Raymond W. Smilor, "Creating a National Festival: The Campaign for a Safe and Sane Fourth, 1903–1916," *Journal of American Culture* 2 (winter 1980): 611–22. Contemporary accounts of the movement include Percy MacKaye, "The New Fourth of July," *The Century,* July 1910, 394–96; Lee F. Hanmer, "Progress of the Sane Fourth," *Journal of Education* 75 (May 9, 1912): 515–16.

55. Letter from Marquis Eaton (president of the SFA) to Henry Crittenden Morris (a trustee), March 24, 1911, Henry Crittenden Morris Papers, correspondence, Chicago Historical Society (hereafter cited as Morris Papers); *Chicago Tribune,* July 2 and July 5, 1911; *Denní Hlasatel,* July 5, 1911, CFLPS. The *Tribune* gave the higher attendance figure, the Czech paper the lower.

56. "Report of the President to the Trustees of the Sane Fourth Association," 1911, Morris Papers, box 2, folder 9; *Chicago Tribune,* July 5, 1911.

57. *Denní Hlasatel,* July 5, 1911, CFLPS; *Dziennik Zwiazkowy,* July 5, 1911, CFLPS; *Abendpost,* July 5, 1911, CFLPS.

58. *Denní Hlasatel,* June 15, 1911, CFLPS; *Chicago Tribune,* July 5, 1911.

59. *Illinois Staats-Zeitung,* May 31, 1893, CFLPS; *Skandinaven,* April 4, 1910, CFLPS; *Chicago Tribune,* July 1, 1911; Eaton to Morris, March 24, 1911, Morris Papers, correspondence.

60. *Dziennik Zwiazkowy,* July 1 and July 3, 1911, CFLPS; *Denní Hlasatel,* June 15 and July 5, 1911, CFLPS.

61. *Chicago Tribune,* July 3 and July 5, 1911; *Dziennik Zwiazkowy,* July 5, 1911, CFLPS.

62. *Denní Hlasatel,* June 14 and July 5, 1911, CFLPS; *Chicago Tribune,* July 5, 1911. *Dziennik Zwiazkowy,* July 5, 1911, CFLPS; *Narod Polski,* July 12, 1911, CFLPS.

63. *Denní Hlasatel,* July 5, 1911, CFLPS; *Chicago Tribune,* July 5, 1911; *Scandia,* July 8, 1911, CFLPS; "Report of the President," Morris Papers. The Czech paper actually reported that the Constitution had been read, but it was almost certainly the Declaration, the reading of which was a longstanding ritual of the Fourth.

64. *Dziennik Zwiazkowy,* July 5, 1911, CFLPS; *Scandia,* July 8, 1911, CFLPS; *Abendpost,* July 5, 1911, CFLPS.

65. Eaton to Morris, June 19, 1912, and James Edgar Brown to Morris, June 28, 1912, Morris Papers, correspondence.

66. Brown to Morris, June 28, 1912, Morris Papers.

67. *Chicago Tribune,* June 14 and June 15, 1918.

68. *Dziennik Zwiazkowy,* February 22, 1917, CFLPS; *Denní Hlasatel,* February 23, 1917, CFLPS.

69. *Denní Hlasatel,* May 31, 1917, CFLPS; *Dziennik Zwiazkowy,* June 14, 1917, CFLPS; Jacobson, *Special Sorrows,* 5–6.

70. "Petition of Ethnic Americans to President Woodrow Wilson, 21 May 1918," in Edward Hale Bierstadt, *Aspects of Americanization* (Cincinnati: Stewart Kidd, 1922), 207–8; Edward George Hartmann, *The Movement to Americanize the Immigrant* (New York: AMS Press, 1967), 202–3, 206–8. A recent book on the CPI does not even mention this celebration, other than to note that Wilson prepared a four-minute speech for Fourth of July exercises in 1918; Stephen Vaughn, *Holding Fast the Inner Lines: Democracy, Nationalism, and the Committee on Public Information* (Chapel Hill: University of North Carolina Press, 1980), 120.

71. *Denní Hlasatel,* June 30, 1918, CFLPS.

72. *Chicago Tribune,* July 1 and July 4, 1918; *Chicago Defender,* June 29, 1918.

73. *Loxias,* June 26, 1918, CFLPS; *Chicago Tribune,* July 2 and July 3, 1918; *Denní Hlasatel,* June 30, 1918, CFLPS.

74. *Sunday Jewish Courier,* June 23, 1918, CFLPS.

75. *Chicago Tribune,* July 3, 1918.

76. *Chicago Tribune,* July 1 and July 4, 1918, Chicago Defender, July 13, 1918.

77. *Chicago Tribune,* July 2, July 3, and July 4, 1918.

78. *Chicago Tribune,* July 3, July 1, and July 5, 1918.

79. *Chicago Tribune,* July 3, July 4, and July 5, 1918; *Denní Hlasatel,* July 5, 1918, CFLPS.

80. *Chicago Tribune,* July 5, 1918; *Denní Hlasatel,* June 25 and July 5, 1918, CFLPS.

81. *Chicago Tribune,* July 3, 1918.

82. *Loxias,* July 11 and June 26, 1918, CFLPS; *Saloniki,* June 29, 1918, CFLPS.

83. *Denní Hlasatel,* June 15, 1918, CFLPS; *Saloniki,* July 6, 1918, CFLPS.

84. *Loxias,* July 11, 1918, CFLPS; *Denní Hlasatel,* July 5, 1918, CFLPS; *Narod Polski,* July 10, 1918, CFLPS.

85. *Sunday Jewish Courier,* June 23, 1918, CFLPS.

About the Contributors

Theodore Caplow is the Commonwealth Professor of Sociology at the University of Virginia. He is the coauthor of *Middletown Families,* along with Howard M. Bahr, Bruce A. Chadwick, Reuben Hill, and Margaret Holmes Williamson, as well as *All Faithful People: Change and Continuity in Middletown's Religion.*

Gary Cross is Distinguished Professor of Modern History at Pennsylvania State University. He is the author or editor of ten books, including *The Cute and the Cool: Wondrous Innocence and Modern American Children's Culture; An All-Consuming Century: Why Commercialism Won in Modern America;* and *Time and Money: The Making of Consumer Culture.*

Matthew Dennis is Professor of History at the University of Oregon. He is the author of *Red, White, and Blue Letter Days: An American Calendar* and coeditor of *Riot and Revelry in Early America.* He is currently working on a book tentatively titled *Bones: A Cultural and Political History of Mortal Remains in America.*

Amitai Etzioni is University Professor at The George Washington University and the founder and director of the Institute for Communitarian Policy Studies. He has taught sociology at Columbia University, Harvard Business School, and the University of California at Berkeley, and he served as president of the American Sociological Association from 1994 to 1995. He is the author of more than twenty books.

John R. Gillis is Professor of History at Rutgers University. He is the author of several books on family history, including a study of the development of Anglo-American family cultures, *A World of Their Own Making: Myth, Ritual, and the Quest for Family Values.* He will soon publish *Islands of the Mind: The Human Imagination in the Shaping of the Atlantic World.*

Ellen M. Litwicki is Associate Professor of History and Chair of the department at SUNY-Fredonia. Her research focuses on the cultural meanings of American rituals. She is the author of *America's Public Holidays, 1865–1920*, and is currently working on a cultural history of gift giving.

Diana Muir is the author of *Thanksgiving: An American Holiday, an American History*; *The Glorious Fourth* (published under the name Diana Karter Appelbaum); and *Reflections in Bullough's Pond: Economy and Ecosystem in New England*.

Elizabeth H. Pleck is Professor of History and Human and Community Development at the University of Illinois at Urbana-Champaign. Her most recent book is *Cinderella Dreams: The Allure of the Lavish Wedding*, which is coauthored by Cele Otnes of the UIUC Business School.

Francesca Polletta is Associate Professor of Sociology at Columbia University. She is the author of *Freedom Is an Endless Meeting: Democracy in American Social Movements* and, with Jeff Goodwin and James Jasper, coeditor of *Passionate Politics: Emotions and Social Movements*. Her current research is on the necessary conditions for effective public participation in urban policymaking.

David E. Procter is Associate Professor and Head of the Department of Speech Communication, Theatre, and Dance at Kansas State University. His research examines language choices that function to sustain and build community. He conducts communication research primarily in rural communities, specifically examining community festivals, strategic planning, and rural heritage museums.

Mary F. Whiteside is a licensed clinical psychologist and a therapist at the Ann Arbor Center for the Family. Her specialties include family counseling and post-divorce mediation. She has published extensively in the areas of divorce, remarriage, and family-owned businesses, and she is the author of *How Families Work Together*.

Anna Day Wilde published "Mainstreaming Kwanzaa" as a senior at Harvard University, where she served as associate managing editor of the *Harvard Crimson*.

Index